T0345170

Big Data Analytics

Big Data Analytics: Digital Marketing and Decision-Making covers the advances related to marketing and business analytics. Investment marketing analytics can create value through the proper allocation of resources and resource orchestration processes. The use of data analytics tools can be used to improve and speed up decision-making processes.

Chapters examining analytics for decision-making cover topics such as:

- Big data analytics for gathering business intelligence
- Data analytics and consumer behavior
- The role of big data analytics in organizational decision-making

This book also looks at digital marketing and focuses on areas such as:

- The prediction of marketing by consumer analytics
- Web analytics for digital marketing
- Smart retailing
- Leveraging web analytics for optimizing digital marketing strategies

Big Data Analytics: Digital Marketing and Decision-Making aims to help organizations increase their profits by making better decisions on time through the use of data analytics. It is written for students, practitioners, industry professionals, researchers, and faculty working in the fields of commerce and marketing, big data analytics, and organizational decision-making.

Big Data Analytics
Digital Marketing and Decision-Making

Edited by
Kiran Chaudhary and Mansaf Alam

CRC Press
Taylor & Francis Group
Boca Raton London New York

CRC Press is an imprint of the
Taylor & Francis Group, an **informa** business
AN AUERBACH BOOK

First edition published 2023
by CRC Press
6000 Broken Sound Parkway NW, Suite 300, Boca Raton, FL 33487-2742

and by CRC Press
4 Park Square, Milton Park, Abingdon, Oxon, OX14 4RN

CRC Press is an imprint of Taylor & Francis Group, LLC

Library of Congress Cataloging-in-Publication Data

Names: Alam, Mansaf, editor. | Chaudhary, Kiran, editor.
Title: Big data analytics : digital marketing and decision-making / edited by Mansaf Alam and Kiran Chaudhary.
Description: 1 Edition. | Boca Raton, FL : Taylor and Francis, 2022. | Includes bibliographical references and index.
Identifiers: LCCN 2022020032 (print) | LCCN 2022020033 (ebook) | ISBN 9781032310305 (hardback) | ISBN 9781032310442 (paperback) | ISBN 9781003307761 (ebook)
Subjects: LCSH: Electronic commerce. | Decision making. | Big data.
Classification: LCC HF5548.32 B54 2022 (print) | LCC HF5548.32 (ebook) | DDC 343.08/1142--dc23/eng/20220729
LC record available at https://lccn.loc.gov/2022020032
LC ebook record available at https://lccn.loc.gov/2022020033

ISBN: 978-1-032-31030-5 (hbk)
ISBN: 978-1-032-31044-2 (pbk)
ISBN: 978-1-003-30776-1 (ebk)

DOI: 10.1201/9781003307761

Typeset in Minion Pro
by KnowledgeWorks Global Ltd.

Contents

List of Figures

List of Tables

Preface

Big Data Analytics: Digital Marketing and Decision-Making focuses on digital marketing and analytics for decision making. This book explores the concept and applications related to digital marketing decision-making. Besides this, it shall also provide future research directions in digital marketing. It is a promising field of research that can be possibly helpful to understand the concept of digital marketing and help in strategic decision-making. This book also helps to enhance the knowledge related to the various concepts of data analytics used in digital marketing. The use of data analytics tools can get better decision-making abilities. This book consists of ten chapters.

Chapter 1 is related to the marketing mode and survival of the entrepreneurial activities of nascent entrepreneurs. Chapter 2 deals with the responsibility of big data analytics in organizational decision-making. Chapter 3 focuses on the decision-making model for medical diagnosis based on some new interval neutrosophic hamacher power choquet integral operators. Chapter 4 describes the concept related to the prediction of marketing by consumer analytics. Chapter 5 deals with web analytics for digital marketing. Chapter 6 includes innovative retailing, a novel approach for retailing business. Chapter 7 focuses on leveraging web analytics for optimizing digital marketing strategies. Chapter 8 is related to smart retailing in digital business. Chapter 9 is based on business analytics and performance management in India. Chapter 10 deals with parameterized fuzzy measures decision-making model based on preference leveled evaluation functions for best signal detection in intelligent antenna. This book includes diverse topics related to digital marketing analytics and decision-making, which helps businesses to increase their profits and wealth by making better decisions on time using data analytics. This book is meant for research scholars, practitioners, industry professionals, researchers, and faculty working in commerce, digital marketing, big data analytics, and comprehensive solutions to organizational decision-making.

Mansaf Alam
Jamia Millia Islamia University
Kiran Chaudhary
University of Delhi

About the Editors

Dr. Kiran Chaudhary is an assistant professor in the Department of Commerce at Shivaji College, University of Delhi. She has 12 years of teaching and research experience. She earned her Ph.D. in Marketing from Kurukshetra University, India. Her areas of research include marketing, human resource management, organizational behavior, and business and corporate law. She is a distinguished student winning various awards of recognition. She is a book author as well as conference and journal paper author.

Dr. Mansaf Alam is a professor in the Department of Computer Science, Faculty of Natural Sciences, at Jamia Millia Islamia University, New Delhi, India. He has also been a Young Faculty Research Fellow for the Ministry of Electronics and Information Technology in India and editor-in-chief of the *Journal of Applied Information Science*. As a journal and conference paper author, he conducts research in such areas as big data analytics, machine learning and deep learning, cloud computing, cloud database management systems, object-oriented database systems, information retrieval, and data mining. His other academic activities include: journal reviewer, member of conference program committees, journal editorial board member, and book author.

Contributors

Firos A.
Rajiv Gandhi University
Itanagar, India

Tarun Krishnan Louie Antony
M.S. Ramaiah Institute of
   Technology
Bengaluru, India

**Ezeifekwuaba Tochukwu
Benedict**
University of Lagos
Lagos, Nigeria
and
South America University
Wilmington, Delaware

Krishnaveer Abhishek Challa
Andhra University
Visakhapatnam, India

Kiran Chaudhary
University of Delhi
New Delhi, India

Iffat Sabir Chaudhry
Al Ain University
Al Ain, United Arab Emirates

Siddhartha Ghosh
Mahatma Gandhi Central
   University
Motihari, India

M. Gunasekaran
Government Arts College
Gandhinagar, India

C.C. Jayasundara
University of Kelaniya
Colombo, Sri Lanka

Seema Khanum
Government Arts College
Gandhinagar, India

Pavnesh Kumar
Mahatma Gandhi Central
   University
Motihari, India

Sandeep B.L.
M.S. Ramaiah Institute of
   Technology
Bengaluru, India

Siddesh G.M.
M.S. Ramaiah Institute of
   Technology
Bengaluru, India

Venkata Rajasekhar Moturu
Indian Institute of Management
Visakhapatnam, India

Farooq Mughal
University of Bath
Bath, United Kingdom

Srinivas Dinakar Nethi
Indian Institute of Management
Visakhapatnam, India

Ghanshyam Parmar
Constituent College of CVM
   University
Natubhai V. Patel College of Pure
   and Applied Sciences
Anand, India

Saifur Rahman
Rajiv Gandhi University
Itanagar, India

Pankaj Kakati
Jagannath Barooah College
Jorhat, India

S.R. Mani Sekhar
M.S. Ramaiah Institute of
   Technology
Bengaluru, India

Sapna Sood
Accenture
Gurgaon, India

Muhammad Nawaz Tunio
Mohammad Ali Jinnah
Karachi, Pakistan

Rajiga S.V.
Government Arts College
Gandhinagar, India

1

Marketing Mode and Survival of the Entrepreneurial Activities of Nascent Entrepreneurs

Muhammad Nawaz Tunio
Mohammad Ali Jinnah University
Karachi, Pakistan

Iffat Sabir Chaudhry
College of Business, Al Ain University
Al Ain, United Arab Emirates

Farooq Mughal
School of Management, University of Bath
Bath, United Kingdom

Erum Shaikh
Department of Business Administration,
Shaheed Benazir Bhutto University,
Sanghar Campus, Pakistan

CONTENTS

DOI: 10.1201/9781003307761-1

1.1 INTRODUCTION

Entrepreneurship is a continuous dynamic process of change that is pushed by new ideas and creative approaches toward establishing new ventures (Raposo & Paco, 2011). In this continuous process, people deploy their skills, abilities, efforts, and available resources to establish a business venture. The concept of entrepreneurship refers to the ability to take the risk and convert it into a successful business enterprise. Thus, it can be described as showing ownership along with the creation of wealth by means of establishing a new enterprise (Hisrich & Kearney, 2014; Bögenhold, 2020). In order to improve economic conditions, it is essential to convert products and services to something commercial. This conversion not only raises income but also creates employment opportunities because entrepreneurship introduces new business ideas and competition. Promoting entrepreneurial ideas is beneficial for unemployed people, and most beneficiaries are the youth who are future handlers for every society. People with broad knowledge, observation power, and interest can easily identify entrepreneurial opportunities and are convinced to pursue an entrepreneurial career (Parastuty & Bögenhold, 2019).

Entrepreneurship is all about recognizing and exploiting the opportunity and playing with the risk skillfully to enter the market and survive (Paul & Feliciano-Cestero, 2020). In line with initiatives taken by the government of Pakistan to promote entrepreneurship, most universities are striving to create an entrepreneurial ecosystem for their students and graduates. These are early days, and the growth rate and progress are very low (Samo & Inayat, 2019). In the context of this chapter, the notion of entrepreneurial journey is helpful in determining the process of the entrepreneurs followed by university graduates for starting and carrying out a business. Hence, this empirical study focuses on exploring the entrepreneurial processes adopted by young people in the backdrop of a developing country, Pakistan. Considering the economic challenges of the country, our research question examines how graduates experience the journey from studentship to entrepreneurship?

1.2 LITERATURE REVIEW

The entrepreneurial process is a phenomenon of the new venture creation from nonexistence to the existence of new business activities, and this journey reflects a series of economic activities in the form of processes with the purpose of value creation. The entrepreneurial process undergoes different phases because of formal and informal changes and challenges (Dvouletý, 2020). The nature of entrepreneurship is always characterized by novelty (Gartner, 1990), new entries (Lumpkin & Dess, 1996), and new combination of resources (Schumpeter, 1947). These characteristics need a change in information, and entrepreneurship is a process in its nature that seeks to amalgamate new information. Aspects of entrepreneurship like process and novelty go together in the sequence of events and activities. Thus, entrepreneurship as a process involves embarking on an entrepreneurial journey that gains momentum as it progresses (McMullen & Dimov, 2013). The entrepreneurial process of starting a business begins with the identification of the opportunity by nascent entrepreneurs. Nascent entrepreneurs are the individuals who are new to a business, either starting it for the very first time or switching from other occupations to a business (Carter et al., 2003). The entrepreneurial journey begins with uncertainty and challenges, and it includes several barriers that are encountered during the entrepreneurial process. Such challenges are responded by innovative qualities and autonomous actions. This journey involves an emerging process, opportunity realization, and potential transformation (Cha & Bae, 2010).

The literature suggests different phases of starting and pursuing a business activity, and according to some studies, university graduates are more likely to follow similar trends and steps to start a business (Hisrich & Ramadani, 2017). However, in the context of our study, the findings indicate that the entrepreneurial process was pursued in four different ways. The first one is market analysis, the second one is personal initiative, the third one is business activity, and the fourth one is the market. Before starting a business, respondents conducted market analysis in which they observed and surveyed the market's strengths and weaknesses, market demand, and market mechanism. Few of the respondents followed this approach and decided on the nature of the business after conducting market analysis (Rasmussen et al., 2011; Sorenson & Stuart, 2008). This market analysis and decision to start any business varies on a gender basis because females have their own concerns and issues while starting business, as they need some support from their family, parents, friends, or teachers. For this purpose, they need to travel and navigate from place to place and interact with a diverse group of people. On the other hand, male respondents were somehow bold in their decisions and choices. Findings suggest that market analysis counts location and checks the placement of the business if it is surrounded and equipped with the required facilities, infrastructure, and support system (Alvarez & Barney, 2000).

1.3 METHODOLOGY

This study draws on qualitative research methods where semistructured interviews are used to collect data. To conduct this study, ten nascent entrepreneurs were identified and recruited (Creswell, 1998). In order to reach participants, the snowball method was used. The interviews were audiotaped with the consent of the participants. A transcription was created from the interviews (Mayring, 2014). The interview data was thematically analyzed to identify new areas of the entrepreneurial process. The analytical strategy includes the processes of summarizing, coding, developing themes, and classifying them into categories that represent similar meanings and analysis (Miles et al., 2014).

The study was conducted in Hyderabad, Pakistan. This area was selected because it was the most suitable region in the country, being the center of education, business, and population concentration. Hyderabad is a geographic location for data collection. Hyderabad is the second-largest city in Sindh province, Pakistan. The target population is comprised of university graduates in the Hyderabad city of Pakistan who were involved in entrepreneurial activities.

1.4 FINDINGS

The findings of the study indicate the themes generated through a thematic analysis, in which four themes have emerged from the codes and that leads to the final category of journey as mentioned in Figure 1.1. Next to Figure 1.1, themes are discussed, respectively.

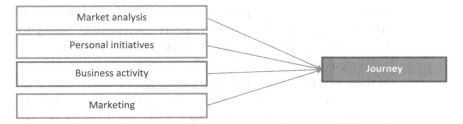

FIGURE 1.1
Entrepreneurial journey. (Source: Created by the author.)

1.5 MARKET ANALYSIS

In the context of entrepreneurship, it is difficult to find their position in the competitive environment, develop the strategies to face the competition, and excel in the competition. This means that entrepreneurs may observe the culture and get the market orientation. It is better and beneficial for both in the interest of entrepreneurs and in the performance of the entrepreneurial activity (Kreiser et al., 2002). Qualities of the entrepreneur, such as creativity and initiative, are useful in the entrepreneurship process. In order to find a plan, the nascent entrepreneur needs to implement a step-by-step approach, so that initiatives may be taken. Such strategies optimize the performance of the entrepreneurial activities in any market and the confidence of the entrepreneur in dealing with the entrepreneurial activities. Such strategies include market analysis, which enables the individual to develop an understanding of the environment. It needs the potential to deal with a diverse and competitive environment. Thus, market orientation, cultural orientation, and market analysis provide support in decision-making and decision implementation (Kemelgor, 2002).

Simultaneously, this theme suggests that young entrepreneurs conduct market analysis in order to know the market mechanisms and structure. In order to develop familiarity, participants suggest that they interact with the local community and communicate with their business fellows. In the process of market analysis, the local market and the business idea matter, and it is important to check the feasibility of the business plan. In this phase, the strengths and weaknesses of the market are observed. Here, not only physical markets but also virtual markets are included in order to start an online business (Kemelgor, 2002; Hult & Ketchen, 2001).

[R1]: We planned a hostel in our private home and conducted interviews from the selected girls in the university and selected those girls who were from very poor family background. Those girls who cannot pay hostel full fees then they participate in routine work of the hostel in order to stay in. Routine work includes cleaning, kitchen, and other necessary work. We have six rooms and three girls can be accommodated in each room, by this way 18 girls can be accommodated.

[R2]: Birds in the hand were our relatives. I conducted a baseline study in which I performed and utilized my SPSS skills so my these skills were also birds in hand.

[R3]: I researched six month earlier before starting my business tried to understanding if my plan works or not. So, I worked on different business ideas, across garments, stores, medical stores, toy shops, and super stores. I thought that which one is best, and my conclusion was that this city needs something of her caliber. So, they need this type of superstore with good quality in an innovative way. So, this idea, I shared with my friends and family. So, they also supported and appreciated this kind of business as compared to other types of business because of the population, location, illiteracy, and so many conceptions here in this city.

[R4]: I have a plan that there are a lot of shops, general stores, and mercantile stores. They do not have such kind of variety of the things and quality available here. For the new and interesting things, one needs to go to another city like Karachi. So, I thought if I start such type of business so that people can enjoy, everything is available in the market in one store. In my city, I am a supplier of many shops as a sole distributor. There are 500 shops here where I supply oil and tea. So, I thought why I should not start a Departmental Store to provide some better facilities to my town.

[R5]: I have done marketing job here in Pakistan and UAE in the bank. During the job, I thought to start my own business, so I returned to Pakistan and started analyzing markets. I was interested in the technology and wanted to involve in the e-commerce.

In view of the arguments of the entrepreneurs about the market analysis and market understanding, it is endorsed and considered important for successful businesses and successful entrepreneurs to analyze the environment, culture, and trends of the market before launching products and services in the market. In this way, enterprises can develop the potential to meet the market needs and challenges offered by the competitors and the environment. The latest research has been recognized as important for entrepreneurship and has improved performance to check market dimensions and social setup (Defourny & Nyssens, 2010).

1.6 A PERSONAL INITIATIVE

The second theme focuses on the personal initiative of young entrepreneurs in this study, and the approaches and methods were undertaken for the entrepreneurial activities by microentrepreneurs. Personal initiative is proactive behavior that is self-starting an initiative in a systematic way, future-oriented, and persistent (Mason et al., 2020). Individuals high in personal initiative show self-initiated behavior with motives to adapt to themselves, change their environment, and go beyond self-starting behavior in considering the future (Frese et al., 2016). A personal initiative indicates that entrepreneurs necessitate the start and practice of the skills in routine work and in every activity. The entrepreneurial environment furnishes several opportunities and challenging tasks. This approach leads to the approach of marketing and convinces to develop innovative marketing strategies (Frese, 2009). Personal initiative is a promising method in the entrepreneurial personal initiative, which is important for successful entrepreneurship. Although the personal initiative has been shown to be entrepreneurial initiative, this is interesting because the proactive behavior can be balanced with changing times and in different situations (Campos et al., 2017).

[R1]: Yes, we are in a group doing business; we are group of friends and they working together with me. I am only in group to do business full time, but other group members are doing as a part-time because they are doing job as well.

[R2]: I have own building of house where we did not need to pay rent. However, everyone participated through bringing extra furniture and other required things from their home to complete the requirements, just like there was one friend who has private tuition center, but it was not in active form therefore, she donated all furniture of tuition center.

[R4]: We started with five members and investors as partners, but two of them are working partners and three of them are silent partners who support us.

[R5]: We introduced a card that is valid on 16 plus brands with different deals that goes from 10% discount to 100% discount, the means of 100% discount is free services or free admission somewhere at the brands or to institutions. For example; an institution is registered with us and gives discount of 3000 rupees to the customers which is an admission fees and he waives the 100% discount.

[R7]: During our study, we were learning about how to bring idea from paper to ground, we were learning about establishing start p which were commercial and more about benefits, it was about breakeven. Basically, that inspirational story pushed us to start this social venture. We were only the people who started such social venture. We made a mechanism through business canon model. We prepared tables which tell us where our partners are, and it has blocks and different resources. We had to present the final project, so we made a business model about social venture and we introduced it to the administration of Institute of Business Administration (IBA), Karachi and they appreciated us. In the result, applied for the incubation for running this venture and we were awarded space as a office at IBA campus.

This theme reflects the entrepreneurial journey of the university graduates, and, in this regard, personal initiative is the first theme of the findings. In this theme, individuals showed different phases and different opinions regarding the initiative and the implementation. This indicates the entrepreneurial ideas of the individuals to bring in the action. Every entrepreneur shared his/her different and new initiative to start their business. Before starting any business activity, they expressed to develop confidence in doing it (Mensmann & Frese, 2019). Personal initiative is a self-starting and proactive initiative of entrepreneurs to exceed and excel in small steps and actions. Personal initiative is undertaken based on the set of goals, information collected, and preset plans. Such personal initiative is an intrinsic motivation of the entrepreneur and self-regulation in the entrepreneurship (Gorostiaga et al., 2019).

1.7 BUSINESS MECHANISM

This theme discusses the process of entrepreneurship and a series of activities undertaken by the entrepreneurs. This theme shows the pivotal role of entrepreneurs in the process of entrepreneurship, in the conduct of the business, how the process is carried out, and what are the phases in the process of entrepreneurship. The entrepreneurial process consists of a number of activities that are interrelated and integrated steps of designing, launching, and running new businesses and play a pivotal role in the framing of business activities. Business processes and business activities are gaining momentum in entrepreneurship because of the different and innovative drives involved (Hsieh & Wu, 2019; Bögenhold et al., 2017).

This theme suggests the entrepreneurial journey of the entrepreneurs, which holds the idea of the process and method of entrepreneurship. The university graduates were engaged in different kinds of business activities, and mobility was according to the nature of their business, whether product-oriented or service-oriented business. Participants mentioned that dealing with the entire process includes the purchase of raw products, workout on products, and employing skills and knowledge. Entrepreneurs working in a team expressed that the entrepreneurial journey is a developmental process of trial and error. In this developmental process, communication, coordination, and correspondence are also involved, which helps them to streamline different sources and resources.

[R1]: I am running my gym for females; I have started as a fitness trainer since last six years. I am doing independently, I am an owner.

[R2]: Our motive was to provide life skills and self-development. In the beginning of two to three months, nobody was ready to join such institute, therefore, we added few other subjects like religion, English language, then registration increased to 28 students but target is 30 for six months.

[R3]: I have learned that for the entrepreneurship to start, you do not need smart amount of money to invest but it is important that what you know and whom you know. So, I had talked to the parents of the children and asked them to donate the money in order to buy basic things. My idea is to collect the children and develop interaction among them. Actually, there is no place where

children can interact with each other and grooming of children takes place; this is a market gape which needs to fill in here.

[R3]: In the starting, I used call and collect children to one place and give them pen, pencil, laptop, and everything of their interest without limiting their activities, without any instructions. Just left them free in their movement and activities. It is taught in the schools that sharing is caring when they open their lunch box, they say they can't share and eat your own. So I decided, let's show them a practical approach of this particular line if you are sharing then it is really caring. When you open your lunch box then you must share it with other friends.

[R6]: I established a venture named IRTA, it is a health sector social venture. Basically, started with the inspiration of a seven-year-old child Abiya, she was a patient of acute lymphoblastic which is a type of blood cancer. I came to know about her from my friend. We went to visit the hospital and ask her for help because we had the social welfare type of mindset. We had intentions to help her parents financially that is what we could do. We went there and ask the duty doctor about her and what the status is. Duty doctor said that she has less chances of survival, so we are going to discharge her, and we have no remedy. So, we said that you want to leave her without any treatment. I mean you leave her to die. So, we thought we should do something to save her, so we collected her medical reports and went to the famous hospitals and ask them if they do something for her., They said that they can admit the patients with initial stages only and at that moment we found a gap in our national health system. Though I had no any background of health-related services or qualifications. I even don't have any experience in the medical treatment also.

[R6]: We have gone through those procedures and we have somehow fulfilled demand, and secondly, we go through aggressively and by law and never fulfilled their demands, we got the results. Forth point, I would like to add here that bank account. Normally, for the profit-based ventures, they have no any problem in creating bank accounts but in social ventures, you have to fulfil all the requirements. There are many restrictions, there so many mandatory procedures you have to pay. It is good but problem is we people we personnel in the banks they are not so much trained. Basically, they do not guide the people who reach the banks for the account opening. When we went there, I don't want to show the name of the bank but the bank officers who were there they were not much informed or trained, they asked us to submit a list of the documents, we submitted on the day, then I received an email to submit additional documents, and after around a year our bank account was opened, after writing three complains to head of the bank then we received a bank account number.

[R7]: I planned an as scheme for the purchaser. I announced of my mart that if you buy something of 3000 rupees you will get 5% discount and if it exceeds 5000 you will get a token. After three months, your token will be put in a box and box will be shaked by a child. The name written on the small paper, who made purchases of 5000 and whose name will be written in the box, he will get a bike. This scheme got popularity in the area and many people came forward. Hence some people came to made shopping of 10,000 rupees to get two token in order to increase the chance to get bike.

[R8]: My business plan is titled with Multi Vendor Place. It is an online business. It is a marketplace where vendors meet their customers. Such as Amazon, Alibaba and Daraz are doing online business. We are dealing with multiple categories. We only charge the sellers and the commission subject to the product, commission varies. Along with that, we also provide delivery service to the sellers. They just have to login in our website and everything comes under our responsibility. We pick up the products from them and deliver to the customers and get the money back to their accounts.

[R9]: My company is registered with name of United Construction. I have run six hostels in the different areas of Hyderabad since 2018. Three hostels for boys and three hostels for the girls. This is for the students and young people coming from the different rural areas for the study, job and business purpose. Around 600 people are accommodated in the hostels as hostels are equipped with all facilities including food and internet.

[R10]: I have started an online mart with name of Sindh Mart. The aim of this business is to promote cultural heritage of the country. As Pakistan contains very diversity in the culture, every different area has its own culture like Sindh culture is quite different than the Punjab culture, simultaneously Punjab, Kashmir, and from all parts of the country, we bring the traditional collection and sell to the local people as well as at international level.

In this way, respondents mentioned that one has introduced an online business by developing a discount card that contains a collaboration of 16 brands famous in the region. Another respondent mentioned that he had established a hostel for poor female students where some residents were paying rent and others by participating in the management of the hostel. Those girls who were unable to pay were offered work such as handling, cooking, cleaning, and looking after overall issues in the hostel. For example, one participant mentioned that while working in the agriculture sector, he developed an app to detect bacteria in fruits, which benefitted the farmers and growers, and led him to earn a lot of money and goodwill from the buyers and users. Simultaneously, one entrepreneur mentioned that he had established a departmental store in a region where there was none, and he provides quality service and opportunity package for customers (Bögenhold & Klinglmair, 2016).

The emerging innovative approaches facilitate the entrepreneurial process and entrepreneurial activities following the strategy and proper implementation. During business activities, creative ideas are beneficial in finding innovative solutions. Such innovative ideas translated into actions and activities are essential to entrepreneurship for the existence of the business. Startups are very essential in the business, and they need skills and innovation in the traits of entrepreneurship. The invisible relationship between entrepreneurship and innovation expands the capacity of the entrepreneurial process. Thus, the entrepreneurial process extends the knowledge across diverse experiences and passes through different kinds of situations. The processes carry ideas to the market and transfer ideas outside the environment as well (Hsieh & Wu, 2019; Bögenhold, 2013).

1.8 MARKETING

The outbreak of academic and research interest revolves around the domains of marketing and entrepreneurship. Entrepreneurship intersects marketing to advance the interests and evolve from their respective boundaries to flourish for the expansion of a business. Traditional marketing in the context of entrepreneurial motives advocates the services and products of the entrepreneurial process. It helps in the promotion of products and services and enhances the capacity of the business. This is not mainly concerned with the size of the business because marketing is equally important for small enterprises as it is for larger companies (Jones & Rowley, 2011). Hence, marketing is not a new area of interest in the research domain, but it has become an interesting case of entrepreneurship. Marketing is a dynamic aspect of entrepreneurship and provides a new perspective on entrepreneurial activities. The business activities of trading products and services accelerate through marketing and networking. However, emerging entrepreneurial marketing helps in identifying opportunities and working in a constantly changing environment (Paul et al., 2020; Bögenhold, 2019).

[R1]: I have wide friend circle; they published my business idea with my name and advertised.

[R1]: It was not possible without social networking and without the support of friends and family.

[R2]: We had one thousand investments only to publish a pamphlet for the advertisement.

[R3]: We are trying to register our products, because without registration, we cannot place it on any display center. As soon we get registration, we will contact a marketing company for the marketing of the product.

[R4]: I am running a social media campaign, and communicating with government officials for different agriculture projects.

[R5]: We started marketing of our product, we started to communicate with the doctors and shared them about use, benefits and purpose. We use social media campaigning and person to person marketing to promote awareness about our app.

[R6]: I advertise on the social media like Facebook with the name Atia Ismael collections and we introduce our products in the different exhibitions conducted in different cities. I have adopted as a career. As we receive online orders on the social media and on mobiles and we try to provide every order on time.

[R7]: Family and friends support in marketing in sharing the products in their further network and it attracts more reliable customers.

This theme determines the marketing tools adopted by the university graduates in their entrepreneurial journey. The concern of the respondents under this theme was to bring knowledge and learning close to the practice and application. Female entrepreneurs who were engaged in the home-based work had a display center, where they used to display their products for the advertisement and marketing. Customers used to visit the display center and order products for home delivery. Social software and social media were also important and emerging marketing tools for male and female entrepreneurs. By adopting these marketing tools, they find out the market demand due to the awareness in the market. However, in this regard, they availed the help of friends and family to run a social media campaign in order to spread the information about products and services to every end of the society. This makes for a more productive approach that brings and triggers innovation in the trade of products and services (Kuhn, 2016; Milanesi, 2018).

1.9 DISCUSSION

The important thing that matters most is the business idea. The feasibility of the business plan is checked with reference to the location and resources available. This is believed to be the most important step in the market analysis. Quality concern is a crucial step in the market analysis, where quality in products and services is observed according to the market demand and the level of the market. In the market, an attraction for customers and clients is created by offering quality and maintaining quality in all business offers. In this case, those entrepreneurs have shared their experiences as well as working experiences in different organizations, and they availed those experiences in order to conduct market analysis (Alvarez & Barney, 2005). The second phase of the entrepreneurial journey is a personal initiative after the market analysis. The initiative is taken individually as well as collectively in the form of groups. Such entrepreneurs have mentioned that in the case of a group, they have divided responsibilities, and everyone have undertaken an individual task and played their own role in starting a business. Some of them were active partners, and some of them were passive partners. Active partners played a full-time role and passive partners played a role as backup support (Alvarez & Busenitz, 2001).

It is found that entrepreneurs started by analyzing the available resources and how to avail them. So, they started to contribute and started from their own contributions such as physical resources, financial resources, human resources, and natural resources. At the start of business, in order to create market attractions, some kinds of offers, discounts, and packages were offered in the initial phase to customers, clients, and consumers.

After the market analysis and personal initiative, the third step of the entrepreneurial journey is a business activity in which carries on business and the growth of the business is focused (Baker & Eesley, 2003). The last phase of the entrepreneurial journey is the marketing of the business. This was a necessary phase to promote trade in the region. Different approaches were used by entrepreneurs. The most convenient methods used were friends, family, and social circle; through them, information about products and services is spread and advertised among personal and social circles. It is acknowledged by few entrepreneurs that without the support of social networking, it was not easy to project and promote the business among the immediate circle and create new channels for the sales of products and services. The second method of the advertisement was to publish pamphlets for the advertisement and distribute them in the local area for promoting awareness and information in order to create market attraction (Baker & Nelson, 2005). The next step of advertisement is very innovative and emerging; it is a social media campaign. Some entrepreneurs mentioned that they advertise their products through a social media campaign; it is very easy, time-saving, convenient, effective, and attractive. In the social media campaign, different social software and applications are used such as Facebook, WhatsApp groups, Instagram, and Snapchat. In contrast to this, one finding indicated that an entrepreneur cannot advertise some products or keep anything on display center because of the cultural and religious barriers, such as a male entrepreneur cannot advertise the female stuff in his business (Cha & Bae, 2010; Tunio, 2020a).

1.10 CONCLUSION

Entrepreneurship is considered a frontier in economic growth and development across different regions and countries. The regional differences may occur in entrepreneurial activities and the entrepreneurial process (Urbano et al., 2019). Individuals inclined to new business get engaged in the entrepreneurial activities of interest and will. Such interest leads them to embark on an entrepreneurial career and oscillate around the entrepreneurial ecosystem. The entrepreneurial attempt resulted in entrepreneurial action and productive outcomes (Slavec et al., 2017; Tunio, 2020b). In this regard, the entrepreneurial process begins with the identification of an opportunity and ends with the exploitation of the opportunity (Davidsson, 2015). The journey goes through several challenges and barriers. But, in the end, there is a different kind of reward in the form of an outcome that is blissful as well as a blessing for the nascent entrepreneurs (Thoumrungroje, 2018; Ramadani et al., 2019).

REFERENCES

Alvarez, S. A., & Barney, J. B. (2000). Entrepreneurial capabilities: A resource-based view. In G. Meyer, & K. Sheppard (Eds.), Entrepreneurship as strategy: Competing on the entrepreneurial edge (pp. 63–82). Thousand Oaks, CA: Sage Publications, Inc.

Alvarez, S. A., & Barney, J. B. (2005). How do entrepreneurs organize firms under conditions of uncertainty? Journal of Management, 31(5), 776–793.

Alvarez, S. A., & Busenitz, L. W. (2001). The entrepreneurship of resource-based theory. Journal of Management, 27, 755–775.

Baker, A. M., & Eesley, D. (2003). Improvising firms: Bricolage, retrospective interpretation and improvisational competencies in the founding process. Research Policy, 32, 255–276.

Baker, A. M., & Nelson, R. E. (2005). Creating something from nothing: Resource construction through entrepreneurial bricolage. Administrative Science Quarterly, 50, 329–366.

Bögenhold, D. (2013). Social network analysis and the sociology of economics: Filling a blind spot with the idea of social embeddedness. American Journal of Economics and Sociology, 72(2), 293–318.

Bögenhold, D. (2019). From hybrid entrepreneurs to entrepreneurial billionaires: Observations on the socioeconomic heterogeneity of self-employment. American Behavioral Scientist, 63(2), 129–146.

Bögenhold, D. (2020). Self-employment and entrepreneurship: Productive, unproductive or destructive? In A. Örtenblad (Ed.), Against entrepreneurship (pp. 19–35). Cham: Palgrave Macmillan.

Bögenhold, D., & Klinglmair, A. (2016). Independent work, modern organizations and entrepreneurial labor: Diversity and hybridity of freelancers and self-employment. Journal of Management & Organization, 22(6), 843–858.

Bögenhold, D., Klinglmair, R., & Kandutsch, F. (2017). Solo self-employment, human capital and hybrid labour in the gig economy. Foresight and STI Governance, 11(4) 23–52.

Campos, F., Frese, M., Goldstein, M., Iacovone, L., Johnson, H., McKenzie, D., & Mensmann, M. (2017). Teaching personal initiative beats traditional business training in boosting small business in West Africa. Science, 357, 1287–1290.

Carter, N. M., Gartner, W. B., Shaver, K. G., & Gatewood, E. J. (2003). The career reasons of nascent entrepreneurs. Journal of Business Venturing, 18(1), 13–39.

Cha, M., & Bae, Z. (2010). The entrepreneurial journey: From entrepreneurial intent to opportunity realization. The Journal of High Technology Management Research, 21(1), 31–42.

Creswell, J. (1998). Qualitative inquiry and research design: Choosing among five traditions. Thousand Oaks, CA: Sage Publications, Inc., pp. 1–403.

Davidsson, P. (2015). Entrepreneurial opportunities and the entrepreneurship nexus: A re-conceptualization. Journal of Business Venturing, 30, 674–695.

Davidsson, P., & Gruenhagen, J. H. (2020). Fulfilling the process promise: A review and agenda for new venture creation process research. Entrepreneurship Theory and Practice, 45(5), 1–36.

Defourny, J., & Nyssens. M. (2010). Social enterprise in Europe: At the crossroads of market, public polices and third sector. Policy and Society, 29(3), 231–242.

Dvouletý, O. (2020). Starting business out of unemployment: How do supported self-employed individuals perform? Entrepreneurship Research Journal, 1(ahead-of-print).

Frese, M. (2009). Towards a psychology of entrepreneurship: An action theory perspective. Foundations and Trends in Entrepreneurship, 5(6), 437–496.

Frese, M., Gielnik, M. M., & Mensmann, M. (2016). Psychological training for entrepreneurs to take action: Contributing to poverty reduction in developing countries. Current Directions in Psychological Science, 25(3), 196–202.

Gartner, W. B. (1990). What are we talking about when we talk about entrepreneurship? Journal of Business Venturing, 5, 15–28.

Gorostiaga, A., Aliri, J., Ulacia, I., Soroa, G., Balluerka, N., Aritzeta, A., & Muela, A. (2019). Assessment of entrepreneurial orientation in vocational training students: Development of a new scale and relationships with self-efficacy and personal initiative. Frontiers in Psychology, 10, 1125.

Hisrich, D. R., & Kearney, C. (2014). Managing innovation and entrepreneurship. Thousand Oaks, CA: Sage Publications, Inc.

Hisrich, R. D., & Ramadani, V. (2017). Entrepreneurial businesses growth. In Effective entrepreneurial management (pp. 135–157). Cham: Springer.

Hsieh, Y. J., & Wu, Y. J. (2019). Entrepreneurship through the platform strategy in the digital era: Insights and research opportunities. Computers in Human Behavior, 95, 315–323.

Hult, G. T. M., & Ketchen, D. J., Jr (2001). Does market orientation matter? A test of the relationship between positional advantage and performance. Strategic Management Journal, 22, 1899–906.

Jones, R., & Rowley, J. (2011). Entrepreneurial marketing in small businesses: A conceptual exploration. International Small Business Journal, 29(1), 25–36.

Kemelgor, B. H. (2002). A comparative analysis of corporate entrepreneurial orientation between selected firms in The Netherlands and the USA. Entrepreneurship and Regional Development, 14, 67–87.

Kreiser, P. M., Marino, L. D., & Weaver, K. M. (2002), Assessing the psychometric properties of the entrepreneurial orientation scale: A multi-country analysis. Entrepreneurship Theory and Practice, 26, 71–92.

Kuhn, K. (2016). The rise of the "gig economy" and implications for understanding work and workers. Industrial and Organizational Psychology, 9(1), 157–162.

Lumpkin, G. T., & Dess, G. G. (1996). Clarifying the entrepreneurial orientation construct and linking it to performance. Academy of Management Review, 21, 135–172.

Mason, C., Anderson, M., Kessl, T., & Hruskova, M. (2020). Promoting student enterprise: Reflections on a university start-up programme. Local Economy, 35(1), 68–79.

Mayring, P. (2014). Qualitative content analysis: Theoretical foundation, basic procedures and software solution (4–136). Klagenfurt.

McMullen, J. S., & Dimov, D. (2013). Time and the entrepreneurial journey: The problems and promise of studying entrepreneurship as a process. Journal of Management Studies, 50(8), 1481–1512.

Mensmann, M., & Frese, M. (2019). Who stays proactive after entrepreneurship training? Need for cognition, personal initiative maintenance, and well-being. Journal of Organizational Behavior, 40(1), 20–37.

Milanesi, M. (2018). Exploring passion in hobby-related entrepreneurship: Evidence from Italian cases. Journal of Business Research, 92, 423–430.

Miles, M. B., Huberman, A. M., & Saldana, J. (2014). Qualitative data analysis: A methods source book, Third edition. Thousand Oaks, CA: Sage Publications, Inc.

Parastuty, Z., & Bögenhold, D. (2019). Paving the way for self-employment: Does society matter? Sustainability, 11(3), 747.

Paul, J., & Feliciano-Cestero, M. M. (2020). Five decades of research on foreign direct investment by MNEs: An overview and research agenda. Journal of Business Research (In press).

Paul, J., Menzies, J., Zutshi, A., & Cai, H. (2020). New and novel business paradigms in and from China and India. European Business Review, 32(5), pp. 785–800.

Ramadani, V., Hisrich, R. D., Abazi-Alili, H., Dana, L. P., Panthi, L., & Abazi-Bexheti, L. (2019). Product innovation and firm performance in transition economies: A multi-stage estimation approach. Technological Forecasting and Social Change, 140, 271–280.

Raposo, M., & Paco, A. (2011). Entrepreneurship education: Relationship between education and entrepreneurial activity. Psicothema, 23(3), 453–457.

Rasmussen, E., Mosey, S., & Wright, M. (2011). The evolution of entrepreneurial competencies: A longitudinal study of university spin-off venture emergence. Journal of Management Studies, 48, 1314–1345.

Samo, A. H, & Inayat, S, (2019). Global University Entrepreneurial Student Spirit Survey (GUESSS), Country Report Pakistan.

Schumpeter, J. A. (1947). The Creative Response in Economic History. The Journal of Economic History, 7(02), 149–159.

Slavec, A., Drnovšek, M., & Hisrich, R. D. (2017). Entrepreneurial openness: Concept development and measure validation. European Management Journal, 35(2), 211–223.

Sorenson, O., & Stuart, T. (2008). Entrepreneurship: A field of dreams? Academy of Management Annals, 2, 517–543.

Thoumrungroje, A. (2018). Entrepreneurial intensity, national culture, and the success of new product developments: The mediating role of information technology. AU Journal of Management, 1(1), 15–23.

Tunio, M. N. (2020a). Academic entrepreneurship in developing countries: Contextualizing recent debate. In J. Gibb, J. M. Scott, M. Akoorie, & P. Sinha (Eds.) Research handbook on entrepreneurship in emerging economies (pp. 130–146). Cheltenham: Edward Elgar Publishing.

Tunio, M. N. (2020b). Role of ICT in promoting entrepreneurial ecosystems in Pakistan. Journal of Business Ecosystems, 1(2), 1–21.

Urbano, D., Aparicio, S., & Audretsch, D. (2019). Twenty-five years of research on institutions, entrepreneurship, and economic growth: What has been learned? Small Business Economics, 53(1), 21–49.

2

The Responsibility of Big Data Analytics in Organization Decision-Making

Ezeifekwuaba Tochukwu Benedict
University of Lagos Lagos, Nigeria
and South America University Wilmington, Delaware

CONTENTS

DOI: 10.1201/9781003307761-2

2.1 INTRODUCTION

As emphasized in the year 2012 by Johnson, 15 out of 17 firms in the United States have more data and information recorded for each company than the US Library of Congress that solely gathered and retrieved 240 terabytes of data and information in 2011. Big Data analytics evaluates a wide array of sources and information (Reddi, 2013) such as the Business Applications, Documents, Public Web, Social Media, Archives and Others. The data sources are applied in analytics to address the aims of business such as development of new services and products, cost reduction, pricing, enhancing sales strategy, enhanced risk management and so many others.

After various researches, we have realized that marketing is still facing a severe and a serious deal of complications as well as the absence of effective internal of the emerging product.

The classical ways are not up to the extent of tackling these challenges as a result of the fact that they are not capable and willing to keep pace with the level or acceleration of knowledge including the channel of information in actual time.

Presently, the Big Data analytics is applied at various domains as the data and information are depicted in excess quantities to be severely understood by the human mind, "Big Data is a term or word that describes and emphasizes vast or huge volumes of high complex, velocity and variable data which require or entails advanced technologies or techniques to enable storage, capture, analysis, management including the distribution of information". Thus, Big Data analytics is viewed to be a perfect technique to assist marketing decision makers to get an effective insight into enhancing the production (output) success.

The exponential growth and the rise of technology have resulted in a modern industry, simply put or state that an organization collects, commercializes and aggregates personal and private information (data). The digital exercises of numerous millions of individuals in the globe can be traced through a variety or a vast of modern approaches varying from credit card/store loyalty to aimed advertisements discovered on social media channels such as Instagram, Twitter, Facebook and many others. Private data, entailing offline and online behavior, are assessed, evaluated and amalgamated and then are sold to various forms of corporations and businesses (Marwick, 2014). Organizations that combine, collect, analyze or evaluate this form of data or information are essential and important and are usually referred to as data brokers. These data brokers depict this wave of transformation that has to do with private data including how it is handled both offline or online. The dramatic change has resulted in new and modern trends toward what is referred to "Big Data". For instance, Big Data basically comprises raw "little data". In major scenarios, these minimal data give an in-depth personal and private insight into an individual consumer and purchasing portfolio including consumer behaviors and habits. Laney Doug, a Tech Analyst, primarily analyzed, explained and emphasized Big Data in 2001 as being "Velocity, High Volume and – Variety Information assets that demand and entail cost effective, innovative (new and modern) of Information (data) processing for improved insight including decision making" (Sicular, 2013). Firms and companies across any organization value these forms of insights that were formerly not available before this technology growth and have become and seem interested in how these analytics are retrieved, collected, gathered and can be applied, which is very necessary and vital for all forms of organization.

The evolution or formation of the service intelligence aligns and amalgamates both the offline and online user behavior to examine and know what consumers or clients are busy with, what they are capable of expending fund on, what form of service they need or require or utmost reason and how to keep them coming back. Organizations use Big Data not only solely to aim their consumers or communities but also to give and provide their consumers precisely what they demand and customize the consumer encounter in a manner which is significant, essential and important to their interests (Byfield, 2014). Big Data customization also permits organizations to discover modern means to trigger the loyalty of customer (consumer), and with the help of Big Data, organizations are willing to simply match up client essential brands/products with the aimed consumer profile and with information-backed decisions. Rather than decisions being focused and concentrated on ordinary feeling and guess, the number or facts are currently present.

Instances of decisions' in-depth analytics outcomes are characterized by corporate-propelled questions; for instance, how should or must we price our services and products? Is there the need or essence for specific new services and products in precise geographical regions? What alternatives or options to consider (Davenport, 2014)? What forms of offers must be provided to customers with various portfolios and profiles (Davenport, 2013)? How much inventory (stock) should be stocked and kept in the warehouse?

Puto and Kościelniak (2015) emphasized that the application of information and data toward decisions making including the manner in which it is organized and coordinated is becoming essential. This perspective is backed up by an outcome of a survey carried out in 2011 by McKinsey (McKinsey & Company, 2011) as it emphasizes that the evaluation of the Big Data is significantly important for innovation, production (output) and competition. The application of the outcomes of the Big Data analytics in business permits organizations to attain competitive benefit (Puto & Kościelniak, 2015). Although applying the traditional information and data to back up decision making is not modern, that is, examining or weighing the best and appropriate product attributes or features in regard to the preferences of users (Ziora, 2015), the information is collected during the phase of product assessment to make decisions in regard to modern goods (Barbacioru, 2014).

However, Big Data is different from traditional data and varies significantly in different selected attributes and features in veracity, variety, velocity and volume (Chen et al., 2014). Presently, value is also included to these features or attributes (Sinha & Wegener, 2015). Therefore, more in-depth and new data can actually be obtained from Big Data for application in organization decision making (Glenys, 2014). Also, a conducted survey by Capgemini in 2012 (Capgemini, 2012) indicates that respondents who have used data analytics have viewed 27% enhancement in business performance, and they anticipate to enhance this statistic to 45% in the nearest future. Also, in a research work carried out by the Common Service Centres in 2014 (Info chimps, 2013) exceeding 350 information technology (IT) staffs (employees), it is emphasized that an estimated 55% of the respondents partake in the Big Data analytics as major five essential items for their organizations.

Yet, a research study by the IDG Enterprise showcased by Columbus (2015) emphasizes that 35% of the involved organizations have plans and motives to maximize their budgets for data- and information-driven ideologies and plans within the company. As major priority, 65% of the respondents emphasized that the major and utmost goal in investing under the data or information-driven plan and initiatives within the firm is enhancing the decision-making quality as they viewed the Big Data analytics as a significant and essential tool to gain as well as accelerate essential business insight including to benefit from the information or data.

From previous research studies, it is glaring that organization decision making including the Big Data analytics is increasing in firms, while no "tangible and reasonable body of knowledge" is presently glaring in the scientific literature. This instance triggered us to carry out a systematic literature review (SLR) so as to seek for some insight. We demanded for four major questions under the major banner of the "role of Big Data Analytics in Organization Decision Making" depicted by various significant and essential points:

- **RQ1** – The involved business functions.
- **RQ2** – The challenges in applying analytics in decision making.
- **RQ3** – The application of analytics outcomes and results in decision making.
- **RQ4** – The impact and effect of analytics on the aspects or areas of the decision-making process.

The major discoveries and findings entail to the following:

- **RQ1:** Various business functions were the results (outcomes) of the Big Data analytics that can be applied and used.
- **RQ2:** (i) Challenges in aligning business strategy with data driven decision making; (ii) collaboration and amalgamation across the business functions.
- **RQ3:** Approaches and techniques on how to apply the outcomes in decision making.
- **RQ4:** The aspects and areas of the Big Data analytics.

Summarily, these findings and discoveries tangibly include the present meager knowledge base in regard to the big analytics roles in organization decision making. Also, the chapter emphasizes on the implications and effects of these research findings and practice. Section 2.2 emphasizes on the research methodology; Section 2.3 emphasizes on the outcomes including the discussions; Section 2.4 emphasizes on the threats including the limitations and Section 2.5 finalizes the chapter.

2.2 METHODOLOGY

This aspect emphasizes on the applied research methodology in the chapter.

2.2.1 Systematic Literature Review

An SLR is a manner of interpreting, assessing and recognizing the research necessary to a specific topic or a research question, phenomenon of interests and areas by applying a research technique or method that is perfect and accurate, better and ensures auditing (Travassos & Mafra, 2006; Kitchenham,2004). There are various reasons for applying an SLR, for instance (Kitchenham & Charters, 2007):

- To recognize any gaps in the present research so as to suggest and emphasize on the necessary areas for further investigation;
- To summarize and evaluate the existing evidence and proof pertaining a particular area;
- To evaluate the extent to which empirical evidence contradicts/ supports theoretical hypothesis as well as to assist yield new and modern techniques (approaches)
- To provide a background/framework so as to accurately position new research exercises and activities

In this research study, we abode and adhered to the suggested guidelines and protocols by Kitchenham and Charters (2007).

2.2.2 Research Questions

We inquire about the following research questions. Also, we address and emphasize on the Big Data analytics role in the decision making of an organization.

- **RQ1:** In which business functions (that is, Project Management, Marketing, Manufacturing, Financial, etc.) are the Big Data analytics outcomes and information's applied? This question assists in attributing business functions as well as recognizing others that could actually take advantage and opportunity of Big Data analytics.

- **RQ2:** What are the challenges of applying Big Data analytics in organization decision making?
  Comprehending the challenges caused by the application of the Big Data analytics in organization decision making?

  Comprehending the challenges caused by applying the Big Data analytics for decision making will assist in ensuring new work processes or technologies.
- **RQ3:** How are the outcomes of the Big Data analytics applied by the management in the organization decision making? The question is so essential for attributing organization decision making in regard to the usage of Big Data.
- **RQ4:** Which aspects or areas of the process of decision making can be influenced by the Big Data analytics?

Liburd-Brown et al. (2015) emphasized that the process of decision making comprises of features such as outcome assessment, accountability and quality of evaluation (analysis) including the numbers of individuals involved. In regard to this, we include some other attributes such as (i) data (e.g., contextual, inputs, timing, constraints, knowhow and deadline) on the hand to be willing to make the decision; (ii) impact and consequences of making decisions including implementing it; and (iii) authority to make decisions, etc.; therefore, which of the elements of the process of decisionmaking are influenced by applying the Big Data analytics.

2.2.3 Search Plan

This section emphasizes on the tactics applied in carrying out the exploration for significant and major studies. We applied both manual (inference proceedings and business journals) and automatic searches (electronic databases).

2.2.3.1 Search Words

In order to ensure and enable that the literature review sticks to the theme of decision making and Big Data analytics, we restricted our search string to the most essential and important words (e.g., Decision, Big Data analytics, Business Functions and Decision-Making Model) that we derived and retrieved from the defined and explained research questions.

We also carried out different tests applying the identified terms. Actually, five aspects and areas of the search string were derived so as to finalize it. The search strings comprised of various terms: (Business Functions, Corporate Decisions, Corporate Decision Making, Decision) returned less or least essential results or outcomes as these terms or words are majorly applied in the business literature (not connected and similar to Big Data analytics).

In order to limit our research to the most essential results or outcomes, we applied the necessary logical operators or terms: ("Decision Making" or "Decision Making Process" or "Decision Making Model") and ("Big Data Analytics" or "Big Data").

Regardless of having the reasons and motives for applying the above search string, the words in it could not have recognized various papers (such as "Larger Scale Complex Systems") that so not apply the search words. Therefore, this is a related threat to this research study (see Section 2.4); the level of which is not recognizable without more and comprehensive exploration.

2.2.3.2 Resources

The applied resources are categorized into Management and Business; Electronic Database and Companies' Technical Reports are also referred to as White Papers and Software Engineering Scientific Journals. Information pertaining to the used (applied) resources is stated in the following:

- **Electronic Databases:** Business Source Complete, Science Direct and ACM Digital Library.
- **Scientific Journals:** Journals of Decision Systems, Journal of Organizational Design, Software Experience and Practice, Leadership and Strategy Journal, Journal of Big Data, Information Systems Engineering and Business Journal and Harvard Business Review.
- **Others:** Published technical reports by famous organizations include Capgemini, McKinsey and IBM.

In regard to automatic explorations, the exploration was conducted by covering and entailing the meta data in regard to the Business Complete Source and a complete text collection (text and meta data) of the literature in regard to both Science Direct and ACM Digital Library including a well-detailed scientific database in business. For electronic storages that index various aspects of knowledge, intellect such as Science Direct solely leads to within the areas of business, computers, account, management including decision science.

2.2.4 Selection Criteria

This aspect emphasizes on the exclusion, the inclusion criteria and the procedures of quality assessment including the process of selection so as to ensure that solely significant and essential literature outcomes are accepted and acknowledged for the evaluation in the SLR.

2.2.4.1 Inclusion Criteria

- **IC1:** Research studies must be written and emphasized in English.
- **IC2:** Research studies must be published between January 2005 and February 2016 as Big Data may or might not have been recognized much earlier than 2005.
- **IC3:** Research was similar or the same to Big Data in the managerial context (the concentration of this SLR).
- **IC4:** Research studies need to be present in complete version.
- **IC5:** For duplicated (copied) works, the most completed and finished one was chosen.

2.2.4.2 Exclusion Criteria

- **EC1:** Dissertations, books and theses (in part as a result of time challenges and limitations in glancing through this voluminous and large literature, while in part, some of the research works need to be anticipated in a research publication form).
- **EC2:** The research paper which did not attain the inclusion criteria was exempted.

2.2.4.3 The Selection Process

The selection stage consists of five protocols and techniques derived from Kitchenham and Charters (2007) and Biolchini et al. (2005).

- **Step 1:** A manual exploration was carried out in management and business journals including conference proceedings. The results and outcomes were actually evaluated by their abstract and title. The research studies necessary to the research context were chosen and the second list or details of the selected and chosen research studies were formed. As suggested by Kitchenham and Charters (2007), the result led to the initial electronic exploration in a vast number of nonessential papers. Following this, nonessential outcomes or details were exempted for more assessment.
- **Step 2:** An automatic and instant research was carried out and conducted. Initially, the results or outcomes were evaluated or assessed by their abstract and title. The research studies seen to be relevant and essential to the research context were chosen, and the primary and major array of the chosen studies was formed.
- **Step 3:** In this stage, the chosen research studies were evaluated by reading and going through their conclusion including the introduction sections. The research studies seen as necessary and essential to the research context were majorly chosen for the next steps; at the end of this stage, the fourth list of end results or outcomes was explained and defined.
- **Step 4:** In this step, the two lists were amalgamated into a sole one.
- **Step 5:** The final stage improved the selection, majorly since the research studies were entirely read, criticized or evaluated in regard to the filter provided and created by the previous steps and of the contextual relevance. In this step, the process of quality assessment was used and adhered to and then the final or last list with chosen results was formed.

2.2.5 Data Extraction

In order to appropriately arrange and coordinate the chosen research papers added to the SLR, a template comprised of the necessary characteristic was applied: Authors, Title, Study ID, Year of Publication, Source, the Designated Questions they referred to, Full Reference including the essential statement to assist to answer and tackle the defined questions.

2.2.6 Quality Assessment

In regard to Kitchenham and Charters (2007), also to the entire exclusion and inclusion condition, it is majorly seen as essential to evaluate the

quality and significance of the primary studies. Also, Kitchenham emphasizes that quality assessment is essential: (i) To guide the interpretation
of findings, (ii) to provide and ensure more detailed and comprehensive
exclusion and inclusion criteria, (iii) to determine the strength of the
interference, as well as (iv) to give recommendations and suggestions for
further and future research.

For this chapter, the necessary questions in regards to quality assessment were defined:

- **QA 1:** Does the research paper handle the use and application of the
  Big Data analytics in decision making?
- **QA 2:** Are the research applications or outcomes described in detail?
- **QA 3:** Are the aims and objectives of the research visibly emphasized?

In regard to the quality assessment, solely papers which addressed and
emphasized the questions of quality assessment including at least one of
the defined research questions in this chapter were chosen to be applied
to this SLR

2.2.7 Descriptive Data and Analysis

During the automatic search (first technique), an aggregate of 1,652 outcomes was recognized. After using the exclusion and inclusion criteria
and studying the abstract as well as the title, solely 50 research studies
were seen to be essential and relevant. Also, an aggregate statistics of
23 papers was chosen during the manual search (second technique and
step) in regard to the exclusion and inclusion criteria. A third list was
explained and emphasized by amalgamating the outcomes from the two
previous lists, making it a total of 73 papers.

After examining the conclusion including the introduction of each article, 49 papers were seen essential as well as chosen for the next procedure
and stage that comprises of reading the entire research work as well as
using the assessment and evaluation technique. Also, scoring principle
and technique was applied in this stage.

The research studies which did not attain the criteria of the evaluation
quality and failed to emphasize at least one of the defined research questions were exempted from the review (29 out of 49). Also, the exempted
research studies emphasized on points that are not similar or connected to
the major aim and objective of this SLR (see Section 2.1). These highlights
entailed: (i) analytics framework, (ii) algorithms and analytics techniques,

(iii) business analytics and intelligence, (iv) execution of tools for the discovery of value, (v) policies and issues for applying Big Data analytics in government and (vi) process for beginning to apply Big Data (information) in organization to list few of them.

At the end of the selection process, 20 research papers were selected for this SLR and considered to be relevant. There were 11 studies; 4studies (20%) were published in the conference proceedings, 11 studies (55%) were published in scientific journals, while 5 (25%) white papers were authored by famous organizations. Also, 25% (five research studies) stressed on the information or data to answer RQ3. Forty-five percent (nine research studies) covered RQ1. RQ4 was addressed and emphasized by 25% (5 research studies) and, lastly, around 65%, which is the majority (13 Studies) of the papers addressed and emphasized RQ2.

Table 2.1 depicts the distribution and the dissemination of the results of the research studies in regard to the questions they emphasized. The

TABLE 2.1

Chosen Major Studies

ID	Authors	Emphasized Research Questions (RQ)
S1	Lavalle et al. (2011)	RQ1, RQ2
S2	Fan et al. (2015)	RQ1, RQ2
S3	Lukiæ (2014)	RQ3, RQ4, RQ2
S4	Colas et al. (2014)	RQ2
S5	Davenport (2013)	RQ3, RQ1
S6	Capgemini (2012)	RQ2
S7	Economist Intelligence Unit (2013)	RQ1, RQ2
S8	Ziora (2015)	RQ1, RQ4
S9	See and Way (2015)	RQ4, RQ2
S10	McKinsey & Company (2011)	RQ4
S11	Brown-Liburd, Lombardi, & Issa (2015)	RQ1, RQ2
S12	Venkatraman and Henry (2015)	RQ4
S13	Puto and Kościelniak (2015)	RQ2
S14	McAfee et al. (2012)	RQ2
S15	Xu, et al. (2015)	RQ1
S16	Probst et al. (2013)	RQ3
S17	Hoskisson and Philips-Wren (2015)	RQ1, RQ2
S18	Schermann et al. (2014)	RQ2
S19	Galbraith (2014)	RQ3, RQ1, RQ2
S20	Davenport (2014)	RQ3

TABLE 2.2

Numbers of Research Studies by Year

Year	2015	2014	2013	2012	2011
Statistics of Papers	8	5	3	2	2

dissemination of papers numerically by research questions can be viewed in Table 2.1. The yearly publication through the distribution of studies is exhibited in Table 2.2. As it can be visibly viewed from the table, the Big Data centric outcomes regarding the concentration of this SLR seem to reappear in the literature around 2011 when this research area started to attract attention in the community.

2.3 RESULTS AND DISCUSSIONS

This section emphasizes on the outcomes derived or obtained for each defined research question in Section 2.2.2.

2.3.1 RQ1: Which of the Business Functions Are the Outcomes of the Big Data Analytics Applied?

Generally, any business functions can majorly apply the Big Data analytics to make and ensure informed decisions. Instances are scampered in the literature. We recognize nine business functions in this SLR and include instances for each of the functions in terms and regarding how the Big Data analytics can be applied in the process of decision making:

- **Audit:** Enhancing the audit protocol efficiency as in evaluating external data or information in the assessment and evaluation of fraud risk, client (customer) business risk and internal control. Actually, it seems that practice is widely taking more hold in regard to the business function diversity, where the results or outcomes of the Big Data analytics are being applied to apply decisions that could emanate and transpire from the SLR discoveries. Also, empirical research studies are visibly required to unveil more information and facts.
- **Risk management (Lavalle et al., 2011):** Have a comprehension on credit risk, market risk including operational risk, e.g., what actions

must be applied so as to minimize the risks? What are the vulnerabilities of our business?

- **Manufacturing/Operations (Economist Intelligence Unit, 2013; Lavalle et al., 2011):** Comprehending variances which could be indicators of quality challenges and constraints. Decisions could entail, e.g., How to define the future strategy to improve our daily activities? How to automate our activities and operations?
- **Financial management/Investment decisions:** Have a proper insight into how to expend or use funds including how to borrow funds such as what can be appropriately done to allocate capital so as to maximize and increase its value? What investment strategy to venture in? How much to borrow?
- **Human resources (Ziora, 2015; Economist Intelligence Unit, 2013):** Recognize attributes of most of the successful employees, apply the predictive modeling to comprehend the workforce, the application of cross-functional data or information with the promotion protocol or procedure, etc. The decisions entail enhancements in the retention and hiring process. Decisions entail process enhancements; which staff to fire, retrench and hire with the information in the human resources department could be applied to form and ensure a larger context. This can be applied to assess the efficiency of employees.
- **Supply Chain (Lavalle et al., 2011):** In supply chain, organization apply Big Data to ascertain and emphasize the outcome of its supply chain including monitoring, evaluating and measuring the supply chain hazards making decision pertaining to product, place, etc. **Questions** such as "What are the quality control techniques to be applied?" can simply be tackled by applying the Big Data analytics.
- **Productivity and sales (Economist Intelligence Unit, 2013; Lavalle et al., 2011; Davenport, 2013) define sales tactics:** For example, How effective is our present sales strategy? Does our present sales staff (employee) require tutoring to maximize sales? How much do we need to invest in training? What can we do to enhance our present sales strategy? Is there a means to minimize that cost with a better tactics? And lastly optimizing sales resources assignments.
- **Marketing management (Hoskisson & Philips-Wrens, 2015; Galbraith, 2014; Davenport, 2013):** Marketing decisions such as client perspectives toward a company, service, product or marketing promotions such as when and where to release the product? How to

define the product marketing tactics or plans? What form of visual assistance must we apply in a product campaign?

- **Product development and research (Ziora, 2015; Xu et al., 2015; Lavalle et al, 2011):** Organizations can apply Big Data to make current product decisions; what attributes must the goods have to attain the customers' preferences? How can we enhance the product design?

2.3.2 RQ2: What Are the Challenges in Applying Big Data Analytics Outcomes for Better Decision Making?

While Big Data analytics provides numerous benefits and advantages to the users, it also brings some obstacles and challenges. In the context of Big Data analytics, organizations experience serious setbacks, both at the technical and managerial levels. While at the technical level, the paradigm of the Big Data imposes various obstacles as a result of majorly unstructured and incoherent data (The Economist, 2013) for which tools are still at the infant stage or infancy (Capgemini, 2012).

At the management stage, an organizational silo can ensure that the decision making is suboptimal if data and information is not pooled or aligned together across the silos, for the purpose of the organization or firm at large. Also, Silos are challenges in effectively and efficiently migrating information and data across the organization, thus resulting in the potential and capability for inconsistent and incoherent reporting among the possible or necessary geographically distributed business categorizations (Capgemini, 2012). Also, the Silos can result to organizations to have challenges of not having relevant and timely data and information across the business functions for an effective and a better decision making.

A study conducted by MIT's Sloan School of Business indicates that organizations that engage and involve in data-driven (propelled) decision making experience a 5–6% rise in productivity and output over the ones that do not (Economist Intelligence Unit, 2013). However, the impediment in aligning and joining business strategy with data decision making (Hoskisson and Philips-Wren, 2015; McAfee et al., 2012) is seen as one of the most major challenges organizations experience in the era of Big Data analytics as it needs and entails an organizational cultural change which entails social, technological and intellectual alignment.

The leveraging of the Big Data usually entails working across functions such as IT, Finance and Engineering, for example (Colas et al., 2014). Also,

TABLE 2.3

Challenges in Applying Big Data Analytics Results in Organizations

Similar Decision-Making Challenges	References
Time to evaluate the information and datasets	Lavalle et al. (2011)
Leadership of analytics initiatives	Hoskisson and Philips-Wren (2015)
Challenges in integrating or aligning their own (personal) data sources within the company or organization	McKinsey & Company (2011)
Talent management	Colas et al. (2014)
Unavailability of clear or vivid business goals	See & Way (2015)
Inconsistent or incoherent information or data reporting among geographies, business organizations and functional operations	McAfee et al. (2012)
Necessary or timely data and information across the organization	Schermann et al. (2014)
Managerial behavior/culture (resistance to transformation, change or development within the firm or company)	Liburd-Brown et al. (2015)
Decentralization or centralization tendencies	Economist Intelligent Unit (2013)
Organizational sales	Schermann et al. (2014)
Aligning and integrating data or information-driven decision making with business development or tactics of the analytics strategy	Puto and Kościelniak (2015)
Special decision making	Galbraith (2014) Puto and Kościelniak (2015)

where the cross-functional techniques are of minimal activity, organizations are not willing to take the benefit and privilege of the power of the Big Data. Table 2.3 states the challenges to applying the results of the Big Data analytics in organizations.

2.3.3 RQ3: How Are the Outcomes of Big Data Analytics Applied by Management in Organization Decision Making?

The SLR analysis indicated that regardless of the identification of the need or essence to apply and comprehend the data (information) in organization decisions (Capgemini, 2012), there has been little or minimal scientific research; five papers since 2013 intended at comprehending how to apply the analytics results in the process of decision making of organizations.

Fourteen of 20 recognized papers address and emphasize on the benefits and advantages of applying the Big Data analytics to support and backup decision making but not on understanding and comprehending on how to apply the results in decision making.

Galbraith (2014) indicates and emphasizes that the analytics results, during the analysis stage, must be carried out in realtime by fast and swift response teams. This can affect and influence decision making. He emphasizes that the analytics results must be applied such that the team needs to discuss the insights as well as decide on the responses in regard to the real-time action.

However, an essential factor needed to be considered is how to organize and coordinate activities in order to facilitate and ensure real-time decisionmaking. A recommendation and suggestion is that organization needs to have multifunctional teams who are in constant and regular contact with the generated data from various sources to respond and react to real-time inputs. The data and information from the various sources are then processed and evaluated by the analytics tools, while the results are applied to make real-time decisions. This process and stage ensures organizations to influence and affect the outcome as well as to prohibit bad outcomes before they transpire.

An instance of how Big Data analytics ensures real-time decisions in managing supply chains is established by Galbraith (2014). At Organization A, there are actually designed and prepared rooms with video screen on the walls as well as computer access and link to different databases. The rooms are designed and prepared to promote cross-functional and real-time decision making. Therefore, when a paper machine's embedded sensors at the Pampers Plant is at a particular location entails that it requires and demands maintenance, a shutdown of plant is scheduled. If it seems that the machine will shut down for a while, then the decision and outcome is made to supply Organization A from the Albany, Georgia Plant. The analytics willingness is applied to know the appropriate way and manner to reroute tracks and also will attain other delivery commitments to clients.

In a research study carried out by Probst (2013), within different IT firms that form and create analytics tools, an essential part of how to handle analytics outcomes was emphasized and printed. Evaluate the information or data as well as generate intuitive and fast reports, the known and named friendly user reports that intend to cater organizations with competitive advantages and to empower organizations decision making as well. The presence of easy and simple to read reports can assist organizations in enhancing their decision-making capability as it results in significant or clear data, thus ensuring that it is simpler for the decision maker to comprehend.

Davenport (2013) forwards six techniques to decision making in regard to Big Data. These techniques entail:

- Identification of a challenge or problem
- Check and evaluate previous findings
- Choose the variables including modeling the solution
- Gather the information (data)
- Evaluate the information (data)
- Present, forward or work on outcomes

In these techniques, for the qualitative decision-making process, the concentration is on the first and second steps including the final procedures of the steps that comprise (i) framing the challenges and problems, recognizing it; (ii) comprehending how others might have solved and tackled it in the past; (iii) modeling the solution;(iv) gathering the data; (v) evaluating the data; and (vi) presenting and forwarding the analytics results as well as acting and working on the results.

For a quality decision making, abiding to the six techniques accordingly is essential, making important and necessary to formulate well-detailed and comprehensive hypotheses, get secondary and primary data on the hypothesized variables and lastly use statistical techniques so as to monitor and evaluate the importance and essence of the information or data. Provided with the size and volume of the Big Data, in these techniques, the Big Data analytics outcomes are applied in a manner where they tell a story to stakeholders and decision makers, and in regard to that story, the outcomes will be provided while action will be carried out upon it. Also, in these techniques, the expertise including the judgment of decision makers is essential as they are applied for the final outcome.

To apply the results of the Big Data analytics in regard to decision making, P&G (described by Colas et al., 2014) created and provided an initiative referred to as the "Decision Cockpits" that can be defined and seen as dashboards that provide and create executives with visual and visible exhibitions of information on market trends and business performance. The notion is to provide and ensure a single and a sole source of truth for the information across business units and geographies. They can provide and ensure a real-time automated information notification as well as customized. In this manner, the results of the Big Data analytics assist in accelerating decision making as well as minimizing time to market (Colas et al., 2014).

2.3.4 RQ4: What Aspects or Areas of the Decision-Making Process can be Affected and Influenced by Big Data Analytics?

In the traditional aspect in regard to the process of decision making, decisions entail human agent experience skills including verdict. In the context of the Big Data, organizational decisions are wholly or partly substituted by automated algorithms such as the data-driven evaluation, which is applied rather than intuition. Thus, this entails that any of the steps and techniques of a human decision-making process (such as gather the information, identify the problem, evaluate the situation, evaluate and develop alternative, select the preferred and necessary action and alternative upon the problem) changes or eliminates in some way, majorly introducing and launching modern steps and techniques for the human agent. In this context, Venkatraman and Henry (2015) emphasize that there is little dependence on subjective managerial inputs as a result to the process of real-time insights from Big Data so as to make and ensure quality data-driven decisions.

Lastly, the cost, time and effort entailed in making a decision as well as evaluating it may be influenced by the application of the Big Data analytics (Ziora, 2015).

2.4 THREATS AND LIMITATIONS

First, we emphasized on some of the SLR limitations, followed by the validity threats. A glaring limitation entails that the interlinkage of organization decisions and Big Data is a major trending theme, with major concentration on Big Data analytics. Therefore, the challenge of discovering relevant and prompt studies must be seen as a limitation and a constraint. Also, not every of the electronic databases provides the exact forms of attributes in applying the emphasized search strings. Therefore, the search strings require a little amendment so that they could effectively be applied.

In regard to threats and impediments to validity, some of the threats were seen when evaluating the results of the SLR:

- **Construction validity:** All the drawn conclusion is exhibited to have been in-depth in precise and a particular core section of this particular chapter. Therefore, there is traceability. However, there can be an emphasis that the extraction of information and data from the chosen papers could be biased. This was emphasized in two forms. One of the applications of two researchers (secondary and primary) including allowing amendments in the interpretation is significant. The second entails the application of information extraction sheet (see Section 2.2.5) applied to gather the necessary data to be applied in this SLR. The outcomes of this chapter are focused and concentrated on organized information.

- **Construction validity:** Pertaining to the search string applied in this SLR (see Sections 2.3.1 and 2.3.3), we applied the considered words which are necessary and appropriate so as to make the string as comprehensive and well detailed and necessary so as to bring out the most essential literature. We carried out different tests applying identified and recognized words and finally five aspects of the search string were formed and derived so as to decide upon the final version. Therefore, this threat was properly and appropriately contained.

- **External validity:** This threat entails whether the discoveries are used in contexts instead of those applied in this research study. An SLR study is not the same thing with a scientific experiment or a case study where this threat is of core and major essence since there are environmental projects (e.g., scopes) outside the researched study where one may intend to use the experiment results and the case study. Since the scope of the chosen data in the SLR study entails the universe to be allowed, this threat is not seen as relevant and essential here. Although collaborative effort or despite care, it is challenging or a constraint to generate or assure that all relevant or necessary concepts and published works pertaining to the theme were added into this SLR.

- **Internal validity:** Presently, the selection stage (see Sections 2.2.4.3 and 2.4) in this SLR was carried out by two researchers at the same time and any form of disagreement was stated and emphasized to reach an agreement from both researchers. In carrying out this, we intended to limit and reduce any threats to the internal validity.

In regard to the manual exploration, it is essential to know that it was carried out solely in a restricted array of sources (e.g., Journals, Magazines, etc.). The other forms of information and data sources were explored by applying automated exploration functions.

2.5 CONCLUSIONS

A systematic literature was carried out so as to answer four research questions (RQ1–RQ4, see Section 2.2) on the interconnection between the decision-making process of organizations and Big Data analytics. The theme is relatively modern and current, and to our understanding, no prior SLR research studies on this theme have been embarked or carried out. The stage and protocol of selection for determining and selecting the studies for evaluation comprises five stages and techniques (see Section 2.2.4). After using the quality assessment process as well as the exclusion and the inclusion criteria, 20 studies were seen as important or significant and chosen to be applied to this SLR (see Table 2.1 for the selected list of studies).

This SLR study provides four major contributions: (1) The comprehension of how the results of Big analytics can contribute to the decision-making process (see Section 2.3.3); (2) the presentation and exhibition of the state-of-the-art on the interlinkage or interconnection between the decision-making process and the Big Data analytics (see Section 2.3.1–2.3.4); (3) the array of obstacles and challenges for applying the analytics in decision making (see Section 2.3.2); and (4) the identification and the recognition of the business functions were the Big Data analytics has been used (see Section 2.3.1). Collectively, their contributions add and include the emerging and the new knowledge base in regard to the decision making and the Big Data analytics. In regard to the study on SLR, we finalize that the outcomes of the Big Data analysis play an essential, multifaceted responsibility in the organization decision making.

In regard to the management position, two essential issues recognized entail: (i) Collaboration across business functions (see Section 2.3.2) and (ii) aligning and amalgamating data decision making with business strategy. Also, in regard to the technical front, Big Data results in some constraints and impediments as a result of the absence of tools to evaluate an array of attributes of the Big Data (such as velocity, volume, veracity including variety).

Without skepticism, analytics and Big Data form the pillars of numerous organizations. Technology has introduced and formed a current and modern digital globe that permits business to trace digital exercises of millions of individuals through an array of multiple procedures that permit organizations a private glance at purchasing habits and consumer behavior. The collection of information has triggered other organizations (firms and industries) to keep them alert to the present situations. Marketing information can provide exact and necessary opportunities by including those in the marketing business to ensure an effective and proper decision.

Gathering and generating Big Data in actual time, 24/7, will provide an in-depth into what individuals are installing, purchasing and dialoguing about. Collected information both offline and online can be aligned and amalgamated to effectively decide and know what the final consumers want and prefer to see, and what consumers or clients are probably determined to purchase. With the client and customer social interactions daily occurring online, the organization can presently perceive and view which of the marketing efforts were effective and which were not and amend their strategies and tactics appropriately.

The rise in analytics and Big Data puts a magnifying and a tremendous glass on the repercussions that emanate from the application of the web in this global and internet age. Current and modern commodities penetrating the markets presently have effective chances of discovering means to differentiate and classify themselves, Kudos to the Big Data upcoming commodities, which usually have a challenging task discovering their target or major customer and client. Presently, with the application of the analytics or data act, it will be much convenient or better to check on how to reach those clients, which ones to completely desist and the most appropriate way to reach there. Big Data ensures the same benefits to be formed and created commodities, but more essentially, it assists these popular and famous brands to stay relevant and popular in their demography and also build and create current consumers that would have never been conscious before.

Also, it is not right and factual that presently organizations do not have the freedom and proper analytic tools to turn and transform the economic volume of information and data into essential and relevant marketing knowledge leading to valid and better decisions that are indirectly affecting and influencing marketing campaigns. They will assist firms (in some form of analytical-qualitative manner or form) to support and backup everyday constant routine marketing activities, sustain and build up strategies and also tactical benefit in business and essentially to aid them in effective planning or execution (referred to as coordination) of future market exercises and activities. From present times, these tools are better and effectively referred to as productive analytics. However, they entail techniques described and emphasized by well known, famous and popular rules derived and obtained from the areas of statistics or econometrics, where the attributes of simulation, modeling as well as forecasting are also used.

It is not factual that organizations are not applying the considerable or necessary investments in ensuring sophisticated analytical systems or techniques so as to better evaluate and assess the saturating external environmental factors that have an impact on profitability (or return) and majorly concentrate on the evaluation and the assessment of consumer groups and profiles, behaviors, styles of living, life time trend values and so on. These organizations identify incredible and tremendous value and a whole lot of privileges and benefits standing for predictive information and solution. Also, they try the best they can to apply and use them so as to better comprehend and appropriately amend future communication with consumers and planning effective price or product levels including the application of necessary means of distribution. Such organizations do not leave such benefits or privileges to unveil opportunities. Unutterably, they require these analytical tools so that they can attest to pure facts and numbers and not just the creativity and intuitions of the manager. For these motives and purposes, they are conscious or convinced of the essential significance of sustaining or developing strong future alliances or connections with clients, but above all, they feel thrilled or excited an urge toward current or new approaches and models of data analysis pertaining consumers. Thus, we attest and believe that their level and extent of interests in pursuing and attaining marketing mix through analytical will be of ascending than descending.

Finally, the results of the SLR also demonstrate and showcase that there has been less and minimal scientific research geared at comprehending how to apply the analytics outcomes or results in the organization's decision-making process. The majority of the important and essential studies address and emphasize on the benefits or advantages of applying the Big Data analytics to support and back up the decision-making process. Thus, a comprehension on how to use and apply the results (outcomes) to make better and decisions is still in its infancy.

REFERENCES

Barbacioru, C.I. (2014). An illustrative and descriptive example of the usage of decision making process for final consumer products output. Retrieved from: https://econ papers.repec.org/article/cbujrnlec/y_3a2014_3av_3aspecial_3ap_3a199-203.htm

Biolchini, J, Mian, G. P., Natali, C., & Candida, A. (2005). Systematic evaluation and review in software engineering. Engineering, 679(May), 165–176.

Byfield, B. (2014). Big data customization: A modern era for the music industry. umbel, https://www.umbel.com/blog/big-data/music-industry-big-data/. Accessed on December 8, 2016.

Capgemini (2012). The deciding and major factor: Decision making & Big Data. London: The Economist Web and Paris: Capgemini.

Chen, M., Liu, Y., & Mao, S. (2014). Big Data: A survey. Mobile Applications and Networks, 19(2), 171–209.

Colas, M. et al. (2014). Cracking the data conundrum: How successful and effective organizations make big data functional and operational, Capgemini Consulting, 1–17, Available at: https://goo.gl/MlDmFT

Columbus, L. (2015). Data analytics dominates enterprises' expending plans and initiatives for 2015. http://www.forbes.com/sites/louiscolumbus/2015/03/15/data-analytics-dominates-enterprises-spending- plans-for-2015/#32355a293eb4. Accessed on August 7, 2016.

Davenport. (2014). How strategists use and apply the 'big data' to support and backup internal business decisions, production and discovery. Leadership & Strategy, 42(4), 45–50.

Davenport. (2013). Keep up with your quant. Harvard Business Review, 91, 7–8.

Economist Intelligence Unit. (2013). The evolving role and responsibility of data and information in decision making. Retrieved from: https://nanopdf.com/download/the-evolving-role-of-data-in-decision-making_pdf

Fan, S., Lau, K.R.Y., & Zhao, L.J. (2015). Demystifying big data analytics for business intelligence through the lens of marketing mix. Big Data Research, 2(1), 28–32. http://dx.doi.org/10.1016/j.bdr.2015.02.006

Galbraith, J.R. (2014). Organization design constraints and limitations emanating from big data. Journal of Organization Design, 3(1), 2–13.

Hoskisson, & Philips-Wren. (2015). An analytical journey and exploration towards big data. Journal of Decision Systems, 125(June), 1–16.

Industrial Internet Insights Report (2015). Accenture. 2015. http://www.accenture.com/SiteCollectionDocuments/PDF/Accenture-Industrial-Internet-Changing-Competitive-Landscape-Industries.pdf. Accessed on February 3, 2017.

Info chimps (2013). Big Data & CIOs: What your IT team needs you to be aware of, Info chimps white paper, 2013.

Johnson, E. J. (2012). Big analytics+ Big opportunity+ Big data, Financial Executive, July/August, 50–53.

Kitchenham, B. (2004). Procedures and protocols for carrying out systematic evaluation and reviews. Technical Report TR/SE-0401, vol. 33, p. 28, Keele University, Keele.

Kitchenham & Charters. (2007). Guidelines and protocols for carrying out systematic literature reviews and assessment in software engineering version 2.3, Engineering, 45(4ve), 1051.

Lavalle, S., Lesser, E., Hopkins, M. S., Shockley, R., & Kruschwitz, N. (2011). Big Data, analytics and the path from insights to value. MIT Sloan Management Review, 52(2), 21.

Brown-Liburd, H., Lombardi, D, & Issa, H. (2015). Behavioral effects and implications of big data's effects on decision making, future research directions and audit judgment. Accounting Horizons, 29(2), 451–468.

Lukiæ. (2014) The impact and implication of information and communication technology (ICT) on relation-centered governance systems. Information Technology for Development, 11(2), 105–122. Doi: 10.1002/itdj.20010.

Marwick, A. (2014), How Your Data Are Being Greatly Mined. New York Books. http://www.nybooks.com/articles/archives/2014/jan/09/how-your-data-are-being-deeply-mined/. Accessed on December 8, 2016.

McAfee, A. et al. (2012). The management revolution: Big Data. Harvard Business Review, 90(10), 60–68.

McKinsey & Company, (2011). The next frontier for competition, productivity and innovation: Big Data. McKinsey Global Institute, Washington, DC, June, p. 156.

Probst, L. et al. (2013). Big Data – Decision Making & Analytics, European Commission, Case study. Retrieved from: https://www.researchgate.net/publication/319662103_The_Role_of_Big_Data_Analytics_in_Corporate_Decision-making

Puto, A., & Kościelniak, H. (2015). Big Data in the processes of decision making of enterprises, Procedia Computer Science, 65(ICCMIT), 1052–1058.

Rothleder, N., Kohavi, R., & Simoudis, E. (2002). Modern trends in business analytics. Communications, 4, 45–48.

Reddi, S. (2013). 4 ways and means in which Big Data will transform and change business, Available at: http://www.csc.com/big_data/publications/89362/964774_ways_big_data_will_transform_business. Accessed on February 21, 2016.

Schermann et al. (2014). An interdisciplinary opportunity and benefits for information systems research. Business and Information Systems Engineering, 6(5), 261–266.

See, S.L., & Way, F. (2015). Big Data Applications: Adaptive User Interfaces to Enhance and Maximize Managerial Decision Making, 3–5. Retrieved from: https://oar.a-star.edu.sg/storage/y/yqd5z5nxnn/icec-14.pdf

Sicular, S. (2013). Gartner's Big Data definition and explanation comprises of three parts, not to be confused and mistaken with three 'V's," Forbes 2013. http://www.forbes.com/sites/gartnergroup/2013/03/27/gartners-big-data-definition-consists-of-three-parts-not-to-be-confused-with-three-vs/. Accessed on December 8, 2016.

Travassos, G.H., & Mafra, S.N. (2006). Estudos Primários e Secundários apoiando a busca por Evidência em Engenharia de Software. Relatório Técnico RT- ES-687/06, Programa de Engenharia de Sistemas e Computação (PESC), COPPE/UFRJ.

Sinha, S.K., & Wegener, J.T. (2015). The value and significance of big data: How analytics differentiates and categorizes winners as a partner with Bain & Company in Atlanta, Global Technology practice.

Glenys, V. (2014). Business analytics in the age of big data. Business Strategy Review, 25(3), 8–9.

Venkatraman, S., & Henry, R. (2015). Big Data analytics, the next big learning benefit and opportunity. Journal of Management Information and Decision Sciences, 18(2), 17–30.

Xu, Z, et al. (2015). Effects and implications of traditional marketing analytics and big data analytics on modern product success: A knowledge fusion perspective. Journal of Business Research, http://dx.doi.org/10.1016/j.jbusres.2015.10.017

Ziora. (2015). The role and responsibility of big data solutions in the management of organizations, review of selected and chosen practical instances. Procedia Computer Science, 65(ICCMIT), 1006–1012.

3

Decision-Making Model for Medical Diagnosis Based on Some New Interval Neutrosophic Hamacher Power Choquet Integral Operators

Pankaj Kakati
Department of Mathematics, Jagannath Barooah College
Jorhat, India

Saifur Rahman
Department of Mathematics, Rajiv Gandhi University
Itanagar, India

CONTENTS

DOI: 10.1201/9781003307761-3

3.1 INTRODUCTION

The fuzzy set (FS) presented by Zadeh [1] copes with vague, conflicting data. Some of the useful extensions of FS for handling imprecision and uncertainty of information are intuitionistic FS (IFS) [2, 3], interval-valued IFS (IVIFS) [4], single-valued neutrosophic set (SVNS) [5], and the interval neutrosophic set (INS) [6]. Recently, the FS and its extensions are widely utilized to model several medical diagnosis processes [7–18].

It is observed that the data accessible to the clinical specialists during the medical diagnosis of the patients are often uncertain, incomplete, and inconsistent due to the constant variation of symptoms in some diseases. Therefore, uncertainty, incompleteness, and inconsistency must be taken into consideration in any medical diagnosis problems. To integrate undetermined and incompatible information, besides vague information, Smarandache [19] proposed the neutrosophic set (NS). The NS [19] is expressed by three self-governing membership grades, namely, the truth, indeterminacy, and falsity memberships. Wang et al. [5, 6] proposed the SVNS and the INS, which are the subcollections of an NS [19]. Ye [20] introduced the single-valued neutrosophic cross-entropy measure. The NS [19] and its extensions also have wide applications in clinical investigation problems. Ye [21] introduced the improved cosine similarity measures for the SVNS and the INS and utilized those for clinical analysis problems. Mondal and Pramanik [22] proposed the tangent similarity measure and the weighted tangent similarity measure for an SVNS and utilized those for clinical diagnosis. However, in some clinical diagnosis problems, indicators and inspection information of several diseases may vary at different time intervals. In such situations, INS [6] is more preferable to SVNS [5] for expressing the diagnosis data.

Aggregation operators have played an important role in clinical diagnosis. Broumi et al. [23] proposed the N-valued INS and studied its application in clinical diagnosis. Ahn et al. [24] applied the interval-valued intuitionistic fuzzy weighted arithmetic average operator to model a medical diagnosis process of headache. Hu et al. [25] established a multicriteria group decision-making (MCGDM) model by utilizing the similarity measure of intuitionistic fuzzy soft sets (IFSS) and the weighted intuitionistic fuzzy soft Bonferroni mean for medical diagnosis. Ngan et al. [26] developed an approach for the clinical diagnosis of X-ray pictures based on aggregation operators. Accuracy is very essential for decision-making during the medical diagnosis process of diseases based on the information from the symptoms. The weighted aggregation operators [27–31] often deal with situations where attributes of the problem are independent of one another. However, during decision-making in a medical diagnosis process, the attributes representing the symptoms of a disease are often interrelated. The Choquet integral (CI) [32] based on the fuzzy measure [33] is an influential aid for expressing correlation between the attributes and it can also provide a robust decision even from limited information. Recently, several decision-making methods [34–39] are developed based on the CI [32] operators under the neutrosophic environment. Trabelsi et al. [40] developed a breast cancer detection system based on the CI [32] for feature selection.

Many conventional aggregation operators don't reflect correlations among the input arguments. Yager [41] proposed some power averaging operators such as the power average (PA) and the power ordered weighted average (POWA) operators, where the weighting vector depends on the input arguments. It has been observed that power averaging operators [41] can allow the aggregated values to boost and strengthen one another. Xu and Yager [42] introduced some geometric power aggregation operators. Zhou and Chen [43] introduced the generalization of the power average operator [41]. Recently, several MCGDM methods [44–46] are proposed based on the power average operator (PAO) [41]. Yang and Li [47] proposed some neutrosophic power average aggregation and developed an MCGDM method. Liu and Tang [48] proposed several generalized power aggregation operators under the interval neutrosophic environment. Peng et al. [49] introduced some new aggregation operators by combining the PAO [41] with the Shapley function-based CI [32] under the SVNS.

Big data analytics is a procedure of investigating large data to reveal hidden information about patterns, relationships, market tendencies, client preferences, etc. Big data analytics can help establishments to take well-versed business decisions. Big data analytics is used for decision-making in numerous areas such as information technology, healthcare, public security, graph mining, social network analysis, health analytics, and medical diagnosis analysis. Raghupathi and Raghupathi [50] provide a review on huge data analysis in the medical sector by describing the capacity and possibility of huge data analysis in medical services. Belle et al. [51] studied three optimistic areas of huge data analysis in medical services such as *Image processing*, *Signal processing*, and *Genomics*. Sun and Reddy [52] discussed the features and associated obstacles in data analysis with big medical data. Mehta and Pandit [53] provided a methodical investigation of the opportunities of large medical data with its applications and challenges. Archenaa and Anita [54] provided an observation of the efficiency of Hadoop on large medical and government data. Chaudhary et al. [55] studied consumer behavior toward social media using big data analytics. Alam [56] introduced the concept of cloud algebra for the cloud-based data management system. Kaur and Alam [57] described the importance of knowledge engineering for the development of a hybrid knowledge-based medical system. Alam and Shakil [58] introduced a background for infrastructural development in a cloud-built system. Alam and Sethi [59] discussed several situations for recognition of probable covert channels and prevent the strikes. Shakil and Alam [60] proposed an approach defining k medians in cloud data management. Alam et al. [61] proposed a five-layered framework for a cloud-based data management scheme. Shakil et al. [62] introduced an efficient environment for accomplishing university information utilizing a cloud environment. Khan et al. [63] proposed a framework that can manage big data in a cloud-based system. Alam et al. [64] studied big data analytics in a cloud system using Hadoop. Kumar et al. [65] introduced an entirely homomorphic encryption system for improved protection in cloud-based computation. Malhotra et al. [66] introduced a method for converting relational database management system (RDBMS) queries into map-reduced codes. Shakil and Alam [67] discussed cloud computing for bioinformatics researchers. Malhotra et al. [68] analyzed big data system architecture and provided a comparison of various big data analytic approaches. Khan et al. [69] introduced a big data analytics tool for the education sector that uses cloud-based technologies. Khan et al. [70] demonstrated the usage of outcome perspective to calculate superiority metrics and generate visual analysis. Khan et al. [71] provided surveys on big data and discussed the data analysis procedure for large data. Shakil et al. [72] provided a prediction model for diseases like dengue with the data mining tool Weka. Shakil et al. [73] proposed a cloud-based system BAM Health Cloud for the management of healthcare data. Khan et al. [74] introduced a scheme to investigate the large data of Twitter. Ali et al. [75] presented a survey on the causes and difficulties related to the massive energy digestion by cloud data sources and formulate a classification of massive energy digestion issues and their associated remedies.

MCGDM can contribute significantly to the healthcare industry with big data to recognize the entire assessment procedure by presenting a decision aid [76]. Palomares et al. [77] introduced an MCGDM model using the fuzzy aggregation functions for data analytics studies in the research areas of web safety and the insider risk problem. Ullah and Noor-E-Alam [78] presented a fuzzy MCGDM method for decision-making under the graphical information generated from big data. Thus, MCGDM in healthcare with big medical data has a huge possibility of enhancement of the standard of medical care, dropping leftover and fault, and minimizing the cost of maintenance.

The medical diagnosis problem is rather complex than many other assessment problems. Therefore, it becomes indispensable to express the patient's diagnosis report from the symptoms appropriately and analyze them accurately. For this purpose, (1) the information about a disease obtained from symptoms can be expressed using INNs; (2) in most of the cases, there will be correlations among symptoms, and then the CI [32] can be utilized to deal with such situation; and (3) also ignoring the relationship among different symptoms may lead to an abnormal impact on the final diagnostic result. To reduce such abnormality of choices, the PA [41] can be combined with the CI [32] operator to propose a new power CI operator for aggregating information from the symptoms of diseases. MCGDM methods are extensively applied in various fields such as transportation, migration, education assessment, investment, data analytics, energy, defense, etc. But the development of MCGDM methods is relatively slow in the healthcare sector. Medical diagnosis is an integral part of healthcare. The complexity of MCGDM in medical diagnosis increases if the patients belong to a big data sample. Especially, during a pandemic situation when medical resources are limited, it becomes essential to provide immediate treatment to the most serious patient, so it is necessary to provide an appropriate decision-making tool such as the aggregation operator. The introduction of an adequate aggregation operator for decision-making in clinical diagnosis depends on the symptoms of diseases. If symptoms of a disease are interrelated, then CI-based aggregation operators are considered more useful as compared to weighted aggregation operators. Also, ignoring the connection between various symptoms might lead to an anomalous influence on the medical diagnosis report. Such anomaly in medical diagnosis can be overcome by combining the PA [41] with the CI [32] operator. This motivates us to propose interval neutrosophic Hamacher power CI (INHPCI) and interval neutrosophic Hamacher power geometric CI (INHPGCI) operators by combining the PA [41] with the CI [32] as an MCGDM tool for aggregating diagnosis information with correlated symptoms of diseases.

The main goal and the contribution of the present study are as follows:

1. To represent the symptoms of diseases in terms of INNs.
2. To introduce two new Choquet-based PAO which deal with the correlation among the symptoms.

3. To develop an MCGDM method using the proposed INHPCI, and INHPGCI operators for decision-making in the medical diagnosis process.
4. To establish the efficiency of the proposed MCGDM model in medical diagnosis by an illustrative example.

The present study can contribute significantly toward complex decision-making procedures in the healthcare sector owing to the influence of the proposed INHPCI and the INHPGCI operators even if the symptoms of the diseases are correlated. The proposed MCGDM method can also contribute to various healthcare sectors such as the selection of medical equipment, X-ray diagnosis, cardiology, and cancer patient's diagnosis, optical disease detection, dental care, etc. The proposed method is expected to be more effective for MCGDM in medical diagnosis for big medical data.

The remaining of our study appears as follows. Certain fundamental concepts and notions have been discussed in Section 3.3.2 and proposed INHPCI, and INHPGCI operators with their desired properties are discussed in Section 3.3.3. An MCGDM model established using the proposed operators for the medical diagnosis of diseases under the interval neutrosophic environment is discussed in Section 3.4. Section 3.5 presents an exemplifying instance to validate the proposed model. The last section contains the final remarks and some future research directions.

3.2 PREREQUISITE

Here, we briefly describe several applicable concepts and notions from the prevailing literary works essential for the progression of the present work.

3.2.1 SVNSs and INSs

The SVNS [5] is defined as follows: Let X be a space of points (objects), and let x be a generic element in X. A single-valued neutrosophic set (SVNS) A in X is an object

$$A = \left\{ \left\langle x, T_A(x), I_A(x), F_A(x) \right\rangle \mid x \in X \right\}$$

where $T_A : X \to [0,1]$ is the truth-membership function, $I_A : X \to [0,1]$ is the indeterminacy-membership function, and $F_A : X \to [0,1]$ is the falsity-membership function. Thus, for each point x in X, we have $0 \leq T_A(x) + I_A(x) + F_A(x) \leq 3$.

As an extension of SVNS, an INS is defined [6] by an object

$$A = \left\{ \left\langle x, \tilde{T}_A(x), \tilde{I}_A(x), \tilde{F}_A(x) \right\rangle \mid x \in X \right\}$$

where $\tilde{T}_A$ is the truth-membership function, $\tilde{I}_A$ is the indeterminacy membership function, and $\tilde{F}_A$ is the falsity-membership function such that for each point x in X, we have that $\tilde{T}_A(x) \subset [0,1], \tilde{I}_A(x) \subset [0,1], \tilde{F}_A(x) \subset [0,1]$.

An INS [6] can provide a value that ranges for the truth, indeterminacy, and falsity rather than single values for each of these quantities. As a particular case of INS, INN has defined as an object $\tilde{\alpha}$ given by the expression $\tilde{\alpha} = \langle [T_{\tilde{\alpha}}^L, T_{\tilde{\alpha}}^U], [I_{\tilde{\alpha}}^L, I_{\tilde{\alpha}}^U], [F_{\tilde{\alpha}}^L, F_{\tilde{\alpha}}^U] \rangle$, where each component of $\tilde{\alpha}$ is an interval number.

3.2.2 The Score, Accuracy, and Certainty Functions of INNs

Sahin [79] proposed a novel score and accuracy functions for the ranking of interval neutrosophic numbers (INNs) and are given as follows:

For an INN $\tilde{\beta} = \langle [T_{\tilde{\beta}}^L, T_{\tilde{\beta}}^U], [I_{\tilde{\beta}}^L, I_{\tilde{\beta}}^U], [F_{\tilde{\beta}}^L, F_{\tilde{\beta}}^U] \rangle$, the score $S(\tilde{\beta})$ and the accuracy $A(\tilde{\beta})$ functions of $\tilde{\beta}$ are, respectively, defined as follows:

$$S(\tilde{\beta}) = \frac{2 + \left(T_{\tilde{\beta}}^L + T_{\tilde{\beta}}^U\right) - 2\left(I_{\tilde{\beta}}^L + I_{\tilde{\beta}}^U\right) - \left(F_{\tilde{\beta}}^L + F_{\tilde{\beta}}^U\right)}{4} \tag{3.1}$$

where $S(\tilde{\beta}) \in [-1, 1]$.

$$A(\tilde{\beta}) = \frac{\left(T_{\tilde{\beta}}^L + T_{\tilde{\beta}}^U\right) - I_{\tilde{\beta}}^U\left(1 - T_{\tilde{\beta}}^U\right) - I_{\tilde{\beta}}^L\left(1 - T_{\tilde{\beta}}^L\right) - F_{\tilde{\beta}}^U\left(1 - I_{\tilde{\beta}}^L\right) - F_{\tilde{\beta}}^L\left(1 - I_{\tilde{\beta}}^U\right)}{2} \tag{3.2}$$

where $A(\tilde{\beta}) \in [-1, 1]$.

We note that if $S(\tilde{u}) > S(\tilde{v})$, then $\tilde{u} \succ \tilde{v}$ and if $S(\tilde{u}) = S(\tilde{v})$ and $A(\tilde{u}) > A(\tilde{v})$, then $\tilde{u} \succ \tilde{v}$ where $\tilde{u}$ and $\tilde{v}$ are INNs. For more details about possibility degree and comparison for INNs, the readers are referring to Zhang et al. [80]

The possibility degree $P(\tilde{u} \geq \tilde{v})$ [31] of interval numbers $\tilde{u} = [u^L, u^U]$ and $\tilde{v} = [v^L, v^U]$ is given as

$$P(\tilde{u} \geq \tilde{v}) = \max\left\{1 - \max\left\{\frac{v^U - u^L}{u^U - u^L + v^U - v^L}, 0\right\}, 0\right\}. \tag{3.3}$$

3.2.3 Hamacher Operations

Hamacher proposed the Hamacher operations [81], which contain Hamacher product $\otimes_H$ and Hamacher sum $\oplus_H$ and are given by

$$T_\gamma(\alpha,\beta) = \alpha \otimes_H \beta = \frac{\alpha\beta}{\gamma + (1-\gamma)(\alpha+\beta-\alpha\beta)}, \gamma > 0 \qquad (3.4)$$

$$S_\gamma(\alpha,\beta) = \alpha \oplus_H \beta = \frac{\alpha+\beta-\alpha\beta-(1-\gamma)\alpha\beta}{1-(1-\gamma)\alpha\beta}, \gamma > 0 \qquad (3.5)$$

when $\gamma=1$ the Hamacher product $\otimes_H$ and Hamacher sum $\oplus_H$ reduce to algebraic product and sum, respectively as

$$T_1(\alpha,\beta) = \alpha\beta \qquad (3.6)$$

$$S_1(\alpha,\beta) = \alpha+\beta-\alpha\beta \qquad (3.7)$$

And if $\gamma=2$, the Hamacher product $\otimes_H$ and Hamacher sum $\oplus_H$ reduce to the Einstein t-norm and t-conorm, respectively, as

$$T_2(\alpha,\beta) = \frac{\alpha\beta}{1+(1-\alpha)(1-\beta)} \qquad (3.8)$$

$$S_2(\alpha,\beta) = \frac{\alpha+\beta}{1+\alpha\beta} \qquad (3.9)$$

Some additive generators [82] for various t-norms and t-conorms with conditions, and based on which additive generators of Hamacher t-norm, and t-conorm [83] are given in Table 3.1.

TABLE 3.1

Additive Generators of Hamacher t-norm and t-conorm

Hamacher	t-Norm/t-Conorm	Additive Generator
t-norm	$T(\alpha,\beta) = \dfrac{\alpha\beta}{\gamma+(1-\gamma)(\alpha+\beta-\alpha\beta)}$	$f(u) = \ln\dfrac{\gamma+(1-\gamma)u}{u}, \gamma > 0;$ $f^{-1}(u) = \dfrac{\gamma}{e^u+\gamma-1}$
t-conorm	$S(\alpha,\beta) = \dfrac{\alpha+\beta-\alpha\beta-(1-\gamma)\alpha\beta}{1-(1-\gamma)\alpha\beta}$	$g(u) = \ln\dfrac{\gamma+(1-\gamma)(1-u)}{1-u}, \gamma > 0;$ $g^{-1}(u) = \dfrac{e^u-1}{e^u+\gamma-1}, \gamma > 0$

3.2.4 The Power Average (PA) Operators

A mapping [41] $PA : R^n \rightarrow R$ defined by

$$PA(\beta_1, \beta_2, \ldots, \beta_n) = \frac{\sum_{i=1}^{n} (1 + T(\beta_i)) \beta_i}{\sum_{i=1}^{n} (1 + T(\beta_i))}$$

is called PA operator, where $T(\beta_i) = \sum_{\substack{j=1 \\ j \neq i}}^{n} Supp(\beta_i, \beta_j)$ and $Supp(\beta_i, \beta_j)$ is the support of β_i from β_j, and $Supp(\beta_i, \beta_j)$ satisfies the following properties:

   i. $Supp(\beta_i, \beta_j) \in [0,1]$,
   ii. $Supp(\beta_i, \beta_j) = Supp(\beta_j, \beta_i)$
   iii. If $|\beta_i - \beta_j| < |\beta_s - \beta_t|$ then $Supp(\beta_i, \beta_j) \geq Supp(\beta_s, \beta_t)$

Similarly, the power geometric (PG) operator [42] is defined by

$$PG(\beta_1, \beta_2, \ldots, \beta_n) = \prod_{i=1}^{n} \beta_i^{\frac{1+T(\beta_i)}{\sum_{i=1}^{n}(1+T(\beta_i))}}, \text{ where } T(\beta_i) = \sum_{\substack{j=1 \\ j \neq i}}^{n} Supp(\beta_i, \beta_j).$$

3.2.5 The Choquet Integral

Definition 3.1: [33] A λ-fuzzy measure $m : P(X) \rightarrow [0,1]$, where $X = \{x_1, x_2, \ldots, x_n\}$ is a finite set of criteria satisfies the following properties:

   i. $m(\phi) = 0, m(X) = 1$
   ii. if $A \subseteq B \subseteq X$, then $m(A) \leq m(B)$
   iii. $m(A \cup B) = m(A) + m(B) + \lambda m(A) m(B)$,
      $\lambda \in (-1, +\infty), \forall A, B \in P(X)$ and $A \cap B = \phi$

The condition (iii) reduces to the axiom of additive measure for $\lambda = 0$:

$$m(A \cup B) = m(A) + m(B), \forall A, B \subseteq X \text{ and } A \cap B = \phi. \tag{3.10}$$

If the elements in X are independent, then

$$m(A) = \sum_{x_i \in A} m(\{x_i\}). \tag{3.11}$$

If $\lambda > 0$ then $\{A, B\}$ has a multiplicative effect and if $\lambda < 0$ then has $\{A, B\}$ a substitutive effect. The interaction between sets or elements of the set can be represented by the parameter λ.

A normalized measure was introduced by Sugeno [33], which can be defined as follows:

$$m(X) = \begin{cases} \dfrac{1}{\lambda}\left(\prod_{i=1}^{n}[1 + \lambda m(x_i)] - 1\right), & \text{if } \lambda \neq 0, \\[3mm] \displaystyle\sum_{i=1}^{n} m(x_i), & \text{if } \lambda = 0 \end{cases} \tag{3.12}$$

If $A \subseteq X$, then

$$m(A) = \begin{cases} \dfrac{1}{\lambda}\left(\prod[1 + \lambda m(x_i)] - 1\right), & \text{if } \lambda \neq 0, \\[3mm] \displaystyle\sum_{i=1}^{n} m(x_i), & \text{if } \lambda = 0. \end{cases} \tag{3.13}$$

Together with Equation (3.12) and the condition $m(X) = 1$, λ can be uniquely determined, which is equivalent to solving the Equation (3.14).

$$\lambda + 1 = \sum_{i=1}^{n}(1 + \lambda m(x_i)). \tag{3.14}$$

The CI [84] based on the fuzzy measure is given as follows:

If f is a positive real-valued function on $X = \{x_1, x_2, \ldots, x_n\}$, and m is a fuzzy measure on X. The discrete CI of f with respect to m, denoted by $C_m(f)$, is defined by the following equation:

$$C_m(f) = \sum_{i=1}^{n} f(x_{(i)})(m(B_{(i)}) - m(B_{(i-1)})), \tag{3.15}$$

here $(\cdot)$ indicates a permutation on X such that $f(x_{(1)}) \geq f(x_{(2)}) \geq \ldots \geq f(x_{(n)})$, with $B_{(i)} = \{x_{(1)}, x_{(2)}, \ldots, x_{(i)}\}$ for $i \geq 1$ and $B_{(0)} = \phi$.

The interval neutrosophic numbers Choquet integral (INNCI) operator [35] for an INN function $f : X \rightarrow L$ on X with respect to a fuzzy measure m on X is given by the following equation:

$$\int f \, dm = \sum_{i=1}^{n} f(x_{(i)})(m(X_{(i)}) - m(X_{(i-1)})), \qquad (3.16)$$

where the notations are defined above.

3.3 SOME INTERVAL NEUTROSOPHIC HAMACHER POWER CHOQUET INTEGRAL OPERATORS

This section introduces some Hamacher operational rules on INNs and proposes some new INHPCI operators for MCGDM in medical diagnosis problems from the information obtained from the symptoms of diseases under the interval neutrosophic environment.

3.3.1 Hamacher Operations on INNs

Based on Hamacher operational rules on SVNNs [85], and IVIFNs [86], some Hamacher operational rules on the INNs are discussed here.

Definition 3.2: If $\tilde{\alpha}$ and $\tilde{\beta}$ are INNs, then for $\gamma, k > 0$, the following rules hold:

i. $\tilde{\alpha} \oplus_H \tilde{\beta} = \left\{ \left[\dfrac{T_{\tilde{\alpha}}^L + T_{\tilde{\beta}}^L - T_{\tilde{\alpha}}^L T_{\tilde{\beta}}^L - (1-\gamma)T_{\tilde{\alpha}}^L T_{\tilde{\beta}}^L}{1 - (1-\gamma)T_{\tilde{\alpha}}^L T_{\tilde{\beta}}^L}, \dfrac{T_{\tilde{\alpha}}^U + T_{\tilde{\beta}}^U - T_{\tilde{\alpha}}^U T_{\tilde{\beta}}^U - (1-\gamma)T_{\tilde{\alpha}}^U T_{\tilde{\beta}}^U}{1 - (1-\gamma)T_{\tilde{\alpha}}^U T_{\tilde{\beta}}^U} \right], \right.$

$\left[\dfrac{I_{\tilde{\alpha}}^L I_{\tilde{\beta}}^L}{\gamma + (1-\gamma)(I_{\tilde{\alpha}}^L + I_{\tilde{\beta}}^L - I_{\tilde{\alpha}}^L I_{\tilde{\beta}}^L)}, \dfrac{I_{\tilde{\alpha}}^U I_{\tilde{\beta}}^U}{\gamma + (1-\gamma)(I_{\tilde{\alpha}}^U + I_{\tilde{\beta}}^U - I_{\tilde{\alpha}}^U I_{\tilde{\beta}}^U)} \right],$

$\left. \left[\dfrac{F_{\tilde{\alpha}}^L F_{\tilde{\beta}}^L}{\gamma + (1-\gamma)(F_{\tilde{\alpha}}^L + F_{\tilde{\beta}}^L - F_{\tilde{\alpha}}^L F_{\tilde{\beta}}^L)}, \dfrac{F_{\tilde{\alpha}}^U F_{\tilde{\beta}}^U}{\gamma + (1-\gamma)(F_{\tilde{\alpha}}^U + F_{\tilde{\beta}}^U - F_{\tilde{\alpha}}^U F_{\tilde{\beta}}^U)} \right] \right\}.$

ii. $\tilde{\alpha} \oplus_H \tilde{\beta} = \left\{ \left[\dfrac{T_{\tilde{\alpha}}^L T_{\tilde{\beta}}^L}{\gamma + (1-\gamma)\left(T_{\tilde{\alpha}}^L + T_{\tilde{\beta}}^L - T_{\tilde{\alpha}}^L T_{\tilde{\beta}}^L\right)}, \dfrac{T_{\tilde{\alpha}}^U T_{\tilde{\beta}}^U}{\gamma + (1-\gamma)\left(T_{\tilde{\alpha}}^U + T_{\tilde{\beta}}^U - T_{\tilde{\alpha}}^U T_{\tilde{\beta}}^U\right)} \right], \right.$

$\left[\dfrac{I_{\tilde{\alpha}}^L + I_{\tilde{\beta}}^L - I_{\tilde{\alpha}}^L I_{\tilde{\beta}}^L - (1-\gamma)I_{\tilde{\alpha}}^L I_{\tilde{\beta}}^L}{1 - (1-\gamma)I_{\tilde{\alpha}}^L I_{\tilde{\beta}}^L}, \dfrac{I_{\tilde{\alpha}}^U + I_{\tilde{\beta}}^U - I_{\tilde{\alpha}}^U I_{\tilde{\beta}}^U - (1-\gamma)I_{\tilde{\alpha}}^U I_{\tilde{\beta}}^U}{1 - (1-\gamma)I_{\tilde{\alpha}}^U I_{\tilde{\beta}}^U} \right],$

$\left. \left[\dfrac{F_{\tilde{\alpha}}^L + F_{\tilde{\beta}}^L - F_{\tilde{\alpha}}^L F_{\tilde{\beta}}^L - (1-\gamma)F_{\tilde{\alpha}}^L F_{\tilde{\beta}}^L}{1 - (1-\gamma)F_{\tilde{\alpha}}^L F_{\tilde{\beta}}^L}, \dfrac{F_{\tilde{\alpha}}^U + F_{\tilde{\beta}}^U - F_{\tilde{\alpha}}^U F_{\tilde{\beta}}^U - (1-\gamma)F_{\tilde{\alpha}}^U F_{\tilde{\beta}}^U}{1 - (1-\gamma)F_{\tilde{\alpha}}^U F_{\tilde{\beta}}^U} \right] \right\}.$

iii. $k\tilde{\alpha} = \left\{ \left[\dfrac{\left(1+(\gamma-1)T_{\tilde{\alpha}}^L\right)^k - \left(1-T_{\tilde{\alpha}}^L\right)^k}{\left(1+(\gamma-1)T_{\tilde{\alpha}}^L\right)^k + (\gamma-1)\left(1-T_{\tilde{\alpha}}^L\right)^k}, \dfrac{\left(1+(\gamma-1)T_{\tilde{\alpha}}^U\right)^k - \left(1-T_{\tilde{\alpha}}^U\right)^k}{\left(1+(\gamma-1)T_{\tilde{\alpha}}^U\right)^k + (\gamma-1)\left(1-T_{\tilde{\alpha}}^U\right)^k} \right], \right.$

$\left[\dfrac{\gamma\left(I_{\tilde{\alpha}}^L\right)^k}{\left(1+(\gamma-1)\left(1-I_{\tilde{\alpha}}^L\right)\right)^k + (\gamma-1)\left(I_{\tilde{\alpha}}^L\right)^k}, \dfrac{\gamma\left(I_{\tilde{\alpha}}^U\right)^k}{\left(1+(\gamma-1)\left(1-I_{\tilde{\alpha}}^U\right)\right)^k + (\gamma-1)\left(I_{\tilde{\alpha}}^U\right)^k} \right],$

$\left. \left[\dfrac{\gamma\left(F_{\tilde{\alpha}}^L\right)^k}{\left(1+(\gamma-1)\left(1-F_{\tilde{\alpha}}^L\right)\right)^k + (\gamma-1)\left(F_{\tilde{\alpha}}^L\right)^k}, \dfrac{\gamma\left(F_{\tilde{\alpha}}^U\right)^k}{\left(1+(\gamma-1)\left(1-F_{\tilde{\alpha}}^U\right)\right)^k + (\gamma-1)\left(F_{\tilde{\alpha}}^U\right)^k} \right] \right\}$

iv. $\tilde{\alpha}^k = \left\{ \left[\dfrac{\gamma\left(T_{\tilde{\alpha}}^L\right)^k}{\left(1+(\gamma-1)\left(1-T_{\tilde{\alpha}}^L\right)\right)^k + (\gamma-1)\left(T_{\tilde{\alpha}}^L\right)^k}, \dfrac{\gamma\left(T_{\tilde{\alpha}}^U\right)^k}{\left(1+(\gamma-1)\left(1-T_{\tilde{\alpha}}^U\right)\right)^k + (\gamma-1)\left(T_{\tilde{\alpha}}^U\right)^k} \right], \right.$

$\left[\dfrac{\left(1+(\gamma-1)I_{\tilde{\alpha}}^L\right)^k - \left(1-I_{\tilde{\alpha}}^L\right)^k}{\left(1+(\gamma-1)I_{\tilde{\alpha}}^L\right)^k + (\gamma-1)\left(1-I_{\tilde{\alpha}}^L\right)^k}, \dfrac{\left(1+(\gamma-1)I_{\tilde{\alpha}}^U\right)^k - \left(1-I_{\tilde{\alpha}}^U\right)^k}{\left(1+(\gamma-1)I_{\tilde{\alpha}}^U\right)^k + (\gamma-1)\left(1-I_{\tilde{\alpha}}^U\right)^k} \right],$

$\left. \left[\dfrac{\left(1+(\gamma-1)F_{\tilde{\alpha}}^L\right)^k - \left(1-F_{\tilde{\alpha}}^L\right)^k}{\left(1+(\gamma-1)F_{\tilde{\alpha}}^L\right)^k + (\gamma-1)\left(1-F_{\tilde{\alpha}}^L\right)^k}, \dfrac{\left(1+(\gamma-1)F_{\tilde{\alpha}}^U\right)^k - \left(1-F_{\tilde{\alpha}}^U\right)^k}{\left(1+(\gamma-1)F_{\tilde{\alpha}}^U\right)^k + (\gamma-1)\left(1-F_{\tilde{\alpha}}^U\right)^k} \right] \right\}.$

Based on the additive generators [82] the Hamacher operational rules of INNs in Definition **3.2** can also be expressed as follows:

i. $\tilde{\alpha} \oplus_H \tilde{\beta} = \left\{ \left[g^{-1}\left(g\left(T_{\tilde{\alpha}}^L\right)+g\left(T_{\tilde{\beta}}^L\right)\right), g^{-1}\left(g\left(T_{\tilde{\alpha}}^U\right)+g\left(T_{\tilde{\beta}}^U\right)\right) \right], \right.$

$$\left[f^{-1}\left(f\left(I_{\tilde{\alpha}}^L\right)+f\left(I_{\tilde{\beta}}^L\right)\right), f^{-1}\left(f\left(I_{\tilde{\alpha}}^U\right)+f\left(I_{\tilde{\beta}}^U\right)\right) \right],$$

$$\left. \left[f^{-1}\left(f\left(F_{\tilde{\alpha}}^L\right)+f\left(F_{\tilde{\beta}}^L\right)\right), f^{-1}\left(f\left(F_{\tilde{\alpha}}^U\right)+f\left(F_{\tilde{\beta}}^U\right)\right) \right] \right\}.$$

ii. $\tilde{\alpha} \oplus_H \tilde{\beta} = \left\{ \left[f^{-1}\left(f\left(T_{\tilde{\alpha}}^L\right)+f\left(T_{\tilde{\beta}}^L\right)\right), f^{-1}\left(f\left(T_{\tilde{\alpha}}^U\right)+f\left(T_{\tilde{\beta}}^U\right)\right) \right], \right.$

$$\left[g^{-1}\left(g\left(I_{\tilde{\alpha}}^L\right)+g\left(I_{\tilde{\beta}}^L\right)\right), g^{-1}\left(g\left(I_{\tilde{\alpha}}^U\right)+g\left(I_{\tilde{\beta}}^U\right)\right) \right],$$

$$\left. \left[g^{-1}\left(g\left(F_{\tilde{\alpha}}^L\right)+g\left(F_{\tilde{\beta}}^L\right)\right), g^{-1}\left(g\left(F_{\tilde{\alpha}}^U\right)+g\left(F_{\tilde{\beta}}^U\right)\right) \right] \right\}.$$

iii. $k\tilde{\alpha} = \left\{ \left[g^{-1}\left(kg\left(T_{\tilde{\alpha}}^L\right)\right), \ g^{-1}\left(kg\left(T_{\tilde{\alpha}}^U\right)\right) \right], \right.$

$$\left[f^{-1}\left(kf\left(I_{\tilde{\alpha}}^L\right)\right), \ f^{-1}\left(kf\left(I_{\tilde{\alpha}}^U\right)\right) \right],$$

$$\left. \left[f^{-1}\left(kf\left(F_{\tilde{\alpha}}^L\right)\right), \ f^{-1}\left(kf\left(F_{\tilde{\alpha}}^U\right)\right) \right] \right\}.$$

iv. $\tilde{\alpha}^k = \left\{ \left[f^{-1}\left(kf\left(T_{\tilde{\alpha}}^L\right)\right), \ f^{-1}\left(kf\left(T_{\tilde{\alpha}}^U\right)\right) \right], \right.$

$$\left[g^{-1}\left(kg\left(I_{\tilde{\alpha}}^L\right)\right), \ g^{-1}\left(kg\left(I_{\tilde{\alpha}}^U\right)\right) \right],$$

$$\left. \left[g^{-1}\left(kg\left(F_{\tilde{\alpha}}^L\right)\right), \ g^{-1}\left(kg\left(F_{\tilde{\alpha}}^U\right)\right) \right] \right\}.$$

3.3.2 The INHPCI and INHPGCI Operators

This subsection proposes the INHPCI and the INHPGCI and discusses their properties.

Definition 3.3: If m is a fuzzy measure on a finite set X and $\tilde{\beta}_j = \{[T_{\tilde{\beta}_j}^L, T_{\tilde{\beta}_j}^U], [I_{\tilde{\beta}_j}^L, I_{\tilde{\beta}_j}^U], [F_{\tilde{\beta}_j}^L, F_{\tilde{\beta}_j}^U]\}$ $(j = 1, 2, \ldots, n)$ are INNs on X, then the INHPCI can be defined as follows:

$$\text{INHPCI}\left(\tilde{\beta}_1, \tilde{\beta}_2, \ldots, \tilde{\beta}_n\right) = \frac{\overset{n}{\underset{j=1}{\oplus}}_H \left(m\left(B_{(j)}\right) - m\left(B_{(j-1)}\right)\right)\left(1 + V\left(\tilde{\beta}_{(j)}\right)\right)\tilde{\beta}_{(j)}}{\sum\limits_{j=1}^{n}\left(m\left(B_{(j)}\right) - m\left(B_{(j-1)}\right)\right)\left(1 + V\left(\tilde{\beta}_{(j)}\right)\right)} \tag{3.17}$$

where $(\cdot)$ indicates a permutation on $\{1, 2, 3, \ldots, n\}$ with $\tilde{\beta}_{(1)} \succ \tilde{\beta}_{(2)} \succ \cdots \succ \tilde{\beta}_{(n)}$ and $B_{(j)} = \{(1), (2), \ldots, (j)\}$, with the convention $B_{(0)} = \phi$, and $\oplus_H$ denotes the Hamacher sum of INNs given by (i) in Definition **3.2**

It is worthy to mention here that $V(\tilde{\beta}_{(i)}) = \sum_{\substack{j=1 \\ j \neq i}}^{n}(m(B_{(j)}) - m(B_{(j-1)}))$ $Supp(\tilde{\beta}_{(i)}, \tilde{\beta}_{(j)})$, where $Supp(\tilde{\beta}_{(i)}, \tilde{\beta}_{(j)})$ denotes the support of $\tilde{\beta}_{(i)}$ from $\tilde{\beta}_{(j)}$ and having the following mentioned properties:

  i. $Supp(\tilde{\beta}_{(i)}, \tilde{\beta}_{(j)}) \in [0,1]$,
  ii. $Supp(\tilde{\beta}_{(i)}, \tilde{\beta}_{(j)}) = Supp(\tilde{\beta}_{(j)}, \tilde{\beta}_{(i)})$,
  iii. $Supp(\tilde{\beta}_{(i)}, \tilde{\beta}_{(j)}) \geq Supp(\tilde{\beta}_{(s)}, \tilde{\beta}_{(t)})$ if $d(\tilde{\beta}_{(i)}, \tilde{\beta}_{(j)}) < d(\tilde{\beta}_{(s)}, \tilde{\beta}_{(t)})$,

where d denotes the Hamming distance [87] of INNs.

Theorem 3.1: *If* $\tilde{\beta}_j = \{[T_{\tilde{\beta}_j}^L, T_{\tilde{\beta}_j}^U], [I_{\tilde{\beta}_j}^L, I_{\tilde{\beta}_j}^U], [F_{\tilde{\beta}_j}^L, F_{\tilde{\beta}_j}^U]\}$ $(j = 1, 2, \ldots, n)$ *are INNs on a finite set* X, *then for a fuzzy measure* m *on* X, *the* INHPCI *can be expressed as*

$$\text{INHPCI}\left(\tilde{\beta}_1, \tilde{\beta}_2, \ldots, \tilde{\beta}_n\right) = \left\{\left[\left[g^{-1}\left(\frac{\sum\limits_{j=1}^{n}\left(m\left(B_{(j)}\right) - m\left(B_{(j-1)}\right)\right)\left(1 + V\left(\tilde{\beta}_{(j)}\right)\right)g\left(T_{\tilde{\beta}_j}^L\right)}{\sum\limits_{j=1}^{n}\left(m\left(B_{(j)}\right) - m\left(B_{(j-1)}\right)\right)\left(1 + V\left(\tilde{\beta}_{(j)}\right)\right)}\right),\right.\right.$$

$$\left.\left.g^{-1}\left(\frac{\sum\limits_{j=1}^{n}\left(m\left(B_{(j)}\right) - m\left(B_{(j-1)}\right)\right)\left(1 + V\left(\tilde{\beta}_{(j)}\right)\right)g\left(T_{\tilde{\beta}_j}^U\right)}{\sum\limits_{j=1}^{n}\left(m\left(B_{(j)}\right) - m\left(B_{(j-1)}\right)\right)\left(1 + V\left(\tilde{\beta}_{(j)}\right)\right)}\right)\right]\right],$$

$$
\left[
\left(
f^{-1}\left[
\frac{\sum_{j=1}^{n}\left(m\left(B_{(j)}\right)-m\left(B_{(j-1)}\right)\right)\left(1+V\left(\tilde{\beta}_{(j)}\right)\right)f\left(I_{\tilde{\beta}_j}^{L}\right)}{\sum_{j=1}^{n}\left(m\left(B_{(j)}\right)-m\left(B_{(j-1)}\right)\right)\left(1+V\left(\tilde{\beta}_{(j)}\right)\right)}
\right],\right.
\right.
$$

$$
\left.
f^{-1}\left[
\frac{\sum_{j=1}^{n}\left(m\left(B_{(j)}\right)-m\left(B_{(j-1)}\right)\right)\left(1+V\left(\tilde{\beta}_{(j)}\right)\right)f\left(I_{\tilde{\beta}_j}^{U}\right)}{\sum_{j=1}^{n}\left(m\left(B_{(j)}\right)-m\left(B_{(j-1)}\right)\right)\left(1+V\left(\tilde{\beta}_{(j)}\right)\right)}
\right]\right],
$$

$$
\left[
f^{-1}\left[
\frac{\sum_{j=1}^{n}\left(m\left(B_{(j)}\right)-m\left(B_{(j-1)}\right)\right)\left(1+V\left(\tilde{\beta}_{(j)}\right)\right)f\left(F_{\tilde{\beta}_j}^{L}\right)}{\sum_{j=1}^{n}\left(m\left(B_{(j)}\right)-m\left(B_{(j-1)}\right)\right)\left(1+V\left(\tilde{\beta}_{(j)}\right)\right)}
\right],
\right.
$$

$$
\left.\left.
f^{-1}\left[
\frac{\sum_{j=1}^{n}\left(m\left(B_{(j)}\right)-m\left(B_{(j-1)}\right)\right)\left(1+V\left(\tilde{\beta}_{(j)}\right)\right)f\left(F_{\tilde{\beta}_j}^{U}\right)}{\sum_{j=1}^{n}\left(m\left(B_{(j)}\right)-m\left(B_{(j-1)}\right)\right)\left(1+V\left(\tilde{\beta}_{(j)}\right)\right)}
\right]\right]\right\}
\tag{3.18}
$$

Equation (3.18) expresses the INHPCI *operator in terms of the additive generators [82], f and g of Hamacher t-norm and t-conorm [83](see Table 3.1).*

Theorem 3.2: *If* $\tilde{\beta}_j = \{[T_{\tilde{\beta}_j}^{L}, T_{\tilde{\beta}_j}^{U}], [I_{\tilde{\beta}_j}^{L}, I_{\tilde{\beta}_j}^{U}], [F_{\tilde{\beta}_j}^{L}, F_{\tilde{\beta}_j}^{U}]\}$ $(j = 1, 2, \ldots, n)$ *are INNs on a finite set X, then for a fuzzy measure m on X, the aggregated result obtained by using the* INHPCI *operator is also an INN.*

Definition 3.4: If $\tilde{\beta}_j = \{[T_{\tilde{\beta}_j}^{L}, T_{\tilde{\beta}_j}^{U}], [I_{\tilde{\beta}_j}^{L}, I_{\tilde{\beta}_j}^{U}], [F_{\tilde{\beta}_j}^{L}, F_{\tilde{\beta}_j}^{U}]\}$ $(j = 1, 2, \ldots, n)$ are INNs on a finite set X, then for a fuzzy measure m on X, the interval neutrosophic Hamacher power geometric Choquet integral operator (INHPGCI) is given as follows:

$$
\text{INHPGCI}\left(\tilde{\beta}_1, \tilde{\beta}_2, \ldots, \tilde{\beta}_n\right) = \otimes_{H}{}_{j=1}^{n} \tilde{\beta}_{(j)}^{\frac{\left(m\left(B_{(j)}\right)-m\left(B_{(j-1)}\right)\right)\left(1+V\left(\tilde{\beta}_{(j)}\right)\right)}{\sum_{j=1}^{n}\left(m\left(B_{(j)}\right)-m\left(B_{(j-1)}\right)\right)\left(1+V\left(\tilde{\beta}_{(j)}\right)\right)}}
\tag{3.19}
$$

where $\otimes_H$ denotes the Hamacher product of INNs given by (ii) in Definition **3.2** and the other notations are the same as with Definition **3.3**

Theorem 3.3: If $\tilde{\beta}_j = \{[T_{\tilde{\beta}_j}^L, T_{\tilde{\beta}_j}^U], [I_{\tilde{\beta}_j}^L, I_{\tilde{\beta}_j}^U], [F_{\tilde{\beta}_j}^L, F_{\tilde{\beta}_j}^U]\}$ $(j=1,2,\ldots,n)$ *are INNs on a finite set* X, *then fuzzy measure* m *on* X, *the* INHPGCI *can be expressed as*

$$
\text{INHPGCI}\left(\tilde{\beta}_1, \tilde{\beta}_2, \ldots, \tilde{\beta}_n\right) = \left\{ \left[\left[f^{-1}\left(\frac{\sum_{j=1}^{n}\left(m\left(B_{(j)}\right)-m\left(B_{(j-1)}\right)\right)\left(1+V\left(\tilde{\beta}_{(j)}\right)\right)f\left(T_{\tilde{\beta}_j}^L\right)}{\sum_{j=1}^{n}\left(m\left(B_{(j)}\right)\right)-m\left(B_{(j-1)}\right)\right)\left(1+V\left(\tilde{\beta}_{(j)}\right)\right)} \right), \right. \right.
$$

$$
\left. f^{-1}\left(\frac{\sum_{j=1}^{n}\left(m\left(B_{(j)}\right)-m\left(B_{(j-1)}\right)\right)\left(1+V\left(\tilde{\beta}_{(j)}\right)\right)f\left(T_{\tilde{\beta}_j}^U\right)}{\sum_{j=1}^{n}\left(m\left(B_{(j)}\right)\right)-m\left(B_{(j-1)}\right)\right)\left(1+V\left(\tilde{\beta}_{(j)}\right)\right)} \right) \right],
$$

$$
\left[g^{-1}\left(\frac{\sum_{j=1}^{n}\left(m\left(B_{(j)}\right)-m\left(B_{(j-1)}\right)\right)\left(1+V\left(\tilde{\beta}_{(j)}\right)\right)g\left(I_{\tilde{\beta}_j}^L\right)}{\sum_{j=1}^{n}\left(m\left(B_{(j)}\right)\right)-m\left(B_{(j-1)}\right)\right)\left(1+V\left(\tilde{\beta}_{(j)}\right)\right)} \right), \right.
$$

$$
\left. g^{-1}\left(\frac{\sum_{j=1}^{n}\left(m\left(B_{(j)}\right)-m\left(B_{(j-1)}\right)\right)\left(1+V\left(\tilde{\beta}_{(j)}\right)\right)g\left(I_{\tilde{\beta}_j}^U\right)}{\sum_{j=1}^{n}\left(m\left(B_{(j)}\right)\right)-m\left(B_{(j-1)}\right)\right)\left(1+V\left(\tilde{\beta}_{(j)}\right)\right)} \right) \right],
$$

$$
\left[g^{-1}\left(\frac{\sum_{j=1}^{n}\left(m\left(B_{(j)}\right)-m\left(B_{(j-1)}\right)\right)\left(1+V\left(\tilde{\beta}_{(j)}\right)\right)g\left(F_{\tilde{\beta}_j}^L\right)}{\sum_{j=1}^{n}\left(m\left(B_{(j)}\right)\right)-m\left(B_{(j-1)}\right)\right)\left(1+V\left(\tilde{\beta}_{(j)}\right)\right)} \right), \right.
$$

$$
\left. \left. \left. g^{-1}\left(\frac{\sum_{j=1}^{n}\left(m\left(B_{(j)}\right)-m\left(B_{(j-1)}\right)\right)\left(1+V\left(\tilde{\beta}_{(j)}\right)\right)g\left(F_{\tilde{\beta}_j}^U\right)}{\sum_{j=1}^{n}\left(m\left(B_{(j)}\right)\right)-m\left(B_{(j-1)}\right)\right)\left(1+V\left(\tilde{\beta}_{(j)}\right)\right)} \right) \right] \right] \right\}.
$$

$$(3.20)$$

Equation (3.20) expresses the INHPGCI *operator in terms of the additive generators [82], f and g of Hamacher t-norm and t-conorm [83].*

Theorem 3.4: *If* $\tilde{\beta}_j = \{[T_{\tilde{\beta}_j}^L, T_{\tilde{\beta}_j}^U], [I_{\tilde{\beta}_j}^L, I_{\tilde{\beta}_j}^U], [F_{\tilde{\beta}_j}^L, F_{\tilde{\beta}_j}^U]\}$ $(j=1,2,\ldots,n)$ *are INNs on a finite set X, then for a fuzzy measure on X, the accumulated result obtained by using the* INHPGCI *operator is also an INN.*

Corollary 3.1: If $\gamma=1$, then the proposed INHPCI operator, given by *Equations (3.17)* and *(3.19)*, converts to the interval neutrosophic power Choquet integral (INPCI), given by

$$\text{INPCI}\left(\tilde{\beta}_1, \tilde{\beta}_2, \ldots, \tilde{\beta}_n\right) = \frac{\overset{n}{\underset{j=1}{\oplus}}\left(m\left(B_{(j)}\right) - m\left(B_{(j-1)}\right)\right)\left(1 + V\left(\tilde{\beta}_{(j)}\right)\right)\tilde{\beta}_{(j)}}{\sum_{j=1}^{n}\left(m\left(B_{(j)}\right) - m\left(B_{(j-1)}\right)\right)\left(1 + V\left(\tilde{\beta}_{(j)}\right)\right)} \tag{3.21}$$

Corollary 3.2: If $\gamma=2$, then the proposed INHPCI operator, given by Equations (3.17) and (3.19), converts to the interval neutrosophic Einstein Power Choquet integral operator (INEPCI), given by

$$\text{INEPCI}\left(\tilde{\beta}_1, \tilde{\beta}_2, \ldots, \tilde{\beta}_n\right) = \frac{\overset{n}{\underset{j=1}{\oplus_E}}\left(m\left(B_{(j)}\right) - m\left(B_{((j-1))}\right)\right)\left(1 + V\left(\tilde{\beta}_{(j)}\right)\right)\tilde{\beta}_{(j)}}{\sum_{j=1}^{n}\left(m\left(B_{(j)}\right) - m\left(B_{((j-1))}\right)\right)\left(1 + V\left(\tilde{\beta}_{(j)}\right)\right)} \tag{3.22}$$

where $\oplus_E$ denotes the Einstein sum of INNs

Corollary 3.3: If $\gamma=1$, then the proposed INHPGCI operator, given by Equations (3.20) and (3.22), reduces to the interval neutrosophic power geometric Choquet integral operator (INPGCI) is given by

$$\text{INPGCI}\left(\tilde{\beta}_1, \tilde{\beta}_2, \ldots, \tilde{\beta}_n\right) = \overset{n}{\underset{j=1}{\otimes_H}} \tilde{\beta}_{(j)}^{\frac{\left(m\left(B_{(j)}\right) - m\left(B_{(j-1)}\right)\right)\left(1 + V\left(\tilde{\beta}_j\right)\right)}{\sum_{j=1}^{n}\left(m\left(B_{(j)}\right) - m\left(B_{(j-1)}\right)\right)\left(1 + V\left(\tilde{\beta}_j\right)\right)}} \tag{3.23}$$

Corollary 3.4: If $\gamma=2$, then the proposed INHPGCI operator, given by Equations (3.17) and (3.19), reduces to the INEPCI, given as

$$\text{INEPGCI}(\tilde{\beta}_1, \tilde{\beta}_2, \ldots, \tilde{\beta}_n) = \overset{n}{\underset{j=1}{\otimes_E}} \tilde{\beta}_{(j)}^{\frac{\left(m\left(B_{(j)}\right) - m\left(B_{(j-1)}\right)\right)\left(1 + V\left(\tilde{\beta}_{(j)}\right)\right)}{\sum_{j=1}^{n}\left(m\left(B_{(j)}\right) - m\left(B_{(j-1)}\right)\right)\left(1 + V\left(\tilde{\beta}_{(j)}\right)\right)}} \tag{3.24}$$

Remark 3.1 From Corollaries **3.1** and **3.3**, it is clear that INHPCI and INHPGCI can be restricted to generate some new Choquet operators such as the INPCI and the INPGCI operators based on the algebraic operations. **Remark 3.2** Corollaries **3.2** and **3.4** show that INHPCI and INHPGCI can be restricted to generate some novel Einstein Choquet operators such as the INEPCI and the INEPGCI operators based on the Einstein operations.

3.3.3 Properties of INHPCI and INHPGCI Operators

This section briefly discusses some of the properties of the INHPCI and INHPGCI operators.

Theorem 3.5: If $\tilde{\beta}_j = \{[T^L_{\tilde{\beta}_j}, T^U_{\tilde{\beta}_j}], [I^L_{\tilde{\beta}_j}, I^U_{\tilde{\beta}_j}], [F^L_{\tilde{\beta}_j}, F^U_{\tilde{\beta}_j}]\}$ $(j=1,2,\ldots,n)$ *are INNs on a finite set X and If all $\tilde{\beta}_l$ are equal, i.e., $\tilde{\beta}_1 = \tilde{\beta}(l=1,2,\ldots,n$, then*

$$\text{INHPCI}\left(\tilde{\beta}_1, \tilde{\beta}_2, \ldots, \tilde{\beta}_n\right) = \tilde{\beta} \tag{3.25}$$

$$\text{INHPGCI}\left(\tilde{\beta}_1, \tilde{\beta}_2, \ldots, \tilde{\beta}_n\right) = \tilde{\beta} \tag{3.26}$$

Theorem 3.6: If $\tilde{\beta}_j = \{[T^L_{\tilde{\beta}_j}, T^U_{\tilde{\beta}_j}], [I^L_{\tilde{\beta}_j}, I^U_{\tilde{\beta}_j}], [F^L_{\tilde{\beta}_j}, F^U_{\tilde{\beta}_j}]\}$ $(j=1,2,\ldots,n)$ *are INNs on a finite set X and $\tilde{\beta}'_l = \{[T^L_{\tilde{\beta}'_l}, T^U_{\tilde{\beta}'_l}], [I^L_{\tilde{\beta}'_l}, I^U_{\tilde{\beta}'_l}], [F^L_{\tilde{\beta}'_l}, F^U_{\tilde{\beta}'_l}]\}$ $(l=1,2,\ldots,n)$ is a permutation of $\tilde{\beta}_l$, then*

$$\text{INHPCI}\left(\tilde{\beta}_1, \tilde{\beta}_2, \ldots, \tilde{\beta}_n\right) = \text{INHPCI}\left(\tilde{\beta}'_1, \tilde{\beta}'_2, \ldots, \tilde{\beta}'_n\right) \tag{3.27}$$

$$\text{INHPGCI}\left(\tilde{\beta}_1, \tilde{\beta}_2, \ldots, \tilde{\beta}_n\right) = \text{INHPGCI}\left(\tilde{\beta}'_1, \tilde{\beta}'_2, \ldots, \tilde{\beta}'_n\right) \tag{3.28}$$

Theorem 3.7: *If two collections* $\tilde{a}_l = \{[T^L_{\tilde{a}_l}, T^U_{\tilde{a}_l}], [I^L_{\tilde{a}_l}, I^U_{\tilde{a}_l}], [F^L_{\tilde{a}_l}, F^U_{\tilde{a}_l}]\}$ $(l=1,2,\ldots,n)$ *and* $\tilde{b}_l = \{[T^L_{\tilde{b}_l}, T^U_{\tilde{b}_l}], [I^L_{\tilde{b}_l}, I^U_{\tilde{b}_l}], [F^L_{\tilde{b}_l}, F^U_{\tilde{b}_l}]\}$ $(l=1,2,\ldots,n)$ *of INNs on a finite set X are comonotonic with*

$$T^L_{\tilde{a}_l} \leq T^L_{\tilde{b}_l}, \ T^U_{\tilde{a}_l} \leq T^U_{\tilde{b}_l}, \ I^L_{\tilde{a}_l} \geq I^L_{\tilde{b}_l}, \ I^U_{\tilde{a}_l} \geq I^U_{\tilde{b}_l}, \ F^L_{\tilde{a}_l} \geq F^L_{\tilde{b}_l}, \ F^U_{\tilde{a}_l} \geq F^U_{\tilde{b}_l}$$

for all l, then

$$\text{INHPCI}\left(\tilde{a}_1, \tilde{a}_2, \ldots, \tilde{a}_n\right) \leq \text{INHPCI}\left(\tilde{b}_1, \tilde{b}_2, \ldots, \tilde{b}_n\right) \tag{3.29}$$

$$\text{INHPGCI}\left(\tilde{a}_1, \tilde{a}_2, \ldots, \tilde{a}_n\right) \leq \text{INHPGCI}\left(\tilde{b}_1, \tilde{b}_2, \ldots, \tilde{b}_n\right) \tag{3.30}$$

Theorem 3.8: *If* $\tilde{\beta}_l = \{[T^L_{\tilde{\beta}_l}, T^U_{\tilde{\beta}_l}], [I^L_{\tilde{\beta}_l}, I^U_{\tilde{\beta}_l}], [F^L_{\tilde{\beta}_l}, F^U_{\tilde{\beta}_l}]\}$ $(l = 1, 2, \ldots, n)$ *are INNs on a finite set X, then*

$$\tilde{\beta}^- \leq INHPCI\left(\tilde{\beta}_1, \tilde{\beta}_2, \ldots, \tilde{\beta}_n\right) \leq \tilde{\beta}^+ \tag{3.31}$$

$$\tilde{\beta}^- \leq INHPGCI\left(\tilde{\beta}_1, \tilde{\beta}_2, \ldots, \tilde{\beta}_n\right) \leq \tilde{\beta}^+ \tag{3.32}$$

where

$$\tilde{\beta}^- = \left\{\left[\min(T^L_{\tilde{\beta}_l}), \min(T^U_{\tilde{\beta}_l})\right], \left[\max(I^L_{\tilde{\beta}_l}), \max(I^U_{\tilde{\beta}_l})\right], \left[\max(F^L_{\tilde{\beta}_l}), \max(F^U_{\tilde{\beta}_l})\right]\right\}$$

$$\tilde{\beta}^+ = \left\{\left[\max(T^L_{\tilde{\beta}_l}), \max(T^U_{\tilde{\beta}_l})\right], \left[\min(I^L_{\tilde{\beta}_l}), \min(I^U_{\tilde{\beta}_l})\right], \left[\min(F^L_{\tilde{\beta}_l}), \min(F^U_{\tilde{\beta}_l})\right]\right\}.$$

3.4 A DECISION-MAKING MODEL FOR MEDICAL DIAGNOSIS WITH THE INHPCI AND INHPGCI OPERATORS

This section introduces a novel MCGDM model for the medical diagnosis of diseases using the INHPCI and the INHPGCI operators. We assume that assessment data of the alternatives are given by INNs and there exists an interrelationship among the attributes.

Assume that $X = \{x_1, x_2, \ldots, x_m\}$ be a collection of patients suffering from various diseases and let $C = \{C_1, C_2, \ldots, C_n\}$ be a collection of symptoms for the selection of patients who must need an immediate diagnosis. The diagnosis report of each patient x_i $(i = 1, 2, \ldots, m)$ corresponding to symptoms C_j $(j = 1, 2, \ldots, n)$ is expressed by the INN decision matrix $\tilde{D} = [\tilde{\beta}_{ij}]_{m \times n}$, where each $\tilde{\beta}_{ij}$ $(i = 1, 2, \ldots, m; j = 1, 2, \ldots, n)$ is an INN and is given by

$$\tilde{\beta}_{ij} = \left\langle \left[T^L_{\tilde{\beta}_{ij}}, T^L_{\tilde{\beta}_{ij}}\right], \left[I^L_{\tilde{\beta}_{ij}}, I^L_{\tilde{\beta}_{ij}}\right], \left[F^L_{\tilde{\beta}_{ij}}, F^L_{\tilde{\beta}_{ij}}\right]\right\rangle \ (i = 1, 2, \ldots, m; \ j = 1, 2, \ldots, n).$$

The selection procedure of patients who required immediate attention includes the following steps:

Step 1 Compute the score value $S(\tilde{\beta}_{ij})$ of each INN using Equation (3.1) to reorder $\tilde{\beta}_{ij}$ $(i = 1, 2, \ldots, m)$ as $\tilde{\beta}_{i(1)} \succ \tilde{\beta}_{i(2)} \succ \ldots \succ \tilde{\beta}_{i(n)}$

Step 2 Evaluate the supports,

$$Supp(\tilde{\beta}_{ij},\tilde{\beta}_{ik})=1-d(\tilde{\beta}_{ij},\tilde{\beta}_{ik}),(i=1,2,\ldots,m;j,k=1,2,\ldots,n;j\neq k), \quad (3.33)$$

where $d(\tilde{\beta}_{ij},\tilde{\beta}_{ik})$ denotes the normalized Hamming distance [87] between any two INNs.

Step 3 Determine the weights associated with the INNs $\tilde{\beta}_{ij}$ $(j=1,2,\ldots,n)$ using

$$w_{ij}=\frac{\left(m\left(B_{(j)}\right)-m\left(B_{(j-1)}\right)\right)\left(1+V\left(\left(\tilde{\beta}_{(ij)}\right)\right)\right)}{\sum_{j=1}^{n}\left(m\left(B_{(j)}\right)-m\left(B_{(j-1)}\right)\right)\left(1+V\left(\tilde{\beta}_{(ij)}\right)\right)} \quad (3.34)$$

where

$$V\left(\tilde{\beta}_{(ij)}\right)=\sum_{\substack{k=1\\k\neq j}}^{n}\left(m\left(B_{(j)}\right)-m\left(B_{(j-1)}\right)\right)Supp\left(\tilde{\beta}_{(ij)},\tilde{\beta}_{(ik)}\right),\ (k=1,2,\ldots,n) \quad (3.35)$$

with $w_{ij}>0$ and $\sum_{j=1}^{n}w_{ij}=1$, $(i=1,2,\ldots,m)$.

Step 4 Recognize the fuzzy measure for each of the symptoms C_j $(j=1,2,\ldots,n)$ and using Equation (3.13), the fuzzy measure $m(A)$ of all $A\subseteq X$ can be determined, where the parameter λ can be determined by using Equation (3.14).

Step 5 Apply the Equation (3.18) of INHPCI or the Equation (3.20) of INHPGCI for evaluation $\tilde{\beta}_i$ of each alternative x_i $(i=1,2,\ldots,m)$.

Step 6 Determine the score and the accuracy values $S(\tilde{\alpha}_i),A(\tilde{\beta}_i)$ $(i=1,2,\ldots,m)$ of the aggregated evaluation values $\tilde{\beta}_i(i=1,2,\ldots,m)$ corresponding to each attribute $x_i(i=1,2,\ldots,m)$ and select the utmost serious patient.

Step 7 End.

3.5 EXPLANATORY EXAMPLE

Here, an illustrative example is presented as a demonstration of the projected MCGDM model for medical diagnosis under the interval neutrosophic environment.

Assume that a medical team of the local hospital performs a diagnosis on four patients $X = \{x_1, x_2, x_3, x_4\}$ based on the following symptoms:

1. C_1: Body temperature
2. C_2: Dry cough
3. C_3: Headache
4. C_4: Body pain.

To detect the patient with the most severe health conditions who need immediate treatment based on the diagnosis report.

Assume that the four patients $x_i (i = 1, 2, 3, 4)$ which need to be diagnosed for symptoms $C_j (j = 1, 2, 3, 4)$ and are expressed as interval neutrosophic decision matrix $\tilde{D} = [\tilde{\alpha}_{ij}]_{4 \times 4}$ as shown in Table 3.2, where each $\tilde{\alpha}_{ij}$ $(i = 1, 2, 3, 4; j = 1, 2, 3)$ is an INN and represents the diagnosis report of the ith patient $x_i (i = 1, 2, 3, 4)$ under the jth symptom $C_j (j = 1, 2, 3, 4)$. The assessment of the ith patient x_i $(i = 1, 2, 3, 4)$ under the jth symptom C_j $(j = 1, 2, 3, 4)$ has been attained according to the doctors' report. The interval neutrosophic decision matrix is generated as revealed in Table 3.2.

Step 1 Recognizing the fuzzy measure $m(C_j)$ for each symptom C_j $(j = 1, 2, \ldots, n)$, that measures the degree of importance of each symptom C_j $(j = 1, 2, \ldots, n)$. Assuming that according to the doctors' estimation, the fuzzy measure of each symptom is given by

$$m(\{C_1\}) = 0.26, \ m(\{C_2\}) = 0.21, \ m(\{C_3\}) = 0.17, \text{ and } m(\{C_4\}) = 0.23.$$

TABLE 3.2

The INN Decision Matrix $\tilde{D} = [\tilde{\alpha}_{ij}]_{4 \times 4}$

	C_1	C_2	C_3	C_4
x_1:	$\langle[0.4, 0.5], [0.3, 0.4], [0.5, 0.6]\rangle$	$\langle[0.4, 0.6], [0.3, 0.5], [0.4, 0.5]\rangle$	$\langle[0.3, 0.5], [0.3, 0.4], [0.6, 0.7]\rangle$	$\langle[0.3, 0.4], [0.2, 0.3], [0.5, 0.6]\rangle$
x_2:	$\langle[0.6, 0.7], [0.2, 0.4], [0.4, 0.6]\rangle$	$\langle[0.6, 0.8], [0.3, 0.6], [0.4, 0.5]\rangle$	$\langle[0.5, 0.6], [0.2, 0.3], [0.4, 0.5]\rangle$	$\langle[0.4, 0.5], [0.1, 0.2], [0.3, 0.4]\rangle$
x_3:	$\langle[0.4, 0.5], [0.3, 0.4], [0.3, 0.5]\rangle$	$\langle[0.5, 0.6], [0.2, 0.3], [0.3, 0.4]\rangle$	$\langle[0.4, 0.7], [0.3, 0.4], [0.2, 0.3]\rangle$	$\langle[0.5, 0.8], [0.3, 0.4], [0.1, 0.3]\rangle$
x_4:	$\langle[0.7, 0.8], [0.2, 0.4], [0.1, 0.3]\rangle$	$\langle[0.5, 0.7], [0.3, 0.5], [0.2, 0.4]\rangle$	$\langle[0.5, 0.8], [0.4, 0.6], [0.5, 0.7]\rangle$	$\langle[0.4, 0.7], [0.4, 0.5], [0.1, 0.3]\rangle$

From Equation (3.14), we obtain the value of $\lambda = 0.43$ and using Equation (3.13), we have

$$m\left(\left\{C_1,C_2\right\}\right)=0.4934, \quad m\left(\left\{C_1,C_3\right\}\right)=0.4490, \quad m\left(\left\{C_1,C_4\right\}\right)=0.5157,$$

$$m\left(\left\{C_2,C_3\right\}\right)=0.3954, \quad m\left(\left\{C_2,C_4\right\}\right)=0.4608, \quad m\left(\left\{C_3,C_4\right\}\right)=0.4168$$

$$m\left(\left\{C_1,C_2,C_3\right\}\right)=0.6996, \quad m\left(\left\{C_1,C_2,C_4\right\}\right)=0.7723, \quad m\left(\left\{C_1,C_3,C_4\right\}\right)=0.7234$$

$$m\left(\left\{C_2,C_3,C_4\right\}\right)=0.6645 \quad m\left(\left\{C_1,C_2,C_3,C_4\right\}\right)=1.$$

Step 2 The score values $S(\tilde{\alpha}_{ij})(i=1,2,3,4; j=1,2,3,4)$ of each $\tilde{\alpha}_{ij}(i=1,2,3,4; j=1,2,3,4)$ are calculated using Equation (3.1) and reordered as revealed in Table 3.3 (Figure 3.1).

Since the score values of $\tilde{\alpha}_{1(j)}(j=1,2,3,4)$ of the first patient, x_1 are $S(\tilde{\alpha}_{1(1)})=0.1000, S(\tilde{\alpha}_{1(2)})=0.1250, S(\tilde{\alpha}_{1(3)})=0.0250$, and $S(\tilde{\alpha}_{1(4)})=0.1500$. Since $S(\tilde{\alpha}_{1(4)})>S(\tilde{\alpha}_{1(2)})>S(\tilde{\alpha}_{1(1)})>S(\tilde{\alpha}_{1(3)})$, therefore for the first patient, x_1 the partial evaluations $\tilde{\alpha}_{1(j)}$ ($j=1,2,3,4$) are reordered as $\tilde{\alpha}_{1(4)} \succ \tilde{\alpha}_{1(2)} \succ \tilde{\alpha}_{1(1)} \succ \tilde{\alpha}_{1(3)}$.

Then, the fuzzy measure for each of the symptom C_j ($j=1,2,3,4$) for the first patient x_1 is given as

$$m\left(A_{1(1)}\right)=m\left(\left\{C_{(4)}\right\}\right)=0.23, \; m\left(A_{1(2)}\right)=m\left(\left\{C_{(4)},C_{(2)}\right\}\right)=0.4608,$$

$$m\left(A_{1(3)}\right)=m\left(\left\{C_{(4)},C_{(2)},C_{(1)}\right\}\right)=0.7723, \; m\left(A_{1(4)}\right)=m\left(\left\{C_{(4)},C_{(2)},C_{(1)},C_{(3)}\right\}\right)=1.$$

Correspondingly, the ranking order of the partial estimations $\tilde{\alpha}_{ij}$ ($i=2, 3,4$; $j=1,2,3,4$) and fuzzy measures of the patients A_i ($i=2,3,4$) based on the symptom C_j ($j=1,2,3,4$) are shown in Table 3.4.

TABLE 3.3

The Score Values of $\tilde{\alpha}_{ij}$ Corresponding to the Decision Matrix $\tilde{D}$

	C_1	C_2	C_3	C_4
x_1:	0.1000	0.1250	0.0250	0.1500
x_2:	0.2750	0.1750	0.3000	0.4000
x_3:	0.1750	0.3500	0.3000	0.3750
x_4:	0.4750	0.2500	0.0250	0.2250

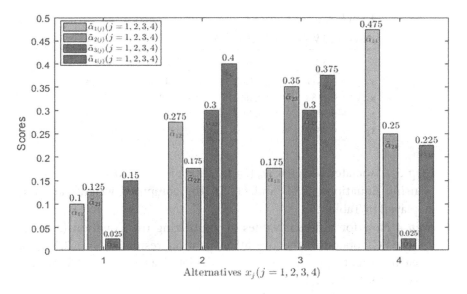

FIGURE 3.1

Score values of $\tilde{\alpha}_{ij}$ corresponding to the decision matrix $\tilde{D}$.

TABLE 3.4

Reordering of the Partial Evaluations

Alternatives	Reordering of the Partial Evaluations	Fuzzy Measures
x_2	$\tilde{\alpha}_{2(4)} \succ \tilde{\alpha}_{2(3)} \succ \tilde{\alpha}_{2(1)} \succ \tilde{\alpha}_{2(2)}$	$m\left(A_{2(1)}\right) = m\left(\{C_{(4)}\}\right) = 0.23,$
		$m\left(A_{2(2)}\right) = m\left(\{C_{(4)}, C_{(3)}\}\right) = 0.4168,$
		$m\left(A_{2(3)}\right) = m\left(\{C_{(4)}, C_{(3)}, C_{(1)}\}\right) = 0.7234,$
		$m\left(A_{2(4)}\right) = m\left(\{C_{(4)}, C_{(3)}, C_{(1)}, C_{(2)}\}\right) = 1$
x_3	$\tilde{\alpha}_{3(4)} \succ \tilde{\alpha}_{3(2)} \succ \tilde{\alpha}_{3(3)} \succ \tilde{\alpha}_{3(1)}$	$m\left(A_{3(1)}\right) = m\left(\{C_{(4)}\}\right) = 0.23,$
		$m\left(A_{3(2)}\right) = m\left(\{C_{(4)}, C_{(2)}\}\right) = 0.4608,$
		$m\left(A_{3(3)}\right) = m\left(\{C_{(4)}, C_{(2)}, C_{(3)}\}\right) = 0.6645,$
		$m\left(A_{3(4)}\right) = m\left(\{C_{(4)}, C_{(2)}, C_{(3)}, C_{(1)}\}\right) = 1$
x_4	$\tilde{\alpha}_{4(1)} \succ \tilde{\alpha}_{4(2)} \succ \tilde{\alpha}_{4(4)} \succ \tilde{\alpha}_{4(3)}$	$m\left(A_{4(1)}\right) = m\left(\{C_{(1)}\}\right) = 0.26,$
		$m\left(A_{4(2)}\right) = m\left(\{C_{(1)}, C_{(2)}\}\right) = 0.4934,$
		$m\left(A_{4(3)}\right) = m\left(\{C_{(1)}, C_{(2)}, C_{(4)}\}\right) = 0.7723,$
		$m\left(A_{4(4)}\right) = m\left(\{C_{(1)}, C_{(2)}, C_{(4)}, C_{(3)}\}\right) = 1$

TABLE 3.5

Associated Weights of Decision Matrix $\tilde{D}$

	C_1	C_2	C_3	C_4
x_1:	0.2817	0.3521	0.1549	0.2113
x_2:	0.1788	0.4632	0.1508	0.2072
x_3:	0.1914	0.4037	0.1866	0.2183
x_4:	0.0817	0.3152	0.3259	0.2772

Step 3 Associated weights w_{ij} $(i=1,2,\ldots,m; j=1,2,\ldots,n)$ are computed using Equations (3.34) and (3.35). The computed weights are displayed in Table 3.5.

Step 4 Now for different values of γ, utilizing the Equation (3.19) of INHPCI operator, the overall evaluation results $\tilde{\alpha}_i(i=1,2,3,4)$ of each patient x_i $(i=1,2,3,4)$ are calculated as shown in Table 3.6 (Figures 3.2 and 3.3).

Step 5 From Table 3.6, it is clear that although the overall assessments of $\tilde{\alpha}_j$ $(j=1,2,3,4)$ corresponding to each patient x_i $(i=1,2,3,4)$ is different, the optimal ranking value is $\tilde{\alpha}_2$. Hence, x_2 is the most serious patient who needs immediate treatment.

TABLE 3.6

Overall Evaluation and Ranking Orders of INNs $\tilde{\alpha}_i$ for Different γ

y	$\tilde{\alpha}_1$	$\tilde{\alpha}_2$	$\tilde{\alpha}_3$	$\tilde{\alpha}_4$	Ranking Orders
0.1	⟨[0.3598, 0.5081], [0.2716, 0.3899], [0.4917, 0.5930]⟩	⟨[0.5474, 0.6951], [0.1818, 0.3402], [0.3722, 0.4978]⟩	⟨[0.4502, 0.6693], [0.2703, 0.3721], [0.2009, 0.3733]⟩	⟨[0.5526, 0.7573], [0.3028, 0.4878], [0.1421, 0.3732]⟩	$\tilde{\alpha}_2 \succ \tilde{\alpha}_3 \succ \tilde{\alpha}_4 \succ \tilde{\alpha}_1$
0.5	⟨[0.3589, 0.5059], [0.2737, 0.3928], [0.4939, 0.5947]⟩	⟨[0.5443, 0.6862], [0.1885, 0.3541], [0.3737, 0.5005]⟩	⟨[0.4492, 0.6586], [0.2724, 0.3736], [0.2111, 0.3779]⟩	⟨[0.5443, 0.7548], [0.3094, 0.4902], [0.1487, 0.3826]⟩	$\tilde{\alpha}_2 \succ \tilde{\alpha}_3 \succ \tilde{\alpha}_4 \succ \tilde{\alpha}_1$
1.0	⟨[0.3582, 0.5045], [0.2745, 0.3944], [0.4954, 0.5961]⟩	⟨[0.5422, 0.6817], [0.1908, 0.3616], [0.3744, 0.5023]⟩	⟨[0.4483, 0.6534], [0.2732, 0.3743], [0.2145, 0.3805]⟩	⟨[0.5393, 0.7538], [0.3123, 0.4918], [0.1510, 0.3891]⟩	$\tilde{\alpha}_2 \succ \tilde{\alpha}_3 \succ \tilde{\alpha}_4 \succ \tilde{\alpha}_1$
1.5	⟨[0.3577, 0.5036], [0.2748, 0.3952], [0.4962, 0.5970]⟩	⟨[0.5409, 0.6795], [0.1917, 0.3656], [0.3748, 0.5034]⟩	⟨[0.4478, 0.6507], [0.2736, 0.3747], [0.2160, 0.3819]⟩	⟨[0.5366, 0.7534], [0.3138, 0.4928], [0.1519, 0.3931]⟩	$\tilde{\alpha}_2 \succ \tilde{\alpha}_3 \succ \tilde{\alpha}_4 \succ \tilde{\alpha}_1$
2.0	⟨[0.3573, 0.5030], [0.2750, 0.3958], [0.4968, 0.5977]⟩	⟨[0.5401, 0.6781], [0.1922, 0.3682], [0.3750, 0.5041]⟩	⟨[0.4475, 0.6490], [0.2738, 0.3749], [0.2168, 0.3828]⟩	⟨[0.5349, 0.7531], [0.3146, 0.4934], [0.1525, 0.3959]⟩	$\tilde{\alpha}_2 \succ \tilde{\alpha}_3 \succ \tilde{\alpha}_4 \succ \tilde{\alpha}_1$

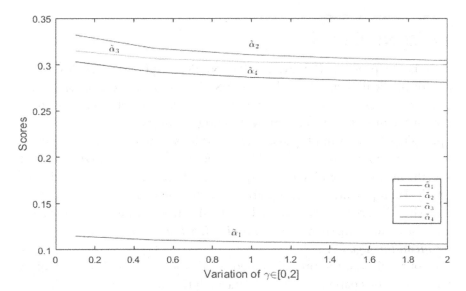

FIGURE 3.2
Overall ranking of the four patients based on the INHPCI operator.

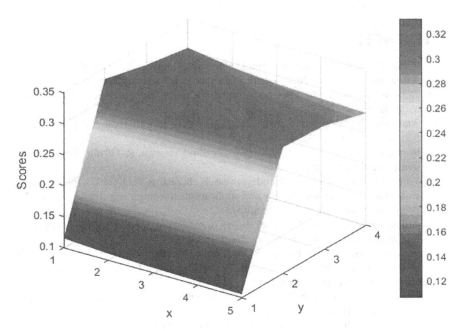

FIGURE 3.3
Overall scores of $\tilde{\alpha}_j$ $(j=1,2,3,4)$.

3.6 CONCLUSION

This chapter proposes INHPCI and the INHPGCI operators as an MCGDM aid for medical diagnosis under the INS environment and discusses their important characteristics. Further, an MCGDM model is developed to obtain the most serious patient by utilizing the proposed operators developed. Finally, an example illustrates the proposed model. For future studies, the proposed operators could be used as a tool for studying several specific health-related issues, X-ray imaging-based diagnosis, selection of medical equipment, population growth, pollution control, hazard control, etc. Also, the present study could be extended to other fields of knowledge and manufacturing such as the *Optimization Theory*, Decision *Theory*, and *Artificial Intelligence*.

In our opinion, the proposed algorithm would be an effective tool to identify serious patients using big data analytics during pandemic-like situations, where the number of healthcare workers is very less compared to the patients so that the most serious patient gets early attention. In doing so, we can minimize the causalities during the pandemic.

REFERENCES

1. Zadeh, L. A. (1965). Fuzzy sets. Information and Control, 8(3): 338–353.
2. Atanassov, K. T. (1986). Intuitionistic fuzzy sets. Fuzzy Sets and Systems, 20(1): 87–96.
3. Atanassov, K. T. (1989). More on intuitionistic fuzzy sets. Fuzzy Sets and Systems, 33(1): 37–45.
4. Atanassov, K., & Gargov, G. (1989). Interval-valued intuitionistic fuzzy sets. Fuzzy Sets and Systems, 31(3): 343–349.
5. Wang, H., Smarandache, F., Zhang, Y., & Sunderraman, R. (2010). Single valued neutrosophic sets. Infinite Study.
6. Wang, H., Smarandache, F., Sunderraman, R., & Zhang, Y. Q. (2005). Interval neutrosophic sets and logic: Theory and applications in computing: Theory and applications in computing. 5, Infinite Study.
7. Adlassnig, K. P. (1986). Fuzzy set theory in medical diagnosis. IEEE Transactions on Systems, Man, and Cybernetics, 16(2): 260–265.
8. Aversa, F., Gronda, E., Pizzuti, S., & Aragno, C. (2002). A fuzzy logic approach to decision support in medicine. In *Proceeding of the Conference on Systemics, Cybernetics, and Informatics*, 1–5.
9. Innocent, P. R., & John, R. I. (2004). Computer-aided fuzzy medical diagnosis. Information Sciences, 162(2): 81–104.
10. Yamada, K. (2004). Diagnosis under compound effects and multiple causes by means of the conditional causal possibility approach. Fuzzy Sets and Systems, 145(2): 183–212.

11. De, S. K., Biswas, R., & Roy, A. R. (2001). An application of intuitionistic fuzzy sets in medical diagnosis. Fuzzy Sets and Systems, 117(2): 209–213.
12. Szmidt, E., & Kacprzyk, J. (2001, October). Intuitionistic fuzzy sets in some medical applications. In International Conference on Computational Intelligence, 148–151.
13. Mondal, K., & Pramanik, S. (2015). Intuitionistic fuzzy similarity measure based on tangent function and its application to multi-attribute decision making. Global Journal of Advanced Research, 2(2): 464–471.
14. Biswas, P., Pramanik, S., & Giri, B. C. (2014). A study on information technology professionals' health problem based on intuitionistic fuzzy cosine similarity measure. Swiss Journal of Statistical and Applied Mathematics, 2(1): 44–50.
15. Das, S., Guha, D., & Dutta, B. (2016). Medical diagnosis with the aid of using fuzzy logic and intuitionistic fuzzy logic. Applied Intelligence, 45(3): 850–867.
16. Khatibi, V., & Montazer, G. A. (2009). Intuitionistic fuzzy set vs. fuzzy set application in medical pattern recognition. Artificial Intelligence in Medicine, 47(1): 43–52.
17. Davvaz, B., & Hassani Sadrabadi, E. (2016). An application of intuitionistic fuzzy sets in medicine. International Journal of Biomathematics, 9(03): 1650037.
18. Hung, K. C., & Tuan, H. W. (2013). Medical diagnosis based on intuitionistic fuzzy sets revisited. Journal of Interdisciplinary Mathematics, 16(6): 385–395.
19. Smarandache, F. (1999). A unifying field in logics: Neutrosophic logic. In Philosophy (pp. 1–141). American Research Press, Rehoboth.
20. Ye, J. (2014). Single valued neutrosophic cross-entropy for multicriteria decision making problems. Applied Mathematical Modelling, 38(3): 1170–1175.
21. Ye, J. (2015). Improved cosine similarity measures of simplified neutrosophic sets for medical diagnoses. Artificial Intelligence in Medicine, 63(3): 171–179.
22. Mondal, K., & Pramanik, S. (2015). Neutrosophic tangent similarity measure and its application to multiple attribute decision making. Neutrosophic Sets and Systems, 9: 80–87.
23. Broumi, S., Deli, I., & Smarandache, F. (2015). N-valued interval neutrosophic sets and their application in medical diagnosis. Critical Review, 10: 45–69.
24. Ahn, J. Y., Han, K. S., Oh, S. Y., & Lee, C. D. (2011). An application of interval-valued intuitionistic fuzzy sets for medical diagnosis of headache. International Journal of Innovative Computing, Information, and Control, 7(5): 2755–2762.
25. Hu, J., Pan, L., Yang, Y., & Chen, H. (2019). A group medical diagnosis model based on intuitionistic fuzzy soft sets. Applied Soft Computing, 77: 453–466.
26. Ngan, T. T., Tuan, T. M., Minh, N. H., & Dey, N. (2016). Decision making based on fuzzy aggregation operators for medical diagnosis from dental X-ray images. Journal of Medical Systems, 40(12): 280.
27. Xu, Z. S. (2007). Models for multiple attribute decision making with intuitionistic fuzzy information. International Journal of Uncertainty, Fuzziness and Knowledge-Based Systems, 15(3): 285–297.
28. Xia, M., Xu, Z., & Zhu, B. (2012). Some issues on intuitionistic fuzzy aggregation operators based on Archimedean t-conorm and t-norm. Knowledge-Based Systems, 31: 78–88.
29. Xu, Z. S., & Da, Q. L. (2002).The uncertain OWA operator. International Journal of Intelligent Systems, 17(6): 569–575.
30. Chen, N., Xu, Z., & Xia, M. (2013). Interval-valued hesitant preference relations and their applications to group decision making. Knowledge-Based Systems, 37: 528–540.

31. Xu, Z. (2005). On method for uncertain multiple attribute decision making problems with uncertain multiplicative preference information on alternatives. Fuzzy Optimization and Decision Making, 4(2): 131–139.
32. Choquet, G. (1954). Theory of capacities. Annales de l'institut Fourier, 5: 131–295.
33. Sugeno, M. (1974). Theory of fuzzy integrals and its applications. PhD Thesis, Tokyo Institute of Technology, Tokyo.
34. Li, X., & Zhang, X. (2018). Single-valued neutrosophic hesitant fuzzy Choquet aggregation operators for multi-attribute decision making. Symmetry, 10(2): 50.
35. Sun, H. X., Yang, H. X., Wu, J. Z., & Ouyang, Y. (2015). Interval neutrosophic numbers Choquet integral operator for multi-criteria decision making. Journal of Intelligent & Fuzzy Systems, 28(6): 2443–2455.
36. Kakati, P., Borkotokey, S., Mesiar, R., & Rahman, S. (2018). Interval neutrosophic hesitant fuzzy Choquet integral in multicriteria decision making. Journal of Intelligent & Fuzzy Systems, 35(3): 3213–3231.
37. Wang, L., Zhang, H. Y., & Wang, J. Q. (2018). Frank Choquet Bonferroni mean operators of bipolar neutrosophic sets and their application to multi-criteria decision-making problems. International Journal of Fuzzy Systems, 20(1): 13–28.
38. Kakati, P., Borkotokey, S., Rahman, S., & Davvaz, B. (2020). Interval neutrosophic hesitant fuzzy Einstein Choquet integral operator for multicriteria decision making. Artificial Intelligence Review, 53(3): 2171–2206.
39. Li, X., Zhang, X., & Park, C. (2018). Generalized interval neutrosophic Choquet aggregation operators and their applications. Symmetry, 10(4): 85.
40. Trabelsi Ben Ameur, S., Sellami, D., Wendling, L., & Cloppet, F. (2019). Breast cancer diagnosis system based on semantic analysis and Choquet integral feature selection for high risk subjects. Big Data and Cognitive Computing, 3(3): 41.
41. Yager, R. R. (2001). The power average operator. IEEE Transactions on Systems, Man, and Cybernetics-Part A: Systems and Humans, 31(6): 724–731.
42. Xu, Z., & Yager, R. R. (2010). Power-geometric operators and their use in group decision making. IEEE Transactions on Fuzzy Systems, 18(1): 94–105.
43. Zhou, L., Chen, H., & Liu, J. (2012). Generalized power aggregation operators and their applications in group decision making. Computers & Industrial Engineering, 62(4): 989–999.
44. Xu, Z. (2011). Approaches to multiple attribute group decision making based on intuitionistic fuzzy power aggregation operators. Knowledge-Based Systems, 24(6): 749–760.
45. Zhang, Z. (2013). Generalized Atanassov's intuitionistic fuzzy power geometric operators and their application to multiple attribute group decision making. Information Fusion, 14(4): 460–486.
46. He, Y. D., Chen, H., Zhou, L., Liu, J., & Tao, Z. (2013). Generalized interval-valued Atanassov's intuitionistic fuzzy power operators and their application to group decision making. International Journal of Fuzzy Systems, 15(4): 401–411.
47. Yang, L., & Li, B. (2016). A multi-criteria decision-making method using power aggregation operators for single-valued neutrosophic sets. International Journal of Database Theory and Application, 9: 23–32.
48. Liu, P., & Tang, G. (2016). Some power generalized aggregation operators based on the interval neutrosophic sets and their application to decision making. Journal of Intelligent & Fuzzy Systems, 30(5): 2517–2528.
49. Peng, J. J., Tian, C., Zhang, Z. Q., Song, H. Y., &Wang, J. Q. (2019). Single-valued neutrosophic power Shapley Choquet average operators and their applications to multi-criteria decision-making. Mathematics, 7(11): 1081.

50. Raghupathi, W., & Raghupathi, V. (2014). Big data analytics in healthcare: promise and potential. Health Information Science and Systems, 2(1): 1–10.
51. Belle, A., Thiagarajan, R., Soroushmehr, S. M., Navidi, F., Beard, D. A., & Najarian, K. (2015). Big data analytics in healthcare. BioMed Research International, 2015 (Article ID 370194): 1–16. DOI: https://doi.org/10.1155/2015/370194.
52. Sun, J., & Reddy, C. K. (2013). Big data analytics for healthcare. In *Proceedings of the 19th ACM SIGKDD International Conference on Knowledge Discovery and Data Mining*, 1525.
53. Mehta, N., & Pandit, A. (2018). Concurrence of big data analytics and healthcare: A systematic review. International Journal of Medical Informatics, 114: 57–65.
54. Archenaa, J., & Anita, E. M. (2015). A survey of big data analytics in healthcare and government. Procedia Computer Science, 50: 408–413.
55. Chaudhary, K., Alam, M., Al-Rakhami, M. S., & Gumaei, A. (2021). Machine learning based mathematical modelling for prediction of social media consumer behaviour using Big Data analytics. Journal of Big Data, 8(1): 1–20.
56. Alam, M. (2012, October). Cloud algebra for cloud database management system. In *Proceedings of the Second International Conference on Computational Science, Engineering and Information Technology*, 26–29.
57. Kaur, A., & Alam, M. (2013). Role of knowledge engineering in the development of a hybrid knowledge based medical information system for atrial fibrillation, American Journal of Industrial and Business Management, 3(1): 36–41.
58. Alam, M., & Shakil, K. A. (2014). A decision matrix and monitoring based framework for infrastructure performance enhancement in a cloud based environment. arXiv preprint arXiv:1412.8029.
59. Alam, M., & Sethi, S. (2013). Covert channel detection techniques. In *Cloud, Confluence 2013: The Next Generation Information Technology Summit (4th International Conference)*, 127–132. DOI: 10.1049/cp.2013.2305.
60. Shakil, K. A., & Alam, M. (2014). Data management in cloud-based environment using k-median clustering technique. International Journal of Computer Applications, 3, 8–13.
61. Alam, B., Doja, M. N., Alam, M., & Mongia, S. (2013). 5-layered architecture of cloud database management system. AASRI Procedia, 5, 194–199.
62. Shakil, K. A., Sethi, S., & Alam, M. (2015, March). An effective framework for managing university data using a cloud based environment. In *2015 2nd International Conference on Computing for Sustainable Global Development (INDIACom)*, 1262–1266.
63. Khan, I., Naqvi, S. K., Alam, M., & Rizvi, S. A. (2015, March). Data model for big data in cloud environment. In *2015 2nd International Conference on Computing for Sustainable Global Development (INDIACom)*, 582–585.
64. Alam, M., & Shakil, K. A. (2016). Big data analytics in cloud environment using Hadoop. *arXiv preprint arXiv:1610.04572*.
65. Kumar, V., Kumar, R., Pandey, S. K., & Alam, M. (2018). Fully homomorphic encryption scheme with probabilistic encryption based on Euler's theorem and application in cloud computing. In V. Aggarwal, V. Bhatnagar, & D. Mishra (Eds.), Big Data Analytics (pp. 605–611). Singapore: Springer.
66. Malhotra, S., Doja, M. N., Alam, B., & Alam, M. (2018). Generalized query processing mechanism in cloud database management system. In V. Aggarwal, V. Bhatnagar, & D. Mishra (Eds.), Big Data Analytics (pp. 641–648). Springer, Singapore.
67. Shakil, K. A., & Alam, M. (2018). Cloud computing in bioinformatics and big data analytics: Current status and future research. In Big Data Analytics (pp. 629–640). Singapore: Springer.

68. Malhotra, S., Doja, M. N., Alam, B., & Alam, M. (2017, May). Big data analysis and comparison of big data analytic approaches. In *2017 International Conference on Computing, Communication, and Automation (ICCCA)*, 309–314.
69. Khan, S., Shakil, K. A., & Alam, M. (2019, February). PABED – A tool for big education data analysis. In *2019 IEEE International Conference on Industrial Technology (ICIT)*, 794–799.
70. Khan, S., Liu, X., Shakil, K. A., & Alam, M. (2019). Big data technology-enabled analytical solution for quality assessment of higher education systems. International Journal of Advanced Computer Science and Applications (IJACSA), 10(6): 292–304.
71. Khan, S., Shakil, K. A., & Alam, M. (2017). Big data computing using cloud-based technologies, challenges, and future perspectives. arXiv preprint arXiv:1712.05233.
72. Shakil, K. A., Anis, S., & Alam, M. (2015). Dengue disease prediction using weka data mining tool. arXiv:1502.05167.
73. Shakil, K. A., Zareen, F. J., Alam, M., & Jabin, S. (2020). BAMHealthCloud: A biometric authentication and data management system for healthcare data in cloud. Journal of King Saud University-Computer and Information Sciences, 32(1): 57–64.
74. Khan, I., Naqvi, S. K., Alam, M., & Rizvi, S. N. A. (2018). A framework for twitter data analysis. In Big Data Analytics (pp. 297–303). Singapore: Springer.
75. Ali, S. A., Affan, M., & Alam, M. (2018). A study of efficient energy management techniques for cloud computing environment. arXiv preprint arXiv:1810.07458.
76. Venkatesh, V. G., Dubey, R., Joy, P., Thomas, M., Vijeesh, V., & Moosa, A. (2015). Supplier selection in blood bags manufacturing industry using TOPSIS model. International Journal of Operational Research, 24(4): 461–488.
77. Palomares, I., Kalutarage, H., Huang, Y., McCausland, P. M. R., & McWilliams, G. (2017, June). A fuzzy multicriteria aggregation method for data analytics: Application to insider threat monitoring. In *2017 Joint 17th World Congress of International Fuzzy Systems Association and 9th International Conference on Soft Computing and Intelligent Systems (IFSA – SCIS)*, 1–6.
78. Ullah, A. S., & Noor-E-Alam, M. (2018). Big data driven graphical information based fuzzy multi-criteria decision making. Applied Soft Computing, 63: 23–38.
79. Sahin, R. (2014). Multi-criteria neutrosophic decision making method based on score and accuracy functions under neutrosophic environment. arXiv preprint arXiv: 1412.5202.
80. Zhang, H. Y., Wang, J. Q., & Chen, X. H. (2014). Interval neutrosophic sets and their application in multicriteria decision making problems. The Scientific World Journal. 2014, ID: 645953.
81. Hamacher, H. (1978). Uber logische verknupfungen unscharfer aussagen und deren zugehörige bewertungsfunktionen. Progress in Cybernetics and Systems Research, 3: 276–288.
82. Dombi, J. (1982). A general class of fuzzy operators, the DeMorgan class of fuzzy operators, and fuzziness measures induced by fuzzy operators. Fuzzy Sets and Systems, 8(2): 149–163.
83. Klement, E. P., Mesiar, R., & Pap, E. (2000). Triangular norms, trends in logic. 8, Dordrecht: Kluwer Academic Publishers.
84. Murofushi, T., & Sugeno, M. (1989). An interpretation of fuzzy measures and the Choquet integral as an integral with respect to a fuzzy measure. Fuzzy Sets and Systems, 29(2): 201–227.

85. Liu, P., Chu, Y., Li, Y., & Chen, Y. (2014). Some generalized neutrosophic number Hamacher aggregation operators and their application to group decision making. International Journal of Fuzzy Systems, 16(2): 242–245.

86. Liu, P. (2013). Some Hamacher aggregation operators based on the interval-valued intuitionistic fuzzy numbers and their application to group decision making. IEEE Transactions on Fuzzy Systems, 22(1): 83–97.

87. Ye, J. (2014). Similarity measures between interval neutrosophic sets and their applications in multicriteria decision-making. Journal of Intelligent & Fuzzy Systems, 26(1): 165–172.

4

Prediction of Marketing by the Consumer Analytics

C.C. Jayasundara
University of Kelaniya
Colombo, Sri Lanka

CONTENTS

DOI: 10.1201/9781003307761-4

4.1 THE MOTIVATION FOR THE STUDY

Marketers have used a variety of methods to understand what customer motivation is related to their products and services. There traditional methods like focus groups, online surveys, etc., were used to find out how customers behaved. Nevertheless, the question for me is whether the above methods are enough to find the motivations of each individual among the millions of customers. Therefore, in this world of "big data" that triggers insights, marketers need to work on everything they know about their customers to maximise their business revenues, optimise sales, increase customer loyalty, and finally to achieve higher customer satisfaction for their products and services. This is consumer analytics, is also referred to by some experts as scientific marketing due to its advanced scientific nature, and is a new subject in the business world. This has led me to present a combination of big data analytics in general and consumer analytics specifically with behavioural marketing practices to make it easier for the scholars interested in understanding how to improve both customers' buying motivations and business decisions through the solutions of scientific marketing. Though the motivation of the study was to increase our basic understanding of consumer analytics, in the long run, this could also contribute to the creation and development of extensions in consumer analytics.

4.2 INTRODUCTION

Corporate data in the form of structured data like traditional databases (e.g., CRM) or nonstructured data is now increasingly being driven by new communication technologies (Lansley & Longley, 2016). Social networks such as Facebook, Instagram, TikTok, and Twitter have had a massive influence on consumer decisiveness for business, brand promotion, and then profit maximisation. Thus, Big data is getting bigger and bigger every day and businesses' attention to big data is also getting improved frequently.

The significance of big data does not always turn around the size of dataset that you have, but it does revolve around what you do with the data. You can analyse data and use them for 1) cost reduction, 2) time reduction, 3) new product development and optimal offers, 4) better decision making and 5) good governance. Customer-related big data plays a significant function in marketing. Thus, we need to understand what 3Vs are in big data. So let's find out what they are. Understanding the 3V of their big data management is essential for businesses to be better equipped to deal with customers. Laney (2001) introduced Vs 3 in big data management: according to him, Vs 3 is volume, variety, and velocity. Recently, two more Vs were added to the big data equation – i.e., variability and value. Gartner's definition of big data in 2012 summarises these five dimensions as "high-volume, high-velocity and/or high-variety information assets that demand cost-effective, innovative forms of information processing that enable enhanced insight, decision making, and process automation" (Fan & Bifet, 2013).

Many scientists have created different methodologies to capture, process, analyse, and finally visualise a vast array of big data with a sport processing time (Khanna et al., 2016). Various disciplines are used to create these novel methodologies such as mathematics, statistics, optimisation techniques, signal processing, machine learning, data visualisation, data mining, and social network analysis (Malhotra et al., 2017; Chen & Zhang, 2014). Every platform of every big data has precise operability, associated with it and a specific focus on it. For example, some big data platforms are designed for group settings such as Apache Hadoop or Pentaho Business Analytics, while the rest are on real-time analytics such as Apache Kafka or Storm (Chen & Zhang, 2014). Logical layers offer a line of attack to organise components when considering the architecture of big data systems. However, from a business perspective, a big data system is important to us only when it is designed to gain the necessary and important skills to sustain business decisions. Predictive analytics applications could be sourced for big data loads, including advanced data loading and advanced machine learning solutions (Hazen et al., 2014). In marketing analytics, decisions are made based on big data, used particularly for selling and promotion goals. It enables marketers to have a strong marketing understanding holistically and technology to solve real marketing problems and maximise the profit margins (Gririgsby, 2015) while retaining customers with the business in the long run (Rajaiah et al., 2020).

4.3 CONSUMERS AND DATA ANALYTICS

Prediction of changing consumer behaviour is one of the biggest challenges facing marketers around the world. But today, as a result of technological advancements, forecasting has become an important element that always comes up with new products, consumer, and market needs. As today's consumers have a wide range of buying options, buying behaviour of customers is constantly changing with the advent of e-commerce and m-commerce, due to many logistical and competitive advantages over traditional marketing mechanisms. However, customers are often left with more choices because they find it usually difficult to decide what the best option is. The wide array of choices has complicated the lives of customers as well as the business decisions of marketers. Therefore, smart marketers now use data analytics to better understand their customer behaviour because marketing is a complex process involving various aspects of the business and its customers, and understanding customer behaviour has become an essential component of strategic marketing. Today, the seller is always behind buyers. This is not to chase after buyers and sell the goods but to market the goods and services that sellers are constantly following customers through the use of electronic technologies. Placing the product on the buyer does not make a sale. To convert customer's interest to buying intention and retain customers with the business, marketers have to struggle more in the digital movement. This is because different businesses offer different options and customers can easily find out what those options are through the Internet and various digital strategies. Thus, it is difficult for customers to evaluate each option as there is a high range of options available and sometimes they can even make a purchase decision based on insignificant factors due to its complexity. Using smart and intuitive data analytic tools, it is comfortable to find the digital footprints of potential buyers. Infrastructure has improved the ability to collect extensive data in the business, which includes consumers' buying data, consumer characteristics, consumer preferences, consumers' sensitivity to price and quality of products, consumer satisfaction, delivery channels, etc. Almost every aspect of a business is open for data collection, operations, products from the supply chain management, and customer behaviour. With the advancement of computer technology, algorithms have been developed and adapted to enable these databases for more comprehensive and in-depth analyses. This large amount of data has led to a growing interest in how to obtain useful information and knowledge from datasets (Kaur & Alam, 2013; Malhotra et al., 2018; Kumar et al., 2018). This leads to the use of data for competitive advantage (Surendro, 2019). Today, cloud computing and combined cloud computing conjoin big data from different technologies that are used for different analytics (Khan et al., 2018; Alam, 2012; Alam & Shakil, 2015; Sethi et al., 2015; Alam et al., 2016). Table 4.1 indicates the potential areas of customer analytics for marketing use.

TABLE 4.1

Potential Areas of Customer Analytics Use

Marketing Capability	Definition	Analytics Use
Pricing	An ability to adjust prices quickly as a response to changes in a market. This capability includes pricing skills, knowledge of competitors' pricing tactics, and also knowledge of the current level of competitor's pricing.	Analytics can be used to optimise pricing by predicting the elasticity of demand and willingness to pay on a customer basis (Rygielski et al., 2002).
Product development	An ability to develop new products and services, to conduct marketing tests of new products, to launch successful new products, and to ensure that they are matching customer needs.	Provide effective targeted product development capabilities, predict features of the product that would meet customer demand (Rygielski et al., 2002).
Channel	An ability to ensure a strong relationship with customers, to attract and retain the best customers, to provide a high level of service support to the customer and end user, to work closely with customers, and to create value for a customer.	Analytics help to identify what product is better to sell through which channel and predict customer lifetime value (CLV) (Rygielski et al., 2002).

Source: Bazylevska (2011).

4.4 BUSINESS INTELLIGENCE AND PREDICTIVE ANALYTICS

The use of business intelligence (BI) to solve problems is now widely accepted. This is in contrast to traditional behavioural patterns analysis. The translation of transaction data into behavioural data for further analysis facilitates clear and quantitative behavioural interventions, patterns, and early effects of behaviour (Cao, 2010; Melnik et al., 2020). This behavioural structure is based on domain knowledge, intelligence, logic, and the conversion of data found by existing data management systems into behavioural information. Accordingly, knowledge of behavioural data analytics is required to discover behavioural intelligence, thereby further developing an understanding of behavioural patterns in the physical world. For example, IBM Center for Big Data Analytics asks a series of questions: Do you produce personalised offers targeted to your customers? Do you know your customers and provide them with real-time, relevant, and ideal products or services grounded on data-based intelligence?

You can build and promote better relationships with your customers, extract information about their behaviour, needs, and preferences, and analyse customer responses and their ratings on a particular product or service. Then, you can find out what they need, what they want, and what they can buy. This information is very important to serve them when they have an intention to buy a product or service. BI helps to achieve business objectives by focusing on continuous operations, and business analytics changes the way that a business operates its tradings. However, the ultimate goal of both seems to be the same. Businesses can provide the product or service that best suits their needs before being expressed the need. Almost savvy providers understand that there is a gap in big data search. They know how important it is to guide customers wisely to know who they are and their priorities to achieve. This is known as financial DNA discovery in data analytics, and this process of self-discovery enables a strong, valid, and structured approach to discover all aspects of a customer's financial personality. Further, financial DNA is an exclusive solution to unearth all the magnitudes of a customer's fiscal personality to make financial decisions using more comprehensive behavioural financial analytics. For example, the stock market manages highly relevant data, especially on prices, volumes, values, and indicators. This data is usually analysed. Then, we can find out the financial personality of some investors in the stock market. This financial personality is a behaviour of a person in terms of investments. These behavioural implications show us that transactional data supports behavioural analysis. Take mobile transactions as an example. Behavioural analysts analyse how consumer behaviour occurs through traditional consumer behavioural data with BI, which helps us determine future consumer behaviour. For instance, network transmissions such as frequency and duration, incoming calls, payment work for bills, nonpayment disconnections period data, time spent to make the payment after disconnection, etc., can be used for behavioural modelling of telecom customers.

Further, imagine what it would be like if you knew what your customers wanted when they entered your store. What do you do if the item the customer is looking for is not in the stock? Therefore, your potential customers may be disturbed and lost. It's easier if you already know what he/she wants and when your customer wants something which is out of stock?

For that, it is important to analyse the behaviour of customers. Thus, by examining the analytics, it can gain insight into:

- Customer database to identify customer behaviour.
- Attract and connect potential customers: target customers with relevant offers by analysing past purchases and profiles.
- Improving customer retention: it enables businesses to use an active retention approach to evaluate customer value and retain customers.

Again, according to big data, forecast analytics can indicate to which customers can be targeted for cross-selling. For example, if a man buys a shirt for $4000, a BMW car would be a better target for him. Cross-marketing and internal product promotion are branches of successful predictive analytic efforts. This is a direct example of predictive analytics. With the advent of big data and the Internet, forecasting has undergone more modern changes. Advanced computer algorithms have made the science of forecasting more accurate and far-reaching than ever before using big data. The difference between BI and data analytics cannot be drawn line by line. However, if we talk about the difference between the two, we can divide the analytics into three parts: descriptive, predictive, and prescriptive. Descriptive analytics takes data and makes it something that business managers can visualise, understand, and interpret. It provides insight into the historical performance and describes what has happened. Predictive analytics provides an insight into future outcomes. Predictive analytics provides advice on actions to take. In simple term, descriptive analytics will give you an answer to "what happened in the past" and predictive analytics will give you the answer to the question of "what may happen in the future". Prescriptive analytics requires knowledge of advanced modelling techniques and many analytical algorithms. In particular, prescriptive analytics helps prevent fraud, limit risk, increase efficiency, achieve business goals, and create customers that are more loyal. For instance, prescriptive analytics can be used by hospitals to improve patient recovery. It is placed in the context of healthcare data to assess the cost effectiveness of various procedures and treatments and to evaluate clinical procedures. It can also be used to analyse hospitalised patients at increased risk of reentry so that health care providers can do more through patient education and medical follow-up to avoid frequent hospitalisation. Big data strategist Van Rijmenam (2019) says that if we see descriptive analytics as the basis of BI and predictive and prescriptive analytics as to the basis of big data today.

4.5 PREDICTIVE ANALYTICS

Customer analytics is an amazing part of marketing science. With regard to continuous, personal/household (consumer level) behavioural data analysis, it provides insights that are particularly useful in identifying and addressing business issues. Data can be obtained online or offline from customer transactions or interactions, or management sources such as customer panels or loyalty panels. These structured data sources are best suited to identify purchasing behaviours in products and services. Analytical parameters-based analytics, group purchasing, asset analysis and behavioural brand loyalty, overlap analysis, crate analysis, profit loss, and new product sales forecasting have the ability to perform over a wide range recurring purchasing standards particularly.

Predictive analytics is not a new subject. This endeavour has been in the businesses for a long time and has been used very successfully in forecasting analysis of organisations ranging from small businesses to large-scale companies. However, the benefits and potential of forecasting analysis are valued because of the big data phenomenon (Ogunleye, 2013). When it comes to the use of predictive analytics, many organisations use it not only to forecast their strategically important corporate judgements but also to inform relevant stakeholders about the current and future trends in the business and to predict future outcomes or events with high accuracy. Defining predictive analytics refers to the use of skills, specificities, and software potentials to excerpt, analyse, and translate data in a clear and consumable manner for organisational planning or a decision-making process. In general, forecasting analytics or predictive analytics are widely used for the prediction of business trends, improvement of employee performance, and usually for making data-driven predictions in the decision-making process in marketing (OPCC, 2012).

Predictive analytics conjoins humanoid skills with data and tools such as machine learning and applications of algorithms to identify data patterns grounded on historical or present data that will predict future probabilities. To make predictions, the analytics uses data mining methods (Shakil et al., 2015), grouping taxonomies, and progression statistics to identify the patterns, and then the predictions are made based upon the identified pattern. However, that is not all. To be the best vendor, shopping is still in the basket left because buyers value the best or most ubiquitous option that suits them best their needs, their economy, and their preferences. In

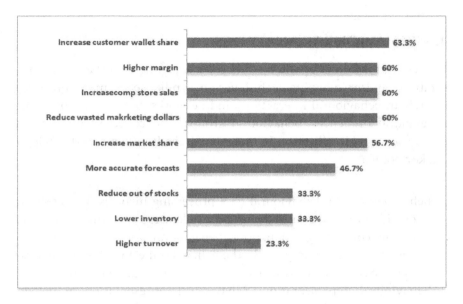

FIGURE 4.1
Hard benefits of up-to-date customer intelligence technology. (RIS News, Sept 2010.)

general, customers do not promote businesses but customers' expectations should be identified by the business and their business should be adapted accordingly. This is where predictive analytics is needed. This is also known as consumer intelligence by some experts and its benefits are reflected in Figure 4.1.

Retailers come up with many hard benefits that are directly related to consumer intelligence technology. They see this as an approach to achieve important business objectives and performance indicators. September 2010 RIS Retailer Survey reveals that 63.3% of people think that consumer intelligence assists them to develop their businesses by increasing customer wallet share. Sixty per cent says it contributes to better profits, increase comp store trades, and diminution of tired marketing dollars. RIS research stresses that 40% of retail winners use customer data to improve the business as a top-3 opportunity for customer programmes, compared with just 7% of laggards. Data-based organisations often use the terms "business intelligence" and "data analytics" interchangeably. BI uses historical data to describe what has happened. Some people distinguish between BI and data analytics to predict what will happen in the future. Both BI and data analytics require a series of analyses in order to make predictions.

4.6 BEHAVIOURAL ANALYTICS

Behavioural informatics and analytics is a scientific field that deals with symbolic and/or mapping techniques to symbolise or map consumer behaviour, behavioural interactions and networks, behavioural patterns, behavioural influences, behavioural groups, and collective intelligence and behavioural intelligence. In more detail, the BA addresses the following key points:

Behavioural Data: behavioural data processing involves the detection of hidden or associated behavioural elements in transaction data, further converting and mapping behavioural-oriented elements into behavioural feature space. In the behavioural element space, behavioural elements are presented in sets of behavioural elements.

Behavioural Representation: Behavioural representation or behavioural modelling is the construction of behavioural-specific specifications to describe the relationship between behavioural elements. Specifications rearrange behavioural elements to fit the presentation and construction of the behavioural sequence. It also provides an integrated mechanism for describing and presenting behavioural models, behavioural elements, behavioural effects, and patterns.

Behavioural Impact Analysis: The focus here is on examining behavioural events that are associated with more impact on business processes and/or business returns. What happens here is that behavioural impact analysis models the behavioural impact.

Behaviour Pattern Analysis: There are generally two methods used for behavioural analysis. One is to find behavioural patterns that do not take into account behavioural effects and the other is to analyse the relationship between behavioural sequences and specific influences.

The Emergence of Behavioural Intelligence: When inquiring about behavioural influences and patterns, it is essential to look for behavioural events, evolution and life cycles, the influence of specific behavioural evolution, and the existence of specific behavioural rules and patterns on intelligence. Here, behavioural rules play an important role in modelling behavioural patterns by defining, demonstrating applying behavioural rules, protocols, and relationships and examining their impact on behavioural evolution and the emergence of intelligence.

Behavioural Network: A behavioural network is a collection of several behavioural sources. Specific human behaviour within such a network is usually emphasised to influence the roles of the behavioural network in a given situation. Behavioural network analysis is the study of intrinsic mechanisms within a network. For example, behavioural laws, interaction protocols, the convergence and divergence of relevant behavioural elements, as well as network location structures, relationships, and influences can affect the constructs of behavioural networks.

Behavioural Simulation: Monitoring dynamics play an important role in understanding all of the above mechanisms that can be present in behavioural data, as well as the influence of rules/protocols/patterns on monitoring dynamics, the emergence of behavioural intelligence, and the building of a social behavioural network.

Behavioural Presentation: From an analytical and BI perspective, this can be seen as the exploration of presentation media and tools that can effectively explain the motivation and interest of stakeholders in specific behavioural data. Visual analytic research on behavioural patterns is currently receiving high attention from researchers. This behavioural information and analysis involve the use of technologies and tools to gain knowledge about behavioural and social behaviour networks. This concept is also introduced by some experts as behavioural computing.

4.7 WHY BEHAVIOUR ANALYTICS

Behaviour in both artificial societies and human societies, such as computerised business support systems, emerges as a key component. Behaviour involves dealing with many institutions and objects in the business, such as corporate objects, behavioural subjects, causes, effects, and opportunities. Besides, many behavioural situations involve a network of social behaviours that include social and institutional factors and collective intelligence. Therefore, behavioural-oriented analytics can provide insight into external information, external business objects, and their occurrences and patterns, as well as causes and effects in particular.

In today's management information systems, factors related to the above behaviour are usually hidden in the transaction data. Transaction data are usually object oriented, and they are linked through the internal keys of an organisation, creating a client-institution space. In the spaces that exist in such client entities, there are behavioural elements embedded in multiple transactions that are weak or lack direct relation. Thus, behaviour affects the transaction data. It is not effective to search only for human behaviour patterns internally by analysing transaction data. In order to effectively and efficiently investigate genuine behaviour patterns, it is important to extract behavioural elements from the transaction data and to study how behavioural orientation and behavioural pattern analysis is affected. Behavioural data presentation is different from normal transaction data presentation. In order to understand and analyse behaviour and its effects, it is important to map a space using the behavioural characteristics and behavioural orientation elements contained in transaction data. Analytical and practical analysis of behavioural patterns and effects can also explain how behaviour changes and transits from the transactional space to the behavioural space. To map from the transactional space to the behavioural space, it is important to develop methods and tools for behavioural representation, processing, and related engineering. That is, the sciences behind this are behavioural information and analytical sciences. Although we can generally use data processing for behavioural elemental-oriented data, it is difficult to distinguish clear behavioural patterns and the causes and effects that influence them. Here, we expect direct behavioural data to meet the behavioural analysis smoothly. In addition, new methods must be used for behaviour and influence patterns and corresponding mechanisms. Within this need, we can understand and investigate problems and their potential and appropriate solutions from a modern perspective that goes far beyond traditional tools, with the development of technologies for business behavioural information analysis. For example, we can do this through mechanisms such as target behaviour and behavioural networks as well as perspectives. Because of the integration of behaviour and its subjects and objects, it is possible to gain a broader understanding of behaviour and gain a better knowledge of what the broad factors surrounding a business problem are and their causes and effects. Examples include human demographics, human activities, as well as environmental and behavioural influences.

4.8 GENERAL BUSINESS INTELLIGENCE ANALYTICS (BIA) PROCESS

With the BIA components, we have presented above, we can show the general functionality of the BIA algorithm as shown below. (Γ) Development of behavioural pattern analysis through behavioural analysis (P (Γ)) and effects (I (Γ)) through behavioural patterns ((Γ)), (Ω) development, presentation of behavioural patterns (V (Γ)), and translate decision-making into business rules (R).

$$\text{BIA}: \Psi(\text{DB})\Theta(\Gamma)- \to \Gamma\Omega, e, c, \text{ti}()- \to P\Lambda, e, c, \text{bi}()- \to R \qquad (4.1)$$

Following the principle of actionable knowledge discovery (Equation 4.1), this process can be further decomposed and modelled in terms of the following steps.

BIA PROCESS: The Process of behaviour Informatics and Analytics
INPUT: original dataset Ψ;
OUTPUT: behaviour patterns P and operationalisable business
rules R;
Step 1: behaviour modeling $\Theta(\Gamma)$;
Given dataset Ψ;
Develop behaviour modeling method θ ($\theta \in \Theta$) with technical interestingness ti();
Employ method θ on the dataset Ψ;
Construct behaviour vector set Γ;
Step 2: Converting to behavioural data $\Phi(\Gamma)$;
Given behaviour modeling method θ; FOR j = 1 to (count(Ψ)) Deploy behaviour modeling method θ on dataset Ψ;
Construct behaviour vector γ; ENDFOR Construct behaviour dataset $\Phi(\Gamma)$;
Step 3: Analysing behavioural patterns P Γ;
Given behaviour data ($\Phi(\Gamma)$);
Design pattern mining method $\omega \in \Omega$;
Employ the method ω on dataset $\Phi \Gamma$;
Extract behaviour pattern set P;
Step 4: Converting behaviour patterns P to operationalisable business rules R;
Given behaviour pattern set P;

Develop behaviour modeling method Λ;

Involve business interestingness bi() and constraints c in the environment e;

Generate business rules R;

Source: Cao (2008).

4.9 RELEVANCE TO MARKETING AND DATA PROFESSIONALS

It is clear from the above discussion that organisations can reap many benefits from the proper implementation of data analytics. Information technology enables marketers to communicate with their potential customers and build stronger customer relationships. Dupre (2013) states that by allowing marketers to take the lead in data analytics, they can use this customer data to better attract positive expectations of customers, increase overall sales efficiency, and optimise marketing Return on Investment (ROI). Furthermore, it was pointed out that marketers can use these tactics to monitor the behaviour of their customers and maintain relationships with them.

Also, Zhong et al. (2004) state that data engineers and data analysts frequently use clustering methods because of their high accuracy rate. Li et al. (2019) report that the Bayesian network is widely used to make predictions from incomplete or missing data. The growing demand for customer analytics has led many companies to try to reach their customers and understand their needs through the programmes they offer and are now dealing with businesses.

While many companies seek to investigate their offerings, it is important to have a strategic understanding of how customers respond to their performance marketing efforts, how their website is experienced, how they test or taste their offers, and ultimately translate into purchase decisions. On the other hand, growth is a constant demand but will slow if innovation stops. Machine learning and artificial intelligence are still essential for data analytics for high-precision and sensitive forecasting. Industry professionals can only talk about the digital marketing experience, but three items are often discussed in the analytics, and it is clear that the marketing future lies in them. They are the following.

Media Mix Modeling (MMM): MMM uses advanced analytics and benchmarks to understand how each marketing channel operates and contributes to a business. Much research has been done on how offline methods such as online banners, stores, and television can be integrated with a wide range of digital data and measured. It is considered the future because campaigns are increasingly integrated by nature. MMM provides a high level of understanding of specific marketing strategies over a long marketing period. This allows marketers to understand a variety of trends and patterns, such as seasonality, weather, holidays, and brand parts. It analyses historical data that is usually two or three years.

Virtual Reality (VR) Analytics: The data obtained from the VR can be used by businesses to better assess risk, understand customer behaviour, and enhance customer interactions. For example, The way a person sees and observes items such as clothes and jewellery through his eyes is done to pick up the customer's behaviour until the moment they finally decide to buy them, which is captured by VR analytic tools. In addition, you can observe how people use hand and body movements to measure how they interact and respond to this object. Companies are experimenting with AR (augmented reality)/ VR offerings, and we see that large traffic is shifting to mobile apps. The obvious trend, however, is that experience in the field of analytics has been a major factor in opening up more technological innovations, especially in the retail industry.

Data-Driven Attribution: Data-driven attribution is a variety of attribution models, such as multitouch attribution that monitors all activities and engagements throughout a customer visit. Active and inactive communication of customers provides insights based on how people interact with various ads and how they decide to become customers. Data from your account is used to determine which ads, keywords, and advertising campaigns have the most impact on business objectives. You can use data-driven attribution to translate Google analytics from websites, store visits, and search network campaigns.

4.10 PREDICTIVE BEHAVIOUR MODELLING

The stage of a customer's behaviour extends from the moment a customer becomes aware of a "need" or "desire" for a purchase transaction for a product/service (Nguyen et al., 2018). It involves three important stages. The consumer journey to becoming aware of, evaluating, and purchasing a new product or service consists of three stages that shape the internal marketing framework. In precise, it is awareness, consideration, and determination. The user, who consumes the product or service is called the payer, buyer, consumer, or customer. Understanding customer behaviour is complicated by the fact that each customer's attitude towards each of the above stages changes. According to Solomon et al. (2009), in addition to these three stages, it is equally important to study the postpurchase stage behaviour, which demonstrates the level of consumer satisfaction that researchers need to focus on. A customer's repetitive buying behaviour usually shows high satisfaction, and sellers need to focus more on completing a product repurchase, which can significantly increase the company's sales and ultimately increase the profit margin. Furthermore, Myers (2001) states that consumer postpurchase behaviour facilitates the collection of appropriate feedback for products and ultimately helps maintain product standards. However, as this is a complex process, it requires a thorough analysis of customers and their preferences, as well as the level of customer involvement in the coplanning process.

Evaluations should not be based solely on customer preferences. Other relevant dynamics should also be taken into consideration. For example, if a customer decides to buy a product or service, how much would he or she be willing to pay to purchase the product or service? Whether it is within the consumer's ability to pay, and by studying consumer behaviour, it is important to inquire how consumers invest resources such as time, money, and effort into their purchasing process. According to Prasad and Jha (2014), the types of products and services to be purchased, the quantity required, the place and time of purchase of that product or service, as well as the method of payment used for purchases are also important. Since the primary purpose of introducing a product or service to the market is to meet the needs and demands of the customer, the product or service must be marketed strategically. From a business point of view, that strategy is to increase the profitability of the business organisation and the purchasing power of that good or service (Pahwa et al., 2017).

Predictive behaviour modelling is the science of applying mathematical and statistical methods, for historical and transactional data to predict future customer behaviour. In the field of consumer analytics, predictive behaviour models consumers, allowing marketers or financial experts to make decisions based on the predicted future of consumers, rather than based on historical data analysis that goes beyond passive analysis. Predictive behaviour modelling is commonly used to select the best marketing strategies to implement in an individual customer group and identify which customers can change their spending levels. An important part of marketing theory is customer behaviour. The literature notes that the study of consumer consumption patterns particularly buying patterns is significantly important in the marketing process (Wang et al., 2020). While consumers' acknowledge that marketing is a major factor influencing greater demand, traditional marketing concepts are not sufficient to test consumer behaviour. Because customer beliefs and behaviours vary from person to person, maintaining the same traditional marketing practices can be a challenge for customers to buy products and services from the same business in the long run. Moreover, by studying the preferences of customers, it is clear that marketing needs to build a strong relationship with the different tastes and preferences of customers.

4.11 PREDICTIVE MODELS

Predictive models are usually used to forecast twofold occurrences. For instance, buying or not buying or trying to make continuous predictions. Accordingly, statistical and data mining methods vary according to analytical objectives. The main mechanisms that we use to forecast a twofold occurrence are logistic regression and artificial neural networks (ANNs). In predicting continuous impacts, such as contributing to the profit margin, we use neural networks (NNs) and regressions. Additional techniques are used for purposes that do not fit into these categories. Regressions on poison distribution could be exercised for forecasting ordinal results (e.g., 0, 1, 2), and hazard models are used to forecast the time for a possible occurrence. The hazard model is a statistical technique for determining "hazardous activity", or the likelihood of a person experiencing an event over a period of time is subject to the individuals potential risk of occurrence. For examples of these are predicting how many reminding phone calls a telecommunication company should make to us to pay our unpaid phone bill and finding out what we can do to optimise the retention of customers who come to our company to purchase certain products. The primary driver is the one who decides which technology to use based on the data miner's experience. Accordingly, there are several different modelling methods for different purposes, and often these methods tend to give similar results. When we choose a technology, we should also pay more attention to the total variables chosen and the practicing background of the model. For example, NNs have a tendency to select a large number variables rather than regressions. In addition, if we use the updated properties, we may have problems with marking or activation of future models. Also, the best models do not deliver the largest rate of return. They contain high-priced upgrades or consumer attributes that are difficult to implement in practice. Therefore, we need to take into account the total implementation cost for the analytical solution when looking for the optimal solution. Optimal transformation of variables and their combination should be considered in model building. Here, the methods of using models vary according to the design technology. Undoubtedly, regression analysis contributes to the better formation of linear connections, and the NN stands out in identifying nonlinear connections. Data conversion and reduction are done to minimise errors and to optimise the correlation between independent variables and dependent variables. Sometimes, the final variables that we find probably are not the most effective single variables. For instance, in forecasting age and earnings because age is closely related to income, which means that income increases with age. Nevertheless, often at a certain age, the income is low or stable. Most of the data gathered by age and earnings are not independent and the resulting overlap causes an error. We need to minimise this error to optimise the model's forecasting power through data reduction methods. In addition, once the final model is selected to measure the predictive accuracy, it should be checked with another dataset and the model verified. This verification database must be the same sample obtained under the same dynamics; otherwise, the model cannot be correctly adapted. However, if possible, it is best to have several verification datasets from different periods. Databases verified by alternative time frames further assure us that the derivative model is a good representation of the customer world. Accordingly, it can be determined whether the model is a generic model or a defective model. A model that adapts to data at different times is error minimised. Here, we can even explore seasonal issues with several verification datasets in different time frames.

4.12 CONSUMER ANALYTICS

4.12.1 Consumer Forecasting Analytics

Behavioural data is the data that a customer goes through after learning that a product has been purchased. It contains the use of these stored interactions to capture customer events and actions over time and to determine the general behaviour and behavioural intentions of customers. Consumer analytics is the process by which consumers' transactional data enquire about unique and functional components of customers and their transactions. That is, it uses customer behaviour data for predictions and so on. These analyses can help the organisation achieve its goals by building specific marketing goals and creating goal-based activities. Customer analytics creates opportunities for effective and advanced CRM in businesses. These analytical methods vary based on the factors such as objectivity, industrial environment, and practical applications.

There are a number of ways in which retailers can benefit from customer analytics. A pioneering example is the Guardagni and Little's paper, whose authors used multitasking to help retailers and manufacturers understand how marketing mixes, specially pricing and promotion decisions, affect the sales and market share of their products. Much of the work in consumer analytics in the retail sector follows the contributions of Guadagni and Little (1983). Let us find out what are the specialties here. Working on CRM and CLV is one unique research path in the modern day. According to Kumar and Petersen (2012), the power of the CLV metric can be used to maximise the profitability of retailers' businesses and to implement a CLV management framework. Many entrepreneurs today find CRM and CLV systems and strategies as powerful mechanisms that bring many benefits to their businesses. These data mining methods can be divided into two parts as described above. Predictive models use the customer's previous interactions with the business to predict future events, while clients with similar behaviours and attributes use the segmentation method to make different groups. Both of these methods allow marketers to maximise their advertising management and the sales targeting process.

One of the key benefits of data in customer sales and behaviour analytics is ROI predictions. Such forecasts are important for budget and strategic planning. The use of predictions generates intelligent and evidence-based sales goal based on sales records for the present as well as the past. The sales manual is used to minimise or eliminate errors based on human activity, which leads to errors in forecasting. Businesses use ROI predictive analytics to maximise their sales and revenue that can be a valuable tool for marketers. When reviewing your strategy in the newly evaluated year, it may be time to consider implementing predictive analytics in your business strategy. Let's look at something that marketers can do when they go with all available data. Predictive analytics can be used for designated seasonal consumer behaviour. This is especially true for online marketing, where the most successful e-commerce websites prevail, that emphasises the products that customers want at a certain time or certain season. Second, can you direct your sales to customers who are likely to buy the cheapest products while focusing on rich customers for luxury products effectively? Next, offer alternatives to customers' buying habits if the product is unavailable. Once the customer approaches you, find out which substitute product may be bought by the customer if the particular product that the customer is looking for is no longer with your business. It seems that problems with the logistics offers occur, based on the forecasting algorithm, to determine whether an alternative option can be sold to the customer. If Mercedes Benz doesn't avail in the market, we may try to sell Audi based on what consumer analytics predicts about the most possible alternative for the said customer. The fifth is customer retention. Therefore, prioritise the client's preferences correspond to the client's previous buying patterns grounded on several factors so that they can make customer retention. Achieve customer satisfaction with easy-to-market marketing, detailed customer data with past purchases and present purchases are important for discovering the potentials of the customers in the context of product or service marketing.

4.12.2 Point of Sale Data (POS)

The unique attraction of POS data is that it is easily accessible from the basic sales tools. Chronological methods are used to find and assess existing patterns in past sales data and use them to predict future demand. However, this forecasting method sometimes appears to be weak because it is a by-product of demand censorship. This means that overdemand increases sales and this excess information on demand are not reported below the existing inventory level. For example, if an inventory has 100 items in one product, the demand is 180, but the excess demand of 80 after 100 is unrecorded, which means that no one in the business knows that there was a demand for 80 items. For these 80 increasing items, the business just says that we run out of goods so there is no way to supply, but it is not recorded that there is an excess demand of 80. Companies do not report demand information in warehousing and report information on inventory exceeding demand. Censorship of such extra requests tends to go downhill and its consequences are poor inventory decisions, further increasing the extent of censorship. This problem can be worsened when companies sell multiple products and when the stock runs out and there are substitute products. Then, the company may end up underrating the demand for bestselling products. Various researchers have shown the problem of demand censorship and how that problem affects demand forecasting (Wecker, 1978), especially how they are adversely affected. But they have also pointed out important consumer features such as price flexibility (Dixon, Seaton, & Waterson, 2014) and vital stock decisions. Scholars specialised in managing an operational business environment have come up with solutions to this problem through several econometric methods, and the problem here is that implementation of such econometric solutions is a very complex process.

The last decade has seen an expansion of payment models in the market, i.e., POS, mPOS, NFC-based m-wallet, other prepaid devices, QR, BBPS, etc. Online markets explore real-time data analytics and censorship chains in conjunction with cognitive learning to mitigate the risks of banking payment systems with increasing digital transactions using many different payment models. Fintech technology has developed adaptive and step-by-step verification solutions for e-commerce transactions. The use of data analytics is a key to growth as it allows players to profile and enhance digital analytics data such as increasing the efficiency of risk management, expansion of banking products and services in financial services, increasing opportunities for top-selling and cross-selling, business models focus on customer orientation, etc. Digital transaction data stimulation, loyalty, and lending decisions are also emerging due to the power of forecasting. Digital transaction data allows banks to establish a predictable pattern for loan repayment schedules, determining loans, loan repayment ability, etc. These data analytics provide a unique service that stimulates a payment grounded on the trading history of merchants on its platforms. Modern point-of-sale systems can capture detailed data on sales times as well as the availability of different products in stock at different times.

This method has traditionally been used as a base for collecting sales data and predicting future demand. Now, cashboxes and readers of credit/ debit cards are already obsolete. POS systems offer the customer a so-called noncritical browsing experience and a transactional data collection system. The POS kiosk, which requires minimal assistance to execute, cuts lines, and speed up checkouts, are now switching to mobile devices with the help of hardware such as NFC-based payments or Square 1 that allow retailers of different ranges to deal with their customers as well as to have different communications with consumers under different conditions. For example, you can contact Apple Inc., to pay for products using Apple Pay, a payment app of Apple on a customer's cell phones at the retail store and enlist the assistance of any retail staff member to inspect the product.

The fact that the POS device is probably a special iPhone is special. In a certain case, Amazon Go 3, for example, says, "No lines. No exit" – the Amazon Go app handles customers' phones for payment and its sensors detect what is in the shopping cart. A POS system is a unique unit that brings together many sales channels, which minimise the difference between customers' physical and online stores today. The main advantage of this system is that all transactions between the customer and the storeowner are integrated into the company's CRM system, either through software applications or through loyalty initiatives (Pratminingsih et al., 2013). It allows us to easily access different types of indexed or encrypted data, which include demographic profiles of customers, product-ordering history, loyalty information, paid discounts, coupon releases, exchange rates, and many more. The second advantage is that modern POS systems integrate with inventory and storage systems to give retailers and customers access to products and consumer access to wider physical and virtual store networks.

4.12.3 Route Data in Storage

With the intention of grasping the buyer behaviour in the digital age, it is also imperative to examine the "non-buying" behaviour of consumers. Many shoppers do not complete purchases even though they have items in their virtual shopping carts. Industry studies show that 88 percent of online shoppers have abandoned their electric carts in the past (Forrester Research, 2005). New storage technologies blur the gap between brick and mortar and the virtual search and purchase experience. Information on consumer search is e-search, the process by which consumers select a specific element of a stimulus to clarify cognitions associated with a brand or product, as well as to satisfy intentions (Howard & Sheth, 1969). Data and purchases (cart collecting, cart abandonment, etc.) that were once only available to large-scale web-based retailers are now also associated with smaller retail stores. (Chaudhary & Kumar, 2016). Beacons link up with the consumer's smartphone through Bluetooth and detect as soon as a potential client enters the shop. Macy's ShopKick app – the application provides examples of this type of activity. It is activated by beacons and integrated with the search experience of the client, storing customer location, pushing store content, offers, and benefits (Tuttle et al., 2014). Kruger,

Inc., one of the largest and most reputable companies in the U.S. retailer, has introduced a new approach to digital rack edges for POS. There, the customer is attached to a personalised information system, including pricing, as they move through the digital rack edges. Another example, one of the high-end retailers like Marks and Spencer is currently experimenting with "virtual rails". Featuring three 46 screens and three physical rails with 50 samples of clothing each, the train will be updated every six weeks to showcase the latest trends. It has a range of order points, iPad screens, and fashion consultants. This innovative e-boutique allows retailers to bring their latest fashions from a very small footprint store, bringing it with mobile and online websites. Current reality applications are used for virtual wardrobes, and there, customers can see if different garments fit them according to different measurements. Infrared sensors, traffic counters, and video cameras can now navigate through customer traffic and storage. They are widely used to reduce check-out lines, to schedule and deploy the workforce and items transportation to customers.

4.12.4 User-Generated Content (UGC)

This is commonly referred to as data generated by unpaid subscribers. It could be Internet searchers like Google search, and it is only available on an overall basis. Alternatively, analysts can clearly identify FB postings, images, video, certificates, blog postings, Twitter messages, and reviews. UGC is a very important factor in finding, researching, and purchasing products. Companies take advantage of UGC, a strategy that seriously stimulates searching, social media, m-marketing, and email-marketing in digital media. In relation to one approximation, by 2021, digital marketing "spending" for U.S. businesses will reach to more than 120 billion dollars, which corresponds to 46 percent of the total sales and promotion expenditure. Companies spend a considerable amount of money on positioning in search engine searches. It not only invests in educating clients but also explores how to use social media platforms to "spread the word" or "word of mouth" with their valued clients. Literature reviews have shown that many such attempts have been successful. It is clear from these empirical findings that UGC brands have a significant impact on the purchasing power of individuals and sales of goods and services (Alam & Khan, 2019; Raji Ridwan et al., 2017; Mohammad et al., 2020). The majority of studies related to trades on UGC exercises statistical data (Netzer et al., 2012), for example, ranking points or number of comments, or a number of retweets. As Lee and Bradlow (2011) point out, this methodology was used to combine different marketing methods and test excavations to determine product citations and brand placement by product.

4.12.5 Granular Sales Data

The inherent demand of consumers for different products as well as the desire to replace them is also interesting. More compact data is available than sales data can be used to learn about customer choices among the various products in a collection. Using inventory data, one can get information on how product sales have changed over time. A more comprehensive understanding of the customer selection process can be gained by looking at how the inventory data is matched with sales transaction data. This has been pointed out by Karabati and Kouvelis (1994) as a multiproduct forecasting system. The sales data of their proposed scheme is divided into different time frames and thus the customers get a different collection of products. These unallocated data are used to measure demand ratios and replacement probabilities for each product. The use of granular sales data for consumer selection models has been used in more recent times for gaining a good knowledge of the consumer selection process. Musalem et al. (2010) developed a multinomial logit (MNL) selection framework. Some researchers have taken into consideration a general rating-based selection model, while granular sales data show how a prelaunched merchandising test can be extensively improved (Aktas & Meng, 2017). In addition to freezing data over time, modern outlets and database systems allow companies to monitor what the basket contains. More precisely, what products have been bought and how frequently they buy, etc. In different segments, including retail, customers purchase several products at once, and it is revealed that the availability of each product has influenced the buying of more different goods in the client' cart. Scholars identified this phenomenon in the construction of various consumer selection models (Chung & Rao, 2003). However, such analysis provides an essential way to predict demand for a particular product. Various data sources have recently made it easier for companies to collect traffic data, link customer behaviour, and transport counter data for predictions. For example, this data helps to obtain information on how many times customers have visited the departmental stores of these institutions. In particular, many retailers today are interested in e-commerce and they have adapted their businesses to it. It is therefore easier to collect and analyse such data. Besides, electronic traffic counters and related technologies have expanded further and are more precise today. Various practices in data related to traffic support businesses' strategic decision-making process, and businesses have understood the practical value of this information to organisations in business decisions such as company promotion and sales, staff training, and warehousing and transportation planning. Traffic data can be used to determine how effective the entrepreneur has been in their business and to what extent the attraction of customers to the business has been achieved through other promotions outside the business. The potential of this data multiplies when combined with sales records. By analysing traffic data and transaction data together, businesses learn about translation tendencies that determine the purchases of a select new customer group, which can provide information on the productivity, efficiency, and effectiveness of drive translation storage components. Not only does it allow companies to predict, but also optimises staff deployments, etc. Another application for traffic data, Lam et al. (2001) have shown to be used to assess the impact of different types of promotions.

4.12.6 Switching Consumer Experience

The higher usage of personal devices such as smartphones or wearable technologies such as smartwatches today has greatly changed the consumer experience. Beacons available in storehouses provide significant opportunities to identify a customer entering a store, to contact customers, to collect data, and to make contacts to purchase based on historical shopping models. Consequently, demand is not only a prediction of any kind for a certain product but also directly affects and changes the customer purchases (Feng & Shanthikumar, 2018; Cohen, 2018). Access to product information, how pricing has affected purchases, and the use of promotional media such as e-coupons can help businesses discover past explorative experiences of their customers and personalise the products and services to clients accordingly.

In any marketing strategy, it is important to deliver a message to your customers at the right time. With the advent of e-commerce in the last decades, it is more important than ever to reach customers ahead of your competitors. In order to provide personalised marketing strategies to consumers, marketers can use this behaviour to reach out to better-targeted groups of businesses, divided into specific subgroups based on geographic distribution or other demographics. With this expertise, it is easy to guide customers to the right products and place them in the right place. The most profitable subgroups can be highlighted by segmentation based on buying behaviour from the past. Customers are subject to change based on the history of the ads viewed, the number of times he or she has visited product sites and advertisements, how much time spent with it, and so on. Accordingly, by displaying advertisements designed to suit the preferences of the users, consumers are encouraged to purchase the products that are displayed.

How do you benefit from using marketing and predictive analytics of sales? First of all, any process or tool that helps marketers identify the buying habits of customers can be helped for their businesses. Predictive analytics helps to ensure that these predictions are accurate. For instance, when a movie viewer buys a ticket, the transaction is captured by the ticket seller's computer system and recorded in a database. Predictive analytics algorithms can instruct the computer to send an email to a customer every time a new cinema is about to launch. To go a step further, certain category algorithms can target ticket buyers with their specific interest generated from the previous cinemas watched, such as musical cinema, mystery cinema, humour cinema, etc., and send out an email when a new cinema matched with their interest comes to the cinema hall.

Businesses can deliver products and sometimes they take customers to these product sites. This is a dynamic research matter in business operations where smart technologies can be used to conduct product research from a consumer's perspective. For example, the customer experience is personalised in many ways, such as searching for reviews, or finding a price of business competitors, or requisitioning a competitive good from the departmental store itself. The demand should be directed to a unique customer with a significantly shorter time frame, and delivery of goods on a plan for his overall needs will be done in the long run by providing services for all needs under one roof. Customers now demand the flexibility of ordering through a product, i.e., they expect to deliver products across different channels to reach orders to different locations including their homes, warehouses, or third-party locations. Omni-channel demand forecasting can be used as part of potential exploration. Integrated supply chain combination enables big data technologies to "communicate" within the supply chain and build an "intelligent" supply chain (Sanders, 2016). Business-oriented messages/promotions can be delivered into the hands of customers. Customer retention can also be further monitored, consumer processes can be monitored online, and businesses can tailor products and services to customer needs. The importance here is that such relationships enable businesses to capture the real needs of customers, thereby tailor supply, and increase customer loyalty. It also has the potential to provide more supply chain feedback to minimise forecasting errors. Confirming customer participation here presents a more feasible testing ground for the predictable community. Provides supply chain programmes such as "Collaborative Planning Forecasting and Replenishment" (CPFR) and "Efficient Customer Response" (ECR) for demand planning and refilling in collaboration with major suppliers. In many cases, companies give the customer the ability to look at inventory from this point of view (Panahifar et al., 2015; Boone & Ganeshan, 2008). The radio frequency identification (RFID) inventory system enhances tracking and maintains consistent service and inventory levels (Bertolini et al., 2010). Promising technologies such as blockchain make the most steady, precise transactions and reporting mechanism much easier.

It facilitates the "track and trace" of the supply chain and provides the applicant with data on refill plans and acquisition delivery times. Equipment supply chains have since improved "yield management" to a higher level through "dynamic price tags (DPT)." Thereby, it improves the functionality of the supply chain. The challenge here is how to integrate these new technologies into the design procedure. For instance, whether the block chain mechanism should be applied to all production in the business, whether they should resort to smart agreements, and whether they should install chain commands. Finding answers to these questions can lead to better visibility and predictions that are more effective.

Sensors collect data on clients related to privacy, partisanship, and discrimination. These types of data, for example, cellular phone data, have no explicit intention. Moreover, these data are not unspecified. These are regularly related to customers' distinctiveness behaviour and use these personal datasets to predict customer behaviour.

4.13 CYCLE ANALYTICS FOR PREDICTIONS

Predictive analytics with low amounts of data is also possible for intelligent decision making and it is still successful. However, while data have reached surprisingly large proportions, the human ability to make wise decisions has been declining. Data-based decision-making is often based on quantitative models that use a closed process, usually called a cycle. The life cycle begins with the identification of problems and then continues with the planning and construction of an analytical framework. You can then move on to data management, reporting, and visualisation. Sample analyses are then performed for cost, activation, and testing. Adaptation to the feedback loop and further access to passive forecast analysis is challenging. It is a powerful technology that can be predicted through the right marketing strategy.

Researchers generally use traditional time series to make various sessional predictions. Automatic feedback is used as a foundation for consumer analytics, which includes a search index for a specific keyword as a predictive attribute to build an improved forecasting model. Verification of the value of the trend variables involves the use of a predictive error prediction window outside the samples of these two models. These predictions are often compared to predictions more advanced. Current studies have found that Google has used tendencies to advance the efficiency of monetary measures such as nonemployment ratios and returns (Choi & Varian, 2012; Smith, 2016), GDP (Castle et al., 2009), and sales. The "automotive, home and retail models (Choi & Varian, 2009; Wu, & Brynjolfsson, 2015) and Mean Absolute Error-enhanced economic models" of Google trends are generally 4–25% smaller than the sample projection errors, which are then the primary models. In addition, "Google-enhanced models" are familiar in hygienics. They frequently monitor events or pandemic (e.g., Ginsberg et al., 2009). Real-time data shows that trend data is also valuable in critical industries. Search query data in financial markets are used to predict retail investor attention (Da et al., 2011), "market volatility" (Dimpfl & Jank, 2016), and "earnings" (Drek et al., 2012). Improved models were employed for the assessment of customer "traffic" to predict tourist arrivals in the tourism industry (Choi & Varian, 2009). Improvements in mean absolute percentage error in most industry-specific models range from 10 to 40% and can be used to improve forecasting by propensity data.

Research into the use of Google trend data to predict sales is not widespread. However, we can identify several related studies that specialise in overall sales forecasting (Choi & Varian, 2009; Schaer et al., 2019). One of the things that we noticed here is that Google simply indexes apps that have a specific level of congestion. Accordingly, "index values" are not built for search terms. Here, another aspect of the uncertainty is the area in which researchers need to pay attention to proxy terms. Search engines identify index generation as a black box, and Google says that the index is grounded on sample data. Thus, it is an outdated method, which raises the question of long-term reliability when using trend variables, followed by search term product life cycles or individual target variables, which is a study area and studies should emphasise how changes in search terms affect demand projection. Schaer et al. (2019) show that if such models perform poorly in predicting the magnitude of the demand, a long-term framework must be built to redesign the supply chain.

Dynamic forecasting can be frustrating as Google uses trending contemporary applications, and these formats are prone to very short forecasts. Research should focus on how these models can be used strategically to plan an organisation's sales and operations. Various research studies are being conducted on how to use the data sources built by social media to understand the predictions related to the data gathered on social media.

From the prevailing literature, it was noted how to use data grounded on social media (Facebook, Twitter, YouTube, etc.) to offer an understanding of social media predictions. As more and more people share these experiences in real time, this data not only informs but also shapes the way users make decisions. From a technical point of view, the main emphasis of many research endeavours in this area is to first validate how entries on social media can be grasped and adjusted to quantitative measurements or indicators. There is a wide range of ideas on how to build these indicators. They have "valence" measurements. They also include posts, part of the positive notes, posters, poster grading, number updates, and "valence" steps related to the background and value of the postings. As the scope is relevant to the post, the "word bag" in the post, the value of the poster, the credibility, impact, the environment in which the post began, etc., are also important here. It aims to easily capture the mood in a marketing process related to the topic, as well as determine how to effectively disseminate product information in the business with social media. For instance, for stock-market forecasts, total progressive tweets could be one of the best indicators such as Dow Jones, S&P 500, and NASDAQ. How these indicators are constructed is an important aspect of research.

The second step in evaluating "customer-generated content" is to upgrade predictive models by social-media parameters and/or indicators to see if the predictions they make are actually in close proximity to the truth. Linear models, as well as many nonlinear models, have been used for social media-related research and Twitter data is widely used for prediction, usually by machine learning methods (Lamb et al., 2013; Broniatowski et al., 2013), stock prices (Zhang et al., 2011), box office earnings (Mishne et al.,

2006; Sanguinet, 2016; Liu et al., 2016), and TV rankings. Many studies (Wakamiya et al., 2011) show that adding social media information can improve predictive errors using data from an online retailer.

4.14 KEY CONCEPTS OF CUSTOMER ANALYTICS

1. Venn Diagram – Hidden relationships are used to find out what connections or disconnections are. This methodology is used to explore customers who have purchased various products as well as to recognise cross-selling openings.
2. Data Profiling – This method identifies consumer traits, selects accounts from "data trees," and searches for the profiles of consumers, to identify the commonalities and performances. Sales and marketing departments use these profiles of consumers to devise what successful selling and promotion tactics are.
3. Forecasting – The "time series analysis based forecasting" method permits the businesses to adjust to the transformations, estimate potential tendencies, and identify cyclical variations. This method can be used to systematically forecast sales periodically; otherwise, you can calculate the expected orders for different periods.
4. Mapping Colour Coding – This is used to identify geographic regions through mapping and it indicates customer behaviour when geographical areas change. A map shared to "polygons" represent geographical areas exhibit, where the Churner hub is located or where specific products are sold.
5. Association Rules – This is called grounds/consequences – analysis of basket. The technology generates a set of rules, which identify relationships or relationship patterns through data. It robotically chooses which ones are more effective for trade acumen. Thus, it examines that which products customers buy at once and when. In addition, you may find which customers are not buying and what the reasons for not buying. Here, you can also find out about new opportunities for cross-selling.
6. Decision Tree – Behaviour, classification, and prediction are done here. It is a prominent technique for categorising different applications of data mining and is a powerful support to the decision-making process. This classification helps you to choose right products

and make predictions about potentials to recommend to a specific segment of customers. The most commonly operated "decision tree algorithms" involve "ID3, C4.5 and CART." Mechanisms for visualising data, such as "polymaps," can be used. Polymaps allows for making interactive and dynamic maps, and it is a joint project between SimpleGio and Steman. This sophisticated mapping method can pile the data from a variety of measures, providing multimagnification activism at all levels of the country to street view. Lurie (2014) uses a JavaScript plot library for jQuery for Floatwich. Float is an application grounded on a browser that is well matched with many corporate browsers, comprising IE, Safari, Chrome, Firefox, and Opera. Float various visualisation options help with the database, interactive graphs, vertical graphs, and other capabilities for panelling and zooming, as well as specific plug-ins for specific functionality (Lurie, 2014). D3.js: A JavaScript library can be used to create data visualisations that emphasise "web standards" with HTML, CSS, and SVG and get a new life to documents with a data-based approach to manipulation of DOM. The SAS Visual Analyser is a mechanism that can be applied to the exploration of any visually diverse dataset for a more detailed and unique analysis. Here, with knowledge of the analyser and automated prediction tools, users of any level will have the opportunity to visualise this SAS visual to find out what the connections behind any dataset are and what the hidden patterns are.

4.15 PRESCRIPTIVE ANALYTICS

Prescriptive analytics is primarily concerned with finding the best course of action from the existing data. This type of analytics applies to both descriptive analytics and predictive analytics and is unique in that it focuses more on functional understanding than data monitoring. Descriptive analytics gives us an insight into what has already happened, while predictive analytics mainly concentrates on the predictions that may occur in the future. Prescriptive analytics presents a variety of choices and seeks to find the best solution. It also allows you to make decisions based on optimising the outcome of future events or risks. However, a prescriptive model is similar to the training process and deeply learns the applications for machine learning. But "deep learning" is grounded on the layered NN in the human brain. Conventional machine learning can identify patterns of human behaviour, but in-depth learning is so sensitive and it can identify patterns. Rathi (2018), Internal Marketing Manager, Netcore Solutions, writes that AI-powered marketing automation does not guarantee the correct communication to the right individual at the right time, but deep learning can take it to the next level, which provides a highly customised and better service to customers, taking into account even the most subtle preferences combined with external factors such as customer preferences, personal preferences, spending patterns, and socioeconomic backdrops as well as natural circumstances such as seasons, disasters, etc. With in-depth learning, for example, you can train a predictive model of all customer activity over the past months and produce an algorithm that can predict which customers will like a particular product. By training the model to predict the likelihood of prospective customers purchasing the product, we can gather information about their purchasing habits and improve conversion rates.

When deploying AI for sales and marketing efforts, allocating customers to the right subgroups is key to optimal targeting. Consumer segmentation based on traditional demographics can be transformed into something different when AI is effectively implemented. Instead of dragging customers into buckets based on age, gender, or sociocultural parameters, we can make a quantum leap beyond those precedents and enrich the marketing strategies of the business with AI that are important only to potential customers who buy the product. It uses data filtration and hole analysis algorithms to provide customers with an understanding of purchasing behaviour. The Future of Consumer Analytics – while scanning the ecosystem, many start-ups have focused on analysing consumer sentiment and buying patterns. Gaining an understanding of customer behaviour helps their enterprise customers understand how to meet demand.

This approach enables businesses to use analytics to provide an understanding of their data and to optimise personalised services, sales, cross-sales, and their business operations to meet customer needs. Tomorrow's successful businesses use analytics to turn the people in society into their customers. Within the scope of consumer intelligence, organisations use such data to better understand their customers and predict the impact on consumer decisions. This will have a positive impact on current inventory businesses. Then, organisations can use data intelligence to create forecast models, customer profiles, and more personalised models. Through this approach, customers learn what they are buying and what influence customer decisions through privatised businesses to achieve timely sales and cross-sales.

We are currently teaming up with evolutionary computing machine learning with genuine game modification technology to create more accurate prediction models. This method permits us to make more accurate predictions using an algorithm called the "white box." This is important to interpret the predictions that we make in marketing analysis and to understand the benefits of relying on data in the decision-making process of the businesses. Marketing multitouch attribution (MTA) is further enhanced by this technology. By technology, we mean the use of genetic algorithms for both features and parameter selection. A genetic algorithm and recurrent neural network (RNN)-based model of gene-regulatory network (GRN) are important technologies that are not commonly used in machine learning (Raza & Alam, 2016). However, it is now playing a more important role. The main challenge we have is to find the best model for a universe with trillions of potentials. Genetic algorithms can be used as an intelligent search engine. However, it is unlikely that a genetic algorithm will always give you the optimal solution. Nevertheless, it does provide a good opportunity to get closer without trying every possible option. In considering its functionality, it generates random solution "populations" and aligns the models according to objective criteria based on them, predicting accuracy as well as minimizing errors.

4.16 CONSUMER ANALYTICS CHALLENGES

Strategically, every business organisation must decide whether or not to utilise technologies related to big data in planning. It hinges on the advantages to the business organisation compared to the cost of collecting and analysing the dataset as needed and whether they outweigh the cost.

Our intention is not to find out how big data can be applied to business processes in organisation and to what extent they contribute to the strategic process. At the changing nature of the supply chain, it is important to look at the challenges that arise when using big data for supply and supply chain planning. Capture and connect big data for conventional SOP procedures, it brings big data with it to advance the prediction of goods and provide an understanding of consumer behaviour. These possible advantages, however, are there with many pragmatic difficulties for the specialists who plan demand in business organisations. First, the size of the data could be enormous. For instance, out of a million customer transactions, Walmart gathers over 2.5 petabytes of data hourly. However, only about 0.5% of the data is analysed. The issue here is determining the type of data to be hoarded and for how long. Second, as Feng and Shanthikumar (2018) explain, theoretically, the more information in general, the better the predictions can be made. The challenge here, however, is what happens when the variables increase abnormally and the relationship becomes unclear.

Large data sets, especially those used for forecasting, are rare and nonreactive and that semi-non-parametric methods for instance machine learning (Cui et al., 2017) are more appropriate for analysis. Application designers need to be prepared to adapt to a wide range of methods in the design process from human judgment to data-based decisions. Studies in industrial applications have repeatedly shown that judgment is a predictive standard based on "gut feeling." Statistical predictions of this usage are made for several factors that are difficult for analysts to measure. These include "promotional activities," "seasonal activities," "demand risk," "demand and supply chain disruptions," etc. Human judgment has the potential to improve predictions, and special attention will often bring it into its own biased process. Often, such judgments adversely affect the accuracy of predictions because their contribution is unequally weighed. Newly available data, at least theoretically, have a prospective for minimising the negative impact of "adjustments" on predictions.

Attempts are made to systematically incorporate new data streams (Sagaert et al., 2018) with forecasts. However, there are important pragmatic challenges. First, recent evaluations (Weller & Crone, 2012) show that such data flows are not straightaway accessible or accessible to the majority of application developers. Second, integration of data with commonly used ERP systems by designers requires important hardware, software, and diagnostic and analytic support. Third, a substantial learning curve is needed to translate the outcomes of new algorithms related to machine learning. On the other hand, research being done for the projection group is to study the possibility of replacing large data streams for specialised professional judgment. Although it is believed that big data can never replace a particular expert opinion, some problems with predictions can be alleviated.

Predictive technology builds insight and makes it easier to derive better business decisions. But without a strong foundation for our project, we will not be able to achieve the desired results. The most important factor in the predictive analytic process is the quality of the data. Data are central to predictive analysis, and we must particularly focus on the quality of the data before using forecasting analysis. Liu et al., (2020) and Yunus et al., (2017) say that poor-quality data can seriously affect the efficiency of business decisions. The less we focus on data quality, the lower the quality of data mining and analytical results. Andrews et al. (2018) found that this can have serious financial or other adverse consequences for the business.

Another factor to consider in consumer analytics is modelling. As Solovyeva and Khominich (2019) explain, modelling needs to be "repetitive, on an industrial scale" to warrant the effective development of many predictive analytical models. Models represent those relationships (Miller, 2014). Therefore, whether predictive models are used, whether retrograde or categorical – the important thing to consider is whether it is at a level acceptable to the user's preference. User preferences, judgment, and experience often affect the results of predictive analytics. Expressly, without product-oriented lifecycle management and production within the system of production or its atmosphere, the forecasting analytics does not preserve the desired outcome (Chu et al., 2007). Legal and ethical considerations for forecasting are especially important if a company is active in different jurisdictions and cultures. Attention should also be paid to how customer information is kept and mined, and whether "data mining protocols are ethical" (Johnson, 2014) in compliance with the ethics. According to Schwartz (2010), it is important for assessing whether the business decision-making process with analytics indicates the "legal, cultural and social norms" of the organisation's activities and when necessary to act under these standards (Johnson, 2013).

Another factor to consider is communication of the return. Data miners and data analysts may be disappointed if it is disbelieved that business users are not serious about implementing the results of analytics, even though the company has invested in a forecasting project (Ogunleye, 2015). Expressly, there may be times when analysts are thrilled about the "insights" provided by them, but this process will not be successful if business management fails to convert the "new insights" value on their part. The introduction of forecasting analytics technology requires a change of attitude and individuals in the business who are accustomed to taking decisions grounded on the intelligence or extrasensory perception that they see as an important aspect of the existing officiation.

In addition, the other important thing is that your data sources, whether internal, external, or third parties may eventually contain errors in this data. This data does not flow properly due to data errors. Errors such as duplicates or individual fields containing incorrect data may be more subtle. New algorithms that do not work as we expect, changes to your coded database, IT failures, or many other things can cause data errors.

4.17 FUTURE RESEARCH

However, many researchers have developed traffic-related sales models, but it is not clear how accurate the traffic data can be. Thus, the prevailing research studies are also based on high aggregate data – little to distinguish between the type of consumers arriving at the departmental store or the assorted arrays of products being sold. Research should explore how this relates to the demand for a specific product as well as potential sales. Current research is mainly based on the number of clients entering the shop and then it doesn't pay proper attention to the time that they spend in the store. Naturally, many customers in a store and the amount of time they spend in it affect purchases. Increase group access to products, access to sellers, and increase "vigilance" at the conclusion of a sales transaction need to be researched because in future research we need to pay more attention to the additional operational dimensions that exist in this customer flow. Data analytics allows a computer to learn a lot from data. Accordingly, machines that are more intelligent will be discovered in the future. Those machines will be able to operate more intelligently in disciplines such as aerospace and medicine.

REFERENCES

Aktas, E., & Meng, Y. (2017). An exploration of big data practices in retail sector. *Logistics*, *1*(2), 12.

Alam, M. (2012). Cloud algebra for cloud database management system. In *Proceedings of the Second International Conference on Computational Science, Engineering and Information Technology* (pp. 26–29).

Alam, M., & Khan, B. M. (2019). The role of social media communication in brand equity creation: An empirical study. *IUP Journal of Brand Management*, *16*(1), 740–747.

Alam, M., & Shakil, K. A. (2015). Recent developments in cloud based systems: State of art. *arXiv preprint arXiv:1501.01323.*

Alam, M., Shakil, K. A., & Sethi, S. (2016, August). Analysis and clustering of workload in google cluster trace based on resource usage. In *2016 IEEE International Conference on Computational Science and Engineering (CSE) and IEEE International Conference on Embedded and Ubiquitous Computing (EUC) and 15th International Symposium on Distributed Computing and Applications for Business Engineering (DCABES)* (pp. 740–747).

Andrews, R., Suriadi, S., Ouyang, C., & Poppe, E. (2018, October). Towards event log querying for data quality. In *OTM Confederated International Conferences "On the Move to Meaningful Internet Systems"* (pp. 116–134).

Bazylevska, O. V. (2011). *Customer analytics as a source of competitive advantage.* Faculty of Technology Policy & Management, Delft University of Technology. Master's thesis. https://d1rkab7tlqy5f1.cloudfront.net/TBM/Over%20faculteit/ Afdelingen/Engineering%20Systems%20and%20Services/People/Professors%20 emeriti/Jan%20van%20den%20Berg/MasterPhdThesis/elena-final-Msc-thesis.pdf. Accessed on 22 November 2020.

Bertolini, M., Bottani, E., Rizzi, A., & Volpi, A. (2010). The Benefits of RFID and EPC in the Supply Chain: Lessons from an Italian pilot study. In *The Internet of Things* (pp. 293–302). New York, NY: Springer.

Boone, T., & Ganeshan, R. (2008). The value of information sharing in the retail supply chain: two case studies. *Foresight: The International Journal of Applied Forecasting, 9,* 12–17.

Broniatowski, D. A., Paul, M. J., & Dredze, M. (2013). National and local influenza surveillance through Twitter: An analysis of the 2012–2013 influenza epidemic. *PLOS One, 8*(12), e83672.

Cao, L. (2008). Behavior informatics and analytics: Let behavior talk. In *2008 IEEE International Conference on Data Mining Workshops* (pp. 87–96).

Cao, L. (2010). In-depth behaviour understanding and use: The behaviour informatics approach. *Information Sciences, 180*(17), 3067–3085.

Castle, J. L., Fawcett, N. W., & Hendry, D. F. (2009). Nowcasting is not just contemporaneous forecasting. *National Institute Economic Review, 210,* 71–89.

Chaudhary, K., & Kumar, S. (2016). Customer satisfaction towards Flipkart and Amazon: A comparative study. *International Journal of Academic Research & Development (JAR&D), 2*(1), 35–42.

Chen, C. P., & Zhang, C. Y. (2014). Data-intensive applications, challenges, techniques and technologies: A survey on Big Data. *Information Sciences, 275,* 314–347.

Choi, H., & Varian, H (2009). Predicting Initial Claims for Unemployment Insurance Using Google Trends. Google Inc. Available at: http://static.googleusercontent. com/media/research.google.com/en//archive/papers/initialclaimsUS.pdf

Choi, H., & Varian, H. (2012). Predicting the present with Google Trends. *Economic Record, 88,* 2–9.

Chu S.-Y., Hsieh P.-C., & Lin L.-L. (2007). Study on the relationship among runoff coefficient, curve number and slope. *Journal of Soil and Water Conservation, 40*(3), 305–314.

Chung, J., & Rao, V. R. (2003). A general choice model for bundles with multiple-category products: Application to market segmentation and optimal pricing for bundles. *Journal of Marketing Research, 40*(2), 115–130.

Cui, L., Huang, S., Wei, F., Tan, C., Duan, C., & Zhou, M. (2017, July). Superagent: A customer service Chatbot for e-commerce websites. In *Proceedings of ACL 2017, System Demonstrations* (pp. 97–102).

Da, Z., Engelberg, J., & Gao, P. (2011). In search of attention. *The Journal of Finance*, 66(5), 1461–1499.

Dimpfl, T., & Jank, S. (2016). Can internet search queries help to predict stock market volatility? *European Financial Management*, 22(2), 171–192.

Dixon, H., Seaton, J. S., & Waterson, M. (2014). *Price flexibility in British supermarkets: Moderation and recession*. University of Warwick, Warwick Economics Research Paper Series. Working Paper No. 2068-2018-1916.

Dupre, E. (2013). "Let data take the lead: Data and analytics help marketers find their lead generation rhythm," *DM News*, p. 32. Available at: http://search.ebscohost.com/login.aspx?direct=true&AuthType=ip, cookie,shib&db=edsggo&AN=edsgcl.3326 55941&site=eds-live&scope=site. Accessed on 2 August 2019.

Fan, W., & Bifet, A. (2013). Mining big data: Current status, and forecast to the future. *ACM SIGKDD Explorations Newsletter*, 14(2), 1–5.

Feng, Q., & Shanthikumar, J. G. (2018). How research in production and operations management may evolve in the era of big data. *Production and Operations Management*, 27(9), 1670–1684.

Forrester Research (2005). *Entertainment grabs youth's online time: Gaming sites get the greatest play with consumers*. http://www.forrester.coni/Research/Document/Excerpt/0,7211,373352,00.html. Accessed on 8 December 2020.

Ginsberg, J., Mohebbi, M. H., Patel, R. S., Brammer, L., Smolinski, M. S., & Brilliant, L. (2009). Detecting influenza epidemics using search engine query data. *Nature*, 457(7232), 1012–1014.

Grigsby, M. (2015). Analytic choices about pricing insights. *Marketing Insights*, 27(2), 38–43.

Guadagni, P. M., & Little, J. D. C. (1983). A logit model of brand choice calibrated on scanner data. *Marketing Science*, 2(3), 203–238.

Hazen, B. T., Boone, C. A., Ezell, J. D., & Jones-Farmer, L. A. (2014). Data quality for data science, predictive analytics, and big data in supply chain management: An introduction to the problem and suggestions for research and applications. *International Journal of Production Economics*, 154, 72–80.

Howard, J., & Sheth, J. (1969). *The Theory of Buyer Behaviour*. New York, NY: Wiley.

Johnson, J. A. (2013). Ethics of Data Mining and Predictive Analytics in Higher Education, Association for Institutional Research Annual Forum, Long Beach, CA, May 19–22. Available at: http://ssrn.com/abstract=2156058 or http://dx.doi.org/10.2139/ssrn.2156058. Accessed on 19 November 2020.

Johnson, J. A. (2014). The Ethics of Big Data in Higher Education, International Review of Information Ethics. http://www.i-r-i-e.net/inhalt/021/IRIE-021-Johnson.pdf. Accessed on 20 November 2020.

Karabati, S., & Kouvelis, P. (1994). The interface of buffer design and cyclic scheduling decisions in deterministic flow lines. *Annals of Operations Research*, 50, 295–317.

Kaur, A., & Alam, M. (2013). Role of knowledge engineering in the development of a hybrid knowledge based medical information system for atrial fibrillation. *American Journal of Industrial and Business Management*, 3(1), DOI: 10.4236/ajibm.2013.31005.

Khan, S., Shakil, K. A., & Alam, M. (2018). Cloud-based big data analytics—a survey of current research and future directions. In Big Data Analytics (595–604). Singapore: Springer.

Khanna, L., Singh, S. N., & Alam, M. (2016, August). Educational data mining and its role in determining factors affecting students academic performance: A systematic review. In *2016 1st India International Conference on Information Processing (IICIP)* (pp. 1–7).

Kumar, V., & Petersen, J. A. (2012). Statistical Methods in Customer Relationship Management. West Sussex: John Wiley & Sons.

Kumar, V., Kumar, R., Pandey, S. K., & Alam, M. (2018). Fully homomorphic encryption scheme with probabilistic encryption based on Euler's theorem and application in cloud computing. In *Big Data Analytics* (pp. 605–611). Singapore: Springer.

Lam, S. Y., Vandenbosch, M., Hulland, J., & Pearce, M. (2001). Evaluating promotions in shopping environments: Decomposing sales response into attraction, conversion, and spending effects. *Marketing Science*, 20(2), 194–215.

Lamb, A., Paul, M. J., & Dredze, M. (2013). Separating fact from fear: Tracking flu infections on Twitter. In *Proceedings of the 2013 Conference of the North American Chapter of the Association for Computational Linguistics: Human Language Technologies* (pp. 789–795).

Laney, D. (2001). 3D Data Management: Controlling Data Volume, Velocity and Variety. Application Delivery Strategies by META Group Inc. disponibile sul sito, available at: https://blogs. gartner. com/doug-laney/files/2012/01/ad949-3D-Data-Management-Controlling-Data-Volume-Velocity-and-Variety. pdf (accessed 10th August 2021.

Lansley, G., & Longley, P. (2016). Deriving age and gender from forenames for consumer analytics. *Journal of Retailing and Consumer Services*, 30, 271–278.

Lee T., & Bradlow E. T. (2011), Automated marketing research using online customer reviews. *Journal of Marketing Research*, 48(5), 881–894.

Li, F., Chen, Y., Wang, J., Zhou, X., & Tang, B. (2019). A reinforcement learning unit matching recurrent neural network for the state trend prediction of rolling bearings. *Measurement*, 145, 191–203.

Liu, T., Ding, X., Chen, Y., Chen, H., & Guo, M. (2016). Predicting movie box-office revenues by exploiting large-scale social media content. *Multimedia Tools and Applications*, 75(3), 1509–1528.

Liu, W., Zhang, J., Wei, S., & Wang, D. (2020). Factors influencing organisational efficiency in a smart-logistics ecological chain under e-commerce platform leadership. *International Journal of Logistics Research and Applications*, 24, 1–28.

Lurie, A. (2014). *Data Visualization Tools for Big Data. Cloud Computing.* Available at: https://blog.profitbricks.com/39-data-visualization-tools-for-big-data. Accessed on 01 September 2020.

Malhotra, S., Doja, M. N., Alam, B., & Alam, M. (2017, May). Big data analysis and comparison of big data analytic approaches. In *2017 International Conference on Computing, Communication and Automation (ICCCA)* (pp. 309–314).

Malhotra, S., Doja, M. N., Alam, B., & Alam, M. (2018). Generalized query processing mechanism in cloud database management system. In *Big Data Analytics* (pp. 641–648). Singapore: Springer.

Melnik, E. V., Korovin, I. S., & Klimenko, A. B. (2020, July). The improvement of the stylometry-based cognitive assistant performance in conditions of big data analysis. In R. Silhavi (Ed.), *Computer Science On-line Conference* (pp. 85–99). Cham: Springer.

Miller, J. A. (2014). Virtual species distribution models using simulated data to evaluate aspects of model performance. *Progress in Physical Geography: Earth and Environment*, 38 (1): 117–128.

Mishne, G., Glance, N. S., et al. (2006). Predicting movie sales from blogger sentiment. In *AAAI Spring Symposium: Computational Approaches to Analyzing Weblogs* (pp. 155–158).

Mohammad, J., Quoquab, F., Thurasamy, R., & Alolayyan, M. N. (2020). The effect of user-generated content quality on brand engagement: The mediating role of functional and emotional values. *Journal of Electronic Commerce Research*, *21*(1), 39–55.

Musalem A., Olivares M., Bradlow E. T., Terwiesch C., & Corsten D. (2010). Structural estimation of the effect of out-of-stocks. *Management Science*, *56*(7), 1180–1197.

Myers, D. G. (2001). *The American Paradox: Spiritual Hunger in an Age of Plenty*. New Haven, CT: Yale University Press.

Netzer, O., Feldman, R., Goldenberg, J., & Fresko, M. (2012). Mine your own business: Market structure surveillance through text mining. *Marketing Science*, *31*(3), 521–543.

Nguyen, D. H., de Leeuw Sander, & Dullaert W. E. H. (2018) Consumer behaviour and order fulfilment in online retailing: A systematic review. *International Journal of Management Reviews*, *20*(2), pp. 255–76. DOI: 10.1111/ijmr.12129. Accessed on 16 November 2020.

Ogunleye, J. (2013). Understand the Difference Business Intelligence and Business Analytics, In IndiaBook, Available at: http://www.indabook.org/d/Understanding-the-Difference-BetweenStructured-and.pdf. Accessed on 15 December 2020.

Ogunleye, J. (2015). Challenges in operationalising predictive analytics. *Research Papers on Knowledge, Innovation and Enterprise*, Volume 3, pp. 69–79.

OPCC (2012). The Age of Predictive Analytics: From Patterns to Predictions. Report prepared by the Research Group of the Office of the Privacy Commissioner of Canada, Available at: https://www.priv.gc.ca/information/research-recherche/2012/pa_201208_e.pdf. Accessed on 18 December 2020.

Pahwa, B., Taruna, S., & Kasliwal, N. (2017). Role of data mining in analyzing consumer's online buying behaviour. *International Journal of Business and Management Invention*, *6*(11), 45–51. Available at: https://www.researchgate.net/publication/324595081_Role_of_Data_mining_in_analyzing_consumer's_online_buying_behaviour. Accessed on 19 December 2020.

Panahifar, F., Heavey, C., Byrne, P. J., & Fazlollahtabar, H. (2015). A framework for collaborative planning, forecasting and replenishment (CPFR). *Journal of Enterprise Information Management*, *28*, 1–36.

Prasad, R. K., & Jha, M. K. (2014). Consumer buying decisions models: A descriptive study. *International Journal of Innovation and Applied Studies*, *6*(3), 335–351. Available at: https://www.researchgate.net/publication/305727378_Consumer_buying_decisions_models_A_d escriptive_study. Accessed on 15 December 2020.

Pratminingsih, S. A., Lipuringtyas, C., & Rimenta, T. (2013). Factors influencing customer loyalty toward online shopping. *International Journal of Trade, Economics and Finance*, *4*(3), 104–110.

Rajaiah, M., Rao, R. N., Nagendra, K. V., Basha, A. M., Rao, B. N., & Vijayakumar, O. (2020). Mathematical modeling on marketing analytics. *Journal of Critical Reviews*, *7*(19), 4189–4198.

Raji Ridwan, A., Mohd Rashid, S., & Ishak, M. S. (2017). User-generated contents in Facebook, functional and hedonic brand image and purchase intention. In *SHS Web of Conferences*, *33*, pp. 1–6.

Rathi, R. (2018). Deep learning and 'hyper-personalization' are the future of marketing automation. Entrepreneur Asia Pacific. https://www.entrepreneur.com/article/317350. Accessed on 15 December 2020.

Raza, K., & Alam, M. (2016). Recurrent neural network based hybrid model for recon-structing gene regulatory network. *Computational Biology and Chemistry, 64,* 322–334.

RIS news. 2010 Cross-Channel Tech Trends Study. https://risnews.com/2010-cross-channel-tech-trends-study. Accessed on 20 December 2020.

Russell, G. J., & Petersen, A. (2000). Analysis of cross category dependence in market basket selection. *Journal of Retailing, 76*(3), 367–392.

Rygielski, C., Wang, J. C., & Yen, D. C. (2002). Data mining techniques for customer rela-tionship management. *Technology in Society, 24*(4), 483–502.

Sagaert, Y. R., Aghezzaf, E. H., Kourentzes, N., & Desmet, B. (2018). Temporal big data for tactical sales forecasting in the tire industry. *Interfaces, 48*(2), 121–129.

Sanders, N. R. (2016). How to use big data to drive your supply chain. *California Management Review, 58*(3), 26–48.

Sanguinet, M. E. (2016). Hashtags, tweets and movie receipts: Social media analytics in predicting box office hits. Doctoral dissertation, San Diego State University.

Schaer, O., Kourentzes, N., & Fildes, R. (2019). Demand forecasting with user-generated online information. *International Journal of Forecasting, 35*(1), 197–212.

Schwartz, M. P. (2010). Data Protection Law and the Ethical Use of Analytics, The Centre for Information Policy Leadership LLP [online] http://www.huntonfiles.com/files/webupload/CIPL_Ethical_Undperinnings_of_ Analytics_Paper.pdf). Accessed on 15 December 2020.

Sethi, S., Shakil, K. A., & Alam, M. (2015, March). Seeking black lining in cloud. In *2015 2nd International Conference on Computing for Sustainable Global Development (INDIACom)* (pp. 1251–1256).

Shakil, K. A., Anis, S., & Alam, M. (2015). Dengue disease prediction using weka data mining tool. *arXiv preprint arXiv:1502.05167.*

Smith, P. (2016). Google's MIDAS touch: Predicting UK unemployment with internet search data. *Journal of Forecasting, 35*(3), 263–284.

Solomon, M., Bamossy, G., Askegaard, S., & Hogg, M. K. (2009). *Consumer Behaviour,* 8th ed. London: Pearson Education.

Solovyeva, Y. A., & Khominich, I. P. (2019, December). The impact of changes in consumer behaviour on the development of insurance company risk models. In *Fourth Workshop on Computer Modelling in Decision Making (CMDM 2019)* (pp. 33–37).

Surendro, K. (2019, March). Predictive analytics for predicting customer behaviour. In *2019 International Conference of Artificial Intelligence and Information Technology (ICAIIT)* (pp. 230–233).

Tuttle, S., Lee, H., Froning, C., & Montgomery, M. (2014). Builders instead of consum-ers: training astronomers in instrumentation & observation. *arXiv preprint arXiv:1410.2856.*

Van Rijmenam, M. (2019). *The Organisation of Tomorrow: How AI, Blockchain and Analytics Turn Your Business into a Data Organisation.* New York, NY: Routledge.

Wakamiya, S., Kitayama, D., & Sumiya, K. (2011). Scene extraction system for video clips using attached comment interval and pointing region. *Multimedia Tools and Applications, 54*(1), 7–25.

Wang, X., Tauni, M. Z., Zhang, Q., Ali, A., & Ali, F. (2020). Does buyer-seller personality match enhance impulsive buying? A green marketing context. *Journal of Marketing Theory and Practice, 28*(4), 436–446.

Wecker, W.E. (1978), Predicting demand from sales data in the presence of stock-outs. *Management Science, 24*(10), 1043–1054.

Weller, M., & Crone, S. F. (2012). Supply chain forecasting: Best practices & benchmarking study. Available at: https://eprints.lancs.ac.uk/id/eprint/135958/1/Weller_Crone_Techical_Report_Supply_Chain_Forecasting_Best_Practices_and_Benchmarking_Study.pdf

Weller, M., & Crone, S. F. (2012). Supply Chain Forecasting: Best Practices & Benchmarking Study. Lancaster Centre for Forecasting. Available at: http://goo.gl/MPbAjz

Wu, L., & Brynjolfsson, E. (2015). The future of prediction: How Google searches foreshadow housing prices and sales. In A. Goldfarb, S. M. Greenstein, and C. E. Tucker (Eds.), *Economic Analysis of the Digital Economy* (pp. 89–118). Chicago, IL: University of Chicago Press.

Yunus, F. M., Magalingam, P., Maarop, N., Samy, G. N., Hooi-Ten Wong, D., Shanmugam, B., & Perumal, S. (2017). Proposed data quality evaluation method for a transportation agency. *Open International Journal of Informatics (OIJI)*, 5(2), 52–63.

Zhang, X., Fuehres, H., & Gloor, P. A. (2011). Predicting stock market indicators through Twitter 'I hope it is not as bad as I fear'. *Procedia-Social and behavioural Sciences*, 26, 55–62.

Zhong, S., Khoshgoftaar, T. M., & Seliya, N. (2004) Analyzing software measurement data with clustering techniques. *IEEE Intelligent Systems*, (2), 20. DOI: 10.1109/MIS.2004.1274907.

5

Web Analytics for Digital Marketing

Srinivas Dinakar Nethi and Venkata Rajasekhar Moturu
Indian Institute of Management
Visakhapatnam, India

Krishnaveer Abhishek Challa
Andhra University
Visakhapatnam, India

CONTENTS

5.1 INTRODUCTION: DIGITAL MARKETING

Smith (2007) described digital marketing as "the use of digital technologies to create an integrated, targeted and measurable communication which helps to acquire and retain customers while building deeper relationships

DOI: 10.1201/9781003307761-5

with them". This shows technology is used as a channel or platform for serving digital or e-marketing activities and positioning, measuring, and crafting the related actions.

Digital marketing is connected to several identical ideas. Probably, the premature idea, direct marketing, connects to digital marketing. It appears as a shift toward measurable and targeted communications, e.g., e-mail, on target groups or specific individuals. Wymbs (2011) details that a key aspect of it is the economical application of databases, which alters campaigners to aim buyers focused on their personal behaviours and characteristics as well as to record responses. As databases were mostly digitized, it can be treated as an initial form of digital marketing. While direct marketing was concentrated on unidirectional communication messages, interactive marketing was aimed with the focus on bidirectional and cross-platform conversations (Zahay, 2014). The vital use of databases remained a key component of interactive marketing, but novel platforms came out for transmitting interactive information exchanges. This translated to the idea of diverse platform marketing, and due to the application of internet raised in prominence, the emphasis on interactive marketing augmented to involve marketing in digital communications (Blasco-Arcas et al., 2014).

At present, digital marketing is rapidly substituted by interactive marketing. Zahay (2014) describes components such as the advancement of conversations and the usage of databases are added to digital marketing. Nevertheless, digital marketing facilitates conversations and increases participation, as the consumer has, to an extent, the balance of conversation via social platforms and retracted the buying option by online surveying prior approaching to a sales representative in the brick-and-mortar store or in a B2B sales (Akgün et al., 2014). In a nutshell, the change to digital marketing from interactive marketing indicates the journey towards one-to-many and many-to-many communications, which are rapidly started off by customers rather than firms.

Chaudhary et al. (2021) in their research used the predictive data analytics technique for understanding consumer behaviour in social media. They have also analysed consumer perception and attitude towards social media marketing. Also, back casting from the digital marketing goals has equally gained momentum with expanding research on cloud database and its interfaces (Alam et al., 2013a). Many factors influence the credibility and accountability of digital marketing including data management

(Shakil & Alam, 2014), security issues in cloud computing (Alam & Alam, 2013), etc. Digital marketing is an umbrella for interdisciplinary research owing to its complex intersection of web analytics, database, and applications. Modelling or structuring the cloud data is realized by the level of complexity, consumer needs for the application, and marketing outcomes. For example, Shakil et al. (2015) have developed a unique cloud-based system model for handling university-level data;, on the other hand, Alam et al. (2013) have developed a five-layer architecture database model that can be applied to a range of digital marketing platforms by changing the model parameters according to the digital applications. On the other hand, the neural network-based hybrid model developed by Raza and Alam (2016) has the faster computation of web analytics.

Digital marketing carters to consumer needs more effectively through various web analytics data such as frequently purchased products, associated products, consumer ratings, etc. Comparative analysis of customer happiness towards Amazon and Flipkart demonstrated that web analytics data features have increased client contentment (Chaudhary & Kumar 2016). The emotional inclination of E-buyers has even greater weightage to the success of digital marketing. Products that are accompanied by a social cause or message are more likely to instigate the emotional response of the consumers (Chaudhary, 2018). Though digital marketing has increased fourfold in its statistics with respect to its usage and demand owing to its abundant consumer-friendly features, it is however faced with greater challenges with respect to consumer protection (Chaudhary et al., 2021) as compared to nondigital platforms. Consumer protection is not just limited to delivering quality products but also there is a greater need for the protection of consumer information. Shakil et al. (2020) have developed a biometric authentication system provided for health care data, while Kumar et al. (2018) have developed a probabilistic encryption system serving the purpose of consumer protection.

The digital marketing infrastructure and features can be enhanced through efficient data analytics systems that can employ different metrics for digital marketing based on the applications. For example, knowledge-based information systems (Kaur & Alam, 2013) emphasize knowledge engineering as an analytics metric, while monitoring-based performance improvement systems use decision matrix (Alam et al., 2013b). On the other hand, metrics from social media communication platforms also have an essential role in conceptualizing frameworks for web analytics and digital marketing. The consumer database analytics from various digital social platforms provide the trends in the range of consumers' needs and demands. For example, Khan et al. (2018) have developed a unique framework for Twitter Data Analysis, wherein consumer needs and requirements have been extracted from their social media communication.

Other ideas associated with digital marketing include e-marketing. By accepting these, ideas are commonly used interchangeably with digital marketing, few differences can be identified. Initially, the phrase internet marketing means only internet. Digital marketing on the other hand is a collection of software that includes mobile apps, MMSs, SMSs, and databases that can be accessed without the use of the internet. Electronic marketing is similar to digital marketing in that it is linked to electronic communication (Chaffey and Smith, 2017).

The phrase "digital marketing" is derived from its wide conceptualization that comprises planning, implementation, tracking, and measuring of marketing with the help of technological applications.

The phrase "digital marketing" has been more popular during the last several years. Google searches for phrases like "interactive marketing" and "internet marketing" outnumber searches for terms like "e-marketing" and "digital marketing." It claims that the term's popularity has progressively risen over the years, and this demonstrates that the terminology shift toward digital marketing has occurred.

5.2 EVOLVING COMMUNICATION PATTERNS

The analysis regarding the evolving communication environment has progressed with the rise of social media channels. In the late1990s, Novak et al. (2000) envisaged how the information exchange environment would change into computer-aided worlds, hypermedia, described as a vital and dynamic disseminated network, possibly worldwide in nature, combined with related software and hardware for retrieving the network that allows firms and customers to (1) arrange and collaboratively use the hypertext format, media collaboration, and (2) exchange communication via the means, i.e., individual collaboration. Although Novak et al. (2000) did not apply the phrase social media channel, they had defined the reason of social media channels and their inferences for specific marketing communications. They defined the change from mass communications, i.e., one-to-many communications, towards parallel communications, many-to-many communications, in which sellers and buyers deliberately participate and engage in conversations via digital media channels. They emphasized that parallel communication patterns would make mass marketing communication, e.g., advertising, styles abortive, as the latter considers that buyers are submissive recipients of information exchanges. Hoffman and Novak trusted buyers were transforming into dynamic members in the communication process by sharing and creating content and ideas in sync with marketers. Also, they estimated that the power parity over the market would move away from traders to buyers, as traders would not be in a position to command the type of marketing messages buyers share and consume. The traders would be left only with an option to adapt to the change by accepting the position of a conversation member rather than a campaigner.

At present, the revolutionary concepts of Hoffman and Novak (1996) have come true. Mass communications are less seen and heard, but mass media campaigning has significantly declined in cost for ad advertising agencies and firms are rapidly shifting their campaigning budgets from the conventional to digital media (Malthouse et al, 2018). Moreover, the impact of direct marketing is into question as it refutes the customer empowerment paradigm, whereas advertisers are being communicated to rather than communicating (Winer, 2009). Nevertheless, direct marketing presumed further modern levels in digital or online media, which allow for behavioural targeting and customization of marketing message, a change which has been found to accelerate the potency and effectiveness of direct marketing (Simonson, 2005).

The growth of parallel communications is apparent in the increasing number of manifestation of choices or opinions linked to brands, services, products, and companies in online or digital media. These manifestations are usually referred to as user-generated content (UGC) (Godes & Mayzlin, 2004), which may include content different from firms or their offerings (Kietzmann et al., 2011) or electronic word-of-mouth (eWOM). In the age of digital media, any individual can exchange eWOM in the way of pictures, videos, and text irrespective of place and time and without formal acceptance or monetary expense by an institution, e.g., publishing firms (Hennig-Thurau et al., 2004). This implies consumers have nearly infinite chances to voice their choices about brand(s), firms, or their products through digital channels, including online communities, discussion forums, blogs, social networking services, and product review sites.

In similarity to the traditional word-of-mouth which happens in a one-to-one or a face-to-face context, eWOM can be exchanged amongst a worldwide structure of internet users who do not inevitably are familiar with each other (Chevalier & Mayzlin, 2006). Also, for the predictable future, eWOM stays in place for individuals seeking data regarding services and products (Kietzmann et al., 2011). In short, the reach and volume of word-of-mouth are increased by social media channels as eWOM receivers and senders have greatly vast choices for consuming and sharing opinions in relation to conventional word-of-mouth (Duan et al., 2008). The significance of e-WOM is multiplied by the fact customers are curious to voice their feedback regarding products or services. For instance, 19% of tweets include a say of a brand, and 20% of such tweets comprise a manifestation inducing an emotion or response towards it (Java et al., 2007).

5.3 EVOLVING PURCHASING PATTERNS

A purchasing pattern has been conventionally interpreted as a simple and linear path in which buyers primarily assume a set of services or products or brands prior to methodically reducing them below at each step of the buying process, but this presumption has met with growing counterattack in the era of digital channels. The novel drive is characterized by a constant spiral in which customers add or remove difficult choices in an iterative manner during the purchasing process, after communicating with other customers through digital media and reading eWOM. Nonetheless, customers may reciprocate amongst the buying decision stages in untraditional ways which are hard to predict.

In the need identification or recognition stage, a buyer perceives a problem or need by an external sign, e.g., an advertisement or an internal sign, e.g., hunger (Zhou et al., 2013). In digital platforms, external signs can be stimulated by marketing triggers, e.g., a display advertisement, but additionally, However, clients may unintentionally come upon E-wom causing them to become aware of new issue (Babić Rosario et al., 2016). For instance, a commercial consumer may require the desire to recruit a new campaigning firm built on a post or suggestion on LinkedIn or Facebook by a friend. Obviously, for a buying process to fasten, a buyer needs to recognize and become conscious of a need, and the rapid increase of eWOM is guiding such a conscious (Chintagunta et al., 2010).

Buyers are becoming conscious and empowered as online or digital media rapidly gives them simpler and instant access to data and information about different suppliers' products and other buyers' reviews and experiences. The position of eWOM is becoming significant in the commercial sector, as detailed by a Chief Marketing Officer: "We see web based 'power evangelists' emerging. Wiersema (2013) opined that people can have very considerable influence, yet with social media, we have no message control. So, we are monitoring chat rooms and blogs, to be aware of what they say about us". The growing role of digital media in commercial customer shopping journeys opens up new opportunities for commercial marketers. For instance, blogging might be an impressive option to demonstrate proficiency and educate customers on how to benefit from firm's services or products. In many-to-many communications, brand communities are especially suitable where buyers may convey their problems and concerns with firm's representative's offerings and could resolve them (Jussila et al., 2014). In a perfect situation, buyers who encountered similar problems may address the concerns of others. Involving and engaging in social networking groups, e.g., Facebook groups and LinkedIn groups, which are particular to specific themes or industries allow firms to enhance dialogue between the potential customers and firm, which might be the best way to find fresh leads (Zarrella, 2009). Online markets in the commercial context, e.g., Amazon or Alibaba, which exhibit different purchasing and trading firms avail a provided platform or website is another way to enable transactions and increase sales and acquire customers (Huang et al., 2017).

5.4 DIGITAL MARKETING OBJECTIVES AND STRATEGIC TRENDS

Marketing goals must guide digital marketing strategies, plans, and evaluation criteria. (Krishnamurthy & Wills, 2006). A firm might have strategic objectives particularly customized to digital marketing, like an increase in sales leads from online media and website traffic rise; however, the key targets of marketing usually merge across platforms, and therefore digital media clearly provides fresh methods to accomplish them. There can be various firm-aimed marketing targets, but the final marketing goal is to kindle net profit and positive cash flow (Ambler & Roberts, 2005). Marketers can influence profit generation by yielding an equal amount of earnings with reduced costs or increasing sales revenue. The former is succeeded in the domain by, for example, improving the efficiency and effectiveness of interchanges in terms of transactions and communications (Siamagka et al, 2015). In terms of expanding sales in the commercial scenario, digital marketing can be deployed to generate vital buyers to a firm's online site and translate into new sales opportunities (Hong, 2007). Moreover, commercial firms use this marketing for cross-selling and upselling purposes, like pushing a fresh variant of a product or providing customer service via electronic mail. As the sales effect of marketing is hard to measure precisely, marketers use transitional goals which are considered as signals of future sales revenue.

Customer relationship goals, such as increasing customer satisfaction and loyalty, and branding goals, such as increasing brand recognition and improving brand value, are two types of transitional goals. Commercial firms go after branding goals in digital channels by focusing on buyers with brand sensitivity. Digital media strategy involves the means and methods by which goals are accomplished (Shuliang & Zheng, 2010). In a different way, while goals define where a firm wants to position itself, the strategy communicates how it gets to that position (Chaffey & Smith, 2017). It is debatable if firms must have targeted digital marketing goals and strategies, or if it must ideally be considered as a toolkit to accomplish overall promotion objectives. In any instance, digital or online promotion goals and strategies should be precisely related to overall business goals and strategies (Wind, 2006) as promotion plays a key role in imparting the rewarding execution of a firm's strategies (Olson et al., 2005).

Research proves that positioning a firm's promotion goals with its business goals delivers enhanced performance in terms of market performance and profitability (Slater & Olson, 2001). As a consequence, a promotion plan that promotes the preferred marketing tactic should be firm related. Due to the obvious firm-specific nature of digital marketing techniques, there is a wealth of compact systemic data on which types of digital marketing strategies are superior to others in specific industrial segments. Nevertheless, digitalization has yielded fresh strategic patterns in marketing due to transformation in purchasing behaviours, news consumption, and communications patterns. Particularly, three strategic developments have arisen in commercial marketing due to progress in digital media: (1) customization of marketing communications, (2) content marketing, and (3) data-driven marketing.

5.5 CUSTOMIZATION OF MARKETING CHANNELS OF COMMUNICATION

Customization of marketing channels of communication is affiliated to content marketing which means delivering appropriate content to the target audience at the right instance requires customization or personalization. The main theme of customization is to look at each person as a distinctive person with individual needs and to assist with personalized solutions; this perspective is affirmed to result in expanded sales earnings (Tam & Ho, 2006). Customization means adapting the components of the marketing mix for affinity at an individual or independent level (Arora et al., 2008). As a result, customization includes improvements to costs, goods, and distribution networks, but the focus is on campaigning contact channels. Customization and personalization are also used interchangeably, but the difference is that customization is triggered by the marketer, while personalization is triggered by the consumer (Arora et al., 2008). To be able to customize marketing communication channels, campaigners need to discover the consumer's specific interests and terms in preferences of the categories of content which the consumer is interested to accept and various individual-targeted characteristics (Wright et al, 2006).

According to Järvinen and Karjaluoto (2015), getting to learn about the consumer can be categorized into passive and active kinds of learning. Passive learning comprises drawing conclusions about the consumer depending on previous transactions and other behaviours, while active learning means asking direct questions to the consumer. Although customization methods forerun the evolution of the internet, social platforms transformed the trader's capacity to estimate consumer needs (White et al., 2008). Hence, the strategic shift toward customization of marketing campaigns has escalated in the past few years. In specific, the ways for unassertive learning have progressed notably.

In a physical environment, the traders' competence to deduce inferences concerning consumer behaviour has been restricted to purchase transaction, i.e., the number of times a product has been purchased, purchases location, and categories of products bought. In the digital world, click-stream information and data are applied to archive each action performed by a consumer in a firm's held social platform, which facilitates market-ers to know about interest levels of a person prior to the buying conclusion happens (McAfee & Brynjolfsson, 2012). As a result, this collection of behavioural data could be used to optimize web content, such as placing content on a network website that is suited to the specifications of the customer. The strength to collate an affluent behavioural data through digital or social channels is a magnificent chance for traders in terms of targeting and customization. Research proves the application of behavioural data, i.e., purchase transactions, to aim marketing communication guides to increasingly greater profits in contrast to the application of demographical data (Reinartz et al., 2004). Of late, it has been exhibited how clickstream, i.e., behavioural, information can be applied to spot consumers who are more willing to go for shopping quickly in their buying process. Paying attention to these consumers via customized communications is expected to grow the prospect that they will end up making a purchase.

5.6 CONTENT MARKETING

Content marketing is defined as an internal marketing technique or a pull method that focuses to attract buyers previously enquiring for specific information pertaining to a firm's catalogue by giving effective content aimed at their targeted needs (Karjaluoto et al., 2015). It includes a vital approach other than a set of practices as it demands an ethnic shift to helping buyers from traders (Rowley, 2008). While the revenue is the ultimate objective, it is achieved through assisting customers rather than by aggressive marketing and selling efforts. As a result, content marketing is a response to concerns about utilizing the least rigid marketing styles possible (White et al., 2008). Although it can use content in conventional forms, e.g., brochures and magazines, the digital world has familiarized the phrase content marketing that for different resources refers solely to content in digital patterns (Handley& Chapman 2010). According to Chaffey (2017), the utmost used digital pattern forms include e-books, videos, pictures, podcasts, animations, white papers, blog texts, info-graphics, webinars, and social media posts. Trainor et al.,2014) proposed that effective content marketing requires an understanding of analytics and the development of a large database that can be used to target and influence content delivery.

5.7 DATA-DRIVEN MARKETING AND DIGITAL MEDIA

Consumer data is becoming more available thanks to digital media, which has contributed to the development of a strategic approach to data-driven marketing (Royle & Laing, 2014). Larivière et al., 2013) defined data-driven marketing as the use of data to update and enhance the execution of promotional activities. The data-driven method can be appreciated as a sign from what do I prefer? toward what do I need? (Rowley, 2008). The approach is based on the use of consumer databases and has roots in both direct and digital marketing (Alba et al., 1997). Customer relationship management (CRM) has become a vital data-driven marketing preference along with the use of customer databases (Garrido-Moreno et al., 2014). In fact, various accepted meanings of CRM highlight using technology in a strategic way and data as the prime component of leading consumer relationships (Reinartz et al., 2004).

Customer database and CRM are important components of marketing-based data; however, the number, frequency, reach, and variety of buyer-related data that can be collected and analysed in real time have increased thanks to web analytics tools. The amount of time it takes to recover data has enticed marketing people to conduct swift checks and analyse their assumptions; data-driven marketers recognize their limitations in estimating the outcome of marketing campaigns and therefore use data and tests to validate their novel concepts (Rowley, 2008). The evaluation can be used to evaluate the efficacy of various promotional activities, as well as positioning eligibility, marketing delivery methods, and pattern format. An example of the second is given in a study by Chandon et al. (2009). Kumar et al. (2018) investigated the impact of weblink positioning on email leaflets on the rate of click and found that weblinks positioned towards the left of email leaflets are highly worthwhile in leading rate of clicks, on a website.

The shift towards marketing based on data and the larger use of analytics is forced by a severe force from senior leadership (Wamba et al., 2015) and is enhanced if the organization is more triumphant with analytics (Kiron et al., 2014). This result implies once leaders appreciate the rewards of the data-driven method; they will persuade marketing campaigners to become efficient and competent with analytics and tools. Executive pressure towards data-driven marketing is backed by experimental findings, highlighting that the application of customer or marketing analytics is associated with escalated firm performance regarding growth, profit, sales, and payoff (, Verhoef & Leeflang, 2009)). Several studies have detailed that high-performing organizations often use analytics five to six times better when compared to least performers (Wamba et al., 2015); also, the application of analytics is a prime origin of competitive advantage by the most (61%) of leaders (Akter,et al., 2016; Ransbotham et al., 2015)

Analytics and databases facilitate firms to generate data-driven marketing goals and strategies with the help of the data of each customer (Vargo & Lusch, 2011; Hausman et al., 2006). The buyer-associated data is assumed to be specifically beneficial in the commercial marketing mix in which a firm's long-term association with its buyers is vital for continuing successful operations (Barac et al., 2017). The efficient and potent use of buyer-related data is further treated as a necessity for triumphing in a rapidly repute management method called as customer experience management, which means analysing and managing customer manifestations or experiences through a series of interactions starting from prebuying to postbuying situations (Lemon & Verhoef, 2016)

5.8 WEB ANALYTICS

Web analytics is the root of the concepts of digital analytics. It is "measurement, collection, analysis and reporting of Internet data for the purposes of understanding and optimizing Web usage" (Kaushik, 2009). Web analytics experts like Kaushik (2009) describe the concept as "the analysis of qualitative and quantitative data from your website and the competition to drive a continuous improvement of the online experience that your customers and potential customers have, which translates to the desired outcomes" in keeping with this description (both online and offline)."

Web analytics serves as a broad terminology for measuring, collecting, analysing, reporting, and maximizing online data for firm's transactions. In the past years, the usage of this term got significantly countered because of its intense relation with website analytics, which does not acceptably consider other online tools, e.g., mobile applications, search browsers, and social media (Järvinen, & Karjaluoto, 2015). Therefore, digital analytics has slowly replaced web analytics as to the comprehensive term as the former comprises the collation and usage of data from all online or digital media. For instance, in 2012, the web analytics association rechristened itself to the digital analytics. Nonetheless, it remains a prime toolkit of digital analytics. The other similarly related phrase is marketing analytics which implies a technology-driven approach to harvest market and customer data to fasten decision making (Verhoef et al., 2016). Going with this, digital analytics and marketing analytics may be treated as substitutes as both involve technology-driven approaches aimed to enhance and easy marketing decisions deploying data. The main contrast is digital analytics prime focus is on behavioural data extracted from online or digital media.

5.9 TECHNIQUES FOR DIGITAL MARKETING

The digital world has produced new possibilities for firms to achieve promoting objectives and actualize techniques via different exercises. Firms exhaust a mean of 10.2% of their yearly income on advertising exercises, and very nearly one-fourth of their last promoting cost is spent on advanced showcasing exercises (Gartner, 2014). As the ideation, arranging, and usage of digital advertising exercises require assets, it is generally hard to anticipate promoting use decisively. This is clear in the space of digitized advertising, where most exercises don't interpret financial speculations, so cost is distinguished by the length spent on the exercises, for example, a discussion through web-based media or composing a post.

The spread of digital channels sets up the subject of which systems firms should choose. While concurring the choice of procedures is guided by advertising objectives, the most broadly utilized digital marketing channels are by and by messages, sites, informal communication administrations, and bulletins (Leeflang et al., 2014). Aside from the firm site, which is required for practically a wide range of firms, there are huge contrasts between firms with respect to the usage of digital marketing procedures. According to the State of Digital Marketing report (Webmarketing123, 2015), email campaigning is the overwhelmingly utilized stunt for mechanical firms while focusing on means of SNSs is the broadly utilized customer marketing tactic. Facebook, inside SNSs, is noted as the indispensable social stage by B2C firms, while LinkedIn is the primary stage for commercial firms.

The fluctuating utilization of formats proposes the apparent viability of focused digital advertising campaigns shifts amongst B2C and mechanical firms. Regardless, a couple of studies have announced the viability of computerized focusing on strategies for conveying deals in B2C conditions (Danaher & Dagger, 2013; Spilker-Attig & Brettel, 2010). Additionally, the outcomes differed relying upon the case firm under investigation, which propose that the general viability of digital aimed strategies is firm explicit. Furthermore, digital marketing techniques are considered to have spill over effects, in which a buyer's openness to one marketing strategy influences the adequacy of openings to other marketing strategies (Verhoef et al., 2016) and Li and Kannan (2014). For example, Kumar et al. (2016) discovered a firm-created content in social channels produces synergistic results with email promoting and TV publicizing. Such sort of impacts trap association's endeavours in estimating the adequacy of a targeted digital marketing strategy.

Generally, it is difficult to explore which marketing strategies are great as adequacy is dependent upon different factors, for example, target group, marketing objectives, and the nature of marketing content. Hence, each firm should test and gauge the presentation of digital campaigning against the firm explicit destinations (Verhoef & Leeflang, 2009), which can be aided by digital analytics tools.

5.10 WEB ANALYTICS TOOLS

Perhaps the earliest advancement called as web analytics that arose as a new methodology for following client conduct on sites. I/PRO Corp, the first vendor, was officially floated in 1994 and was immediately trailed by various others (Järvinen & Karjaluoto, 2015). When Google Analytics was launched in 2005, it had already become a popular method for tracking visitor behaviour on websites, and it is still the most widely used digital analytic tool today. Further to the rise of web analytics, the amount and assortment of tools have detonated. Existence of marketing campaigning tools to customize advertising content and overseeing prospective customer testing devices to lead digital examinations, e.g., Apptimize, checking tools to follow online news and conversations, e.g., Cision, text mining tool to extricate data from text sources, e.g., RapidMiner, site review instruments to get client criticism, e.g., SurveyMonkey, online boards to acquire a comprehension of target crowd conduct on Web, e.g., Adobe Analytics, and online insight tools to measure contender execution, e.g., Synthesio.

Few digital analytics tools are custom-made for a particular stage, e.g., Facebook examination, while the rest are intended for a specific strategy or action. In the area of search advertising, for example, tools are accessible for examining catchphrases, distinguishing search rankings, encouraging third-party referencing, and slithering and reviewing the site to discover issues applicable to site design improvement. In contrast to traditional marketing analytics, which has provided information on customers' inaccessible partnerships and profiles, e.g. segment data, digital analytics provides additional information by incorporating customers' digital footprints. (Germann et al., 2013; Hauser, 2007).

To expound, there are numerous components that have composed digital analytics strikingly ground breaking from the advertisers' point of view. To begin with, digital analytics offers significantly more definite information on client conduct as the clickstream information records all the activities attempted by clients in an advanced climate, while conventional showcasing investigation normally catches just the results of conduct, like exchanges. Second, although clients' inclinations and goals can be peddled through overviews and meetings, digital analytics catches certified conduct and articulations of assessment in clients' indigenous habitat. Third, digital analytics tracks the conduct, everything being equal, and not simply clients, which is gainful as far as client obtaining. Fourth, the conduct information incorporates locational data that encourages the conveyance of customized and context-oriented showcasing messages. At last, the experiences from digital analytics data can be stretched out to disconnected settings. For instance, advertisers can audit how disconnected publicizing builds the quantity of site guests and improves the subsequent results. As the utilization of cell phones keeps on expanding, offline environment and digital environment are becoming more interlaced, which moreover builds the force of digital analytics.

Web analytics tools are programmes that monitor the identity of visitors to a website, monitor clients' route ways dependent on labels, and treats and present the data in an important structure (Wang et al., 2016; Nakatani & Chuang, 2011). In practice, it can be utilized for realizing which showcasing channels and tools drive guests to organization sites, the pages visited, duration spent, and the ensuing after-effects of their visits (e.g., pamphlet downloads, contact solicitations, or exchanges). The most significant justification for using web data is to enhance the customer experience on the site in order to maximize the business benefits received from site users (Wilson, 2010). Web analytics can separate visitors into segments or conduct sections, but since these tools usually generate total level information about site visitors, they are constrained in terms of identifying visitors and tracking their visits over time. Advertisers would only be able to merge online data with individual data until they have figured out how to do so, e.g., by means of site logins would they be able to follow communications with explicit guests for a longer duration and design further, exact marketing activities aimed at them (Jansen, 2006; Phippen et al., 2004).

While web investigation gives quantitative information on clients' site conduct, web-based media observing empower firms to mine clients' appearances of sentiments and encounters identified with the organization and its items across digital media (Liu, 2006). Assessment mining has gotten more doable because of the expanded measure of eWOM (Pang & Lee, 2008). The ascent of eWOM has made client discourse and conversation more perceptible and quantifiable given that the online environment permits the assortment of genuine exchange of data between people (Hennig-Thurau et al., 2004). In fact, web-based media monitoring catches the volume and valence of eWOM data with respect to explicit catchphrases (Godes & Mayzlin, 2004). The volume of eWOM shows the number of notices of the chose keyword(s) in an online environment inside a predetermined time span (Sponder, 2012). The valence of eWOM estimates the tone of conversations and shows whether the chosen search word is referenced in a positive, unbiased, or negative setting (Pang & Lee, 2008). However, social media tools are restricted as far as their capacity to order the tone of conversations, with one investigation showing a precision pace of 60% (Liu, 2006). In usage, social media tracking can be utilized for following the useful and pessimistic buzz about an organization and analysing what individuals say about it. Moreover, following industry-related conversations might be a decent methodology for distinguishing client concerns and new freedoms in the business.

5.10.1 Automating Marketing

Marketing automation depends on comparative analytics methods to web analytics as it tracks client conduct on sites using treats, logins, IP addresses, and personalized joints. Nonetheless, two significant highlights recognize showcasing web analytics provides marketing automation. Based on the requirement that customers identify themselves by completing a website contact form, marketing automation can potentially track their behaviour over longer periods of time. Second, marketing automation goes past following client conduct as it very well may be utilized to customize site components and substance conveyed to a client dependent on explicit standards set by programming clients (Kantrowitz, 2014). The goal is to draw in, form, and keep up trust with current and imminent clients via consequently customizing significant and helpful substances to meet their necessities (Moncrief & Marshall, 2005). Nevertheless, vendors such Eloqua and Hubspot guarantee that the tool permits organizations to enhance and quicken lead capability measures. Given that prospecting and lead capability are the most difficult undertakings of the modern selling measure (Heimbach et al., 2015), It's not surprising that encouraging marketing automation has piqued the mechanical community's interest. To be sure, one of the crucial developments in the commercial sector, according to Wiersema (2013), is the creative automation of manual activities conducted by advertisers. Wilson (2010) utilized clickstream information to exhibit how web examination can be utilized for upgrading mechanical online business site execution as far as diminishing shopping basket surrender. Outstandingly, the two examinations were directed regarding internet business organizations that had the benefit of having the option to follow client conduct from starting openness to advertising action right to the last exchange in correlation; mechanical organizations portrayed by mind boggling and protracted selling measures are known to battle in their endeavours to set up a connection between promoting exercises and deals sway (Webster et al., 2005). In its entirety, digital analytics empower organizations to follow client conduct in advanced channels and assess client reactions to promoting improvements. Advertisers use data tools to determine the success of marketing strategies, ascertain which methods work better for unique client groups, and boost future activities. The majority of current data on the use of digital analytics is based on studies from market research organizations and is, in general, controlling in nature (Pickton, 2005; Waisberg & Kaushik, 2009). Thus, it stays indistinct how much firms can utilize digital analytics for estimating showcasing execution or what decides the business benefits acquired from digital analytics.

5.11 IMPLICATIONS

Marketing aficionados should start preparing their use of digital analytics by identifying digital marketing goals. The objectives should be obviously defined, quantifiable, and connected to business strategy. When marketing executives start with sales-related objective, they are bound to have the option to show solid advantages to leadership and consequently gain more assets for building up a more all-encompassing MPM framework. After defining the goals, the following stage is to choose appropriate measurements and make a significant measurement system. The measurement system ought to have an unmistakable construction that shows how the measurements are identified with one another and which there are in any event two reasonable approaches to structure a measurement structure.

Another option is to divide the measurement scheme into sections based on the main marketing goal into different stages of the buying process for clients or different stages of the sale interaction (e.g., traffic age, site conduct, deals income, etc.). The issues in the utilization of digital analytics occur when the measurement framework is set in motion, on the grounds that an excessive number of associations do not have a deliberate cycle for overseeing measurement information. They should treat data alignment and which tools are utilized for this reason. The determination of proper devices ought to be guided by what information are required for the measurements framework; however, it is, for the most part, suggested that advertisers begin with web analytic devices, Google Analytics, which offer data about client conduct and coming about results. They are likewise simple to utilize and do not need direct financial ventures.

In addition, web analytical tools offer highlights for marketers to imagine and communicate findings to the management. It's indeed critical to report the results to leadership on a regular basis in a meaningful way and to be able to comprehend the report in a reasonable amount of time while considering the reports. Presentation or reporting is vital to conveying the input of marketing to the firm's execution, which is truly important for improving the competence of marketing within an organization and rationalizing an expanded budget and number of assets. At last, the most key assessment related to the estimation method is to brief how the data is dissected, processed, and deciphered. Except if the data is investigated properly, nor can they make rational choices regarding how to refine it.

5.12 CONCLUSION

The basis of any optimization effort is web analytics. Its task is to figure out which digital marketing activities are the most important execution facilitators and which zones underperform in relation to achieving digital marketing goals. Producing ideas on how to improve main activities that are currently struggling to reach standards is a requirement of the analytical work. The tasks may be related to the option of digital marketing strategies or their current implementation.

REFERENCES

Akgün, A. E., İmamoğlu, S. Z., Koçoğlu, İ., İnce, H., & Keskin, H. 2014. Bridging organizational learning capability and firm performance through customer relationship management. *Procedia-Social and Behavioral Sciences*, 150, 531–540.

Akter, S., Wamba, S. F., Gunasekaran, A., Dubey, R., & Childe, S. J. 2016. How to improve firm performance using big data analytics capability and business strategy alignment? *International Journal of Production Economics*, 182, 113–131.

Alam, M., & Alam, B. (2013, June). Cloud query language for cloud database. In *Proceedings of the International Conference on Recent Trends in Computing and Communication Engineering–RTCCE 2013* (pp. 108–112).

Alam, B., Doja, M. N., Alam, M., & Malhotra, S. 2013a. Security issues analysis for cloud computing. *International Journal of Computer Science and Information Security*, 11(9), 117.

Alam, B., Doja, M. N., Alam, M., & Mongia, S. 2013b. 5-layered architecture of cloud database management system. *AASRI Procedia*, 5, 194–199.

Alam, M., & Shakil, K. A. (2014). A decision matrix and monitoring based framework for infrastructure performance enhancement in a cloud based environment. *arXiv preprint arXiv:1412.8029*.

Alba, J., Lynch, J., Weitz, B., Janiszewski, C., Lutz, R., Sawyer, A., & Wood, S. 1997. Interactive home shopping: Consumer, retailer, and manufacturer incentives to participate in electronic marketplaces. *Journal of Marketing*, 61(3), 38–53.

Ambler, T., & Roberts, J. 2005. Beware the silver metric: Marketing performance measurement has to be multidimensional, London Business School. Center for Marketing, London.

Arora, N., Dreze, X., Ghose, A., Hess, J. D., Iyengar, R., Jing, B., ... & Zhang, Z. J. 2008. Putting one-to-one marketing to work: Personalization, customization, and choice. *Marketing Letters*, 19(3), 305–321.

Babić Rosario, A., Sotgiu, F., De Valck, K., & Bijmolt, T. H. 2016. The effect of electronic word of mouth on sales: A meta-analytic review of platform, product, and metric factors. *Journal of Marketing Research*, 53(3), 297–318.

Barac, D., Ratkovic-Živanovic, V., Labus, M., Milinovic, S., & Labus, A. 2017. Fostering partner relationship management in B2B ecosystems of electronic media. *Journal of Business & Industrial Marketing*, 32(8), 1203–1216.

Blasco-Arcas, L., Hernandez-Ortega, B. I., & Jimenez-Martinez, J. 2014. Collaborating online: The roles of interactivity and personalization. *The Service Industries Journal*, 34(8), 677–698.

Chaffey, D., & Smith, P. R. 2017. *Digital marketing excellence: Planning, optimizing and integrating online marketing*. Oxfordshire: Taylor & Francis Group.

Chaffey, D., Smith, P.R. and Smith, P.R. 2013. *eMarketing excellence: Planning and optimizing your digital marketing*. Oxfordshire: Routledge.

Chandon, P., Hutchinson, J. W., Bradlow, E. T., & Young, S. H. 2009. Does in-store marketing work? Effects of the number and position of shelf facings on brand attention and evaluation at the point of purchase. *Journal of Marketing*, 73(6), 1–17.

Chaudhary, K. 2018. Impact of emotional state of E-buyers on E-satisfaction: An empirical study. *Shanlax International Journals of Management*, 5, 83–88.

Chaudhary, K., & Kumar, S. 2016. Customer satisfaction towards Flipkart and Amazon: A comparative study. *International Journal of Academic Research & Development (JAR&D)*, 2, 35–42.

Chaudhary, K., Alam, M., Al-Rakhami, M. S., & Gumaei, A. 2021. Machine learning based mathematical modelling for prediction of social media consumer behaviour using Big Data analytics.

Chaudhry, K., Chandhiok, T., & Dewan, P. 2011. Consumer protection and consumerism in India. *ZENITH-International Journal of Multidisciplinary Research*, 1(1), 83–94.

Chevalier, J. A., & Mayzlin, D. 2006. The effect of word of mouth on sales: Online book reviews. *Journal of Marketing Research*, 43(3), 345–354.

Chintagunta, P. K., Gopinath, S., & Venkataraman, S. 2010. The effects of online user reviews on movie box office performance: Accounting for sequential rollout and aggregation across local markets. *Marketing Science*, 29(5), 944–957.

Court, D., Elzinga, D., Mulder, S. and Vetvik, O. J., 2009. The consumer decision journey. *McKinsey Quarterly*, 3(3), 96–107.

Danaher, P. J., & Dagger, T. S. 2013. Comparing the relative effectiveness of advertising channels: A case study of a multimedia blitz campaign. *Journal of Marketing Research*, 50(4), 517–534.

Duan, W., Gu, B., & Whinston, A. B. 2008. Do online reviews matter? – An empirical investigation of panel data. *Decision Support Systems*, 45(4), 1007–1016.

Garrido-Moreno, A., Lockett, N., & García-Morales, V. 2014. Paving the way for CRM success: The mediating role of knowledge management and organizational commitment. *Information & Management*, 51(8), 1031–1042.

Gartner 2014. Gartner Survey Reveals Digital Marketing Budgets Will Increase By 10 Percent in 2014. https://www.gartner.com/en/newsroom/press-releases/2014-04-29-gartner-survey-reveals-digital-marketing-budgets-will-increase-by-10-percent-in-2014. Accessed on March 14, 2021.

Germann, F., Lilien, G. L., & Rangaswamy, A. 2013. Performance implications of deploying marketing analytics. *International Journal of Research in Marketing*, 30(2), 114–128.

Godes, D., & Mayzlin, D. 2004. Using online conversations to study word-of-mouth communication. *Marketing Science*, 23(4), 545–560.

Handley, A., & Chapman, C. C. (2010). *Content rules: How to create killer blogs, podcasts, videos, ebooks, webinars (and more) that engage customers and ignite your business* (Vol. 5). New Jersey: John Wiley & Sons.

Hauser, W. J. 2007. Marketing analytics: The evolution of marketing research in the twenty-first century. *Direct Marketing: An International Journal*, 1(1), 38–54.

Hausman, A., Johnston, W. J., Gundlach, G. T., Bolumole, Y. A., Eltantawy, R. A., & Frankel, R. (2006). The changing landscape of supply chain management, marketing channels of distribution, logistics and purchasing. *Journal of Business & Industrial Marketing*, 21(7), 428–438.

Heimbach, I., Gottschlich, J., & Hinz, O. 2015. The value of user's Facebook profile data for product recommendation generation. *Electronic Markets*, 25(2), 125–138.

Hennig-Thurau, T., Gwinner, K. P., Walsh, G., & Gremler, D. D. 2004. Electronic word-of-mouth via consumer-opinion platforms: What motivates consumers to articulate themselves on the internet? *Journal of Interactive Marketing*, 18(1), 38–52.

Hoffman, D.L. and Novak, T.P., 1996. Marketing in hypermedia computer-mediated environments: Conceptual foundations. *Journal of Marketing*, 60(3), 50–68.

Hong, I. B. 2007. A survey of web site success metrics used by Internet-dependent organizations in Korea. *Internet Research*, 17(3), 272–290.

Huang, Q., Chen, X., Ou, C. X., Davison, R. M., & Hua, Z. 2017. Understanding buyers' loyalty to a C2C platform: The roles of social capital, satisfaction and perceived effectiveness of e-commerce institutional mechanisms. *Information Systems Journal*, 27(1), 91–119.

Jansen, B. J. 2006. Search log analysis: What it is, what's been done, how to do it. *Library & Information Science Research*, 28(3), 407–432.

Järvinen, J., & Karjaluoto, H. 2015. The use of web analytics for digital marketing performance measurement. *Industrial Marketing Management*. 50, 117–127.

Java, A., Song, X., Finin, T., & Tseng, B. 2007. Why we twitter: Understanding microblogging usage and communities. In *Proceedings of the 9th WebKDD and 1st SNA-KDD 2007 Workshop on Web Mining and Social Network Analysis*, pp. 56–65.

Jussila, J. J., Kärkkäinen, H., & Aramo-Immonen, H. 2014. Social media utilization in business-to-business relationships of technology industry firms. *Computers in Human Behavior*, 30, 606–613.

Kantrowitz, A. 2014. The CMO's guide to marketing automation. *Advertising Age*, 85(17), 24.

Karjaluoto, H., Ulkuniemi, P., & Mustonen, N. 2015. The role of digital channels in industrial marketing communications. *Journal of Business & Industrial Marketing*, 30(6), 703–710.

Kaur, A., & Alam, M. 2013. Role of knowledge engineering in the development of a hybrid knowledge based medical information system for atrial fibrillation. *American Journal of Industrial and Business Management*, 3(1), 36–41.

Kaushik, A. (2009). *Web analytics 2.0: The art of online accountability and science of customer centricity*. John Wiley & Sons. https://www.webanalyticsassociation.com/

Khan, I., Naqvi, S. K., Alam, M., & Rizvi, S. N. A. 2018. A framework for twitter data analysis. In *Big data analytics* (297–303). Singapore: Springer.

Kietzmann, J. H., Hermkens, K., McCarthy, I. P., & Silvestre, B. S. 2011. Social media? Get serious! Understanding the functional building blocks of social media. *Business Horizons*, 54(3), 241–251.

Kiron, D., Prentice, P. K., & Ferguson, R. B. (2014). Raising the bar with analytics. *MIT Sloan Management Review*, 55(2), 29.

Krishnamurthy, B., & Wills, C. E. 2006. Generating a privacy footprint on the internet. In *Proceedings of the 6th ACM SIGCOMM Conference on Internet Measurement*, pp. 65–70.

Kumar, A., Bezawada, R., Rishika, R., Janakiraman, R., & Kannan, P. K. 2016. From social to sale: The effects of firm-generated content in social media on customer behavior. *Journal of Marketing*, 80(1), 7–25.

Kumar, V., Kumar, R., Pandey, S. K., & Alam, M. 2018. Fully homomorphic encryption scheme with probabilistic encryption based on Euler's theorem and application in cloud computing. In V. B. Aggarwal, V., Bhatnagar, & D. K. Mishra (Eds.), *Big data analytics* (pp. 605–611). Singapore: Springer.

Larivière, B., Joosten, H., Malthouse, E. C., Birgelen, M. V., Aksoy, P., Kunz, W. H., & Huang, M. H. 2013. Value fusion: The blending of consumer and firm value in the distinct context of mobile technologies and social media. *Journal of Service Management*, 24(3), 268–293.

Leeflang, P. S. H., Verhoef, P. C., Dahlström, P., & Freundt, T. 2014. Challenges and solutions for marketing in a digital era. *European Management Journal*, 32(1), 1–12.

Lemon, K. N., & Verhoef, P. C. 2016. Understanding customer experience throughout the customer journey. *Journal of Marketing*, 80(6), 69–96.

Li, H., & Kannan, P. K. 2014. Attributing conversions in a multichannel online marketing environment: An empirical model and a field experiment. *Journal of Marketing Research*, 51(1), 40–56.

Liu, Y. 2006. Word of mouth for movies: Its dynamics and impact on box office revenue. *Journal of Marketing*, 70(3), 74–89.

Malthouse, E. C., Maslowska, E., & Franks, J. U. 2018. Understanding programmatic TV advertising. *International Journal of Advertising*, 37(5), 769–784.

McAfee, Andrew & Brynjolfsson, Erik. 2012. Big data: The management revolution. *Harvard Business Review*, 90, 60-6, 68, 128.

Moncrief, W. C., & Marshall, G. W. 2005. The evolution of the seven steps of selling. *Industrial Marketing Management*, 34(1), 13–22.

Nakatani, K., & Chuang, T. T. 2011. A web analytics tool selection method: An analytical hierarchy process approach. *Internet Research*, 21(2), 171–186.

Novak, T. P., Hoffman, D. L., & Yung, Y. F. 2000. Measuring the customer experience in online environments: A structural modeling approach. *Marketing Science*, 19(1), 22–42.

Olson, E. M., Slater, S. F., & Hult, G. T. M. 2005. The performance implications of fit among business strategy, marketing organization structure, and strategic behavior. *Journal of Marketing*, 69(3), 49–65.

Pang, B., & Lee, L. 2008 Opinion mining and sentiment analysis. *Foundations and Trends in Information Retrieval*, 2(1), 1–35.

Phippen, A., Sheppard, L., & Furnell, S. 2004. A practical evaluation of web analytics. *Internet Research*, 14(4), 284–293.

Pickton, D. (2005). Left brain marketing planning: A Forrester Research® viewpoint. *Marketing Intelligence & Planning*, 23, 537–542.

Ransbotham, S., Kiron, D., & Prentice, P. K. 2015. Minding the analytics gap. *MIT Sloan Management Review*, 56(3), 63–68.

Raza, K., & Alam, M. 2016. Recurrent neural network based hybrid model for reconstructing gene regulatory network. *Computational Biology and Chemistry*, 64, 322–334.

Reinartz, W., Krafft, M., & Hoyer, W. D. 2004. The customer relationship management process: Its measurement and impact on performance. *Journal of Marketing Research*, 41(3), 293–305.

Rowley, J. 2008. Understanding digital content marketing. *Journal of Marketing Management*, 24(5-6), 517–540.

Royle, J., & Laing, A. 2014. The digital marketing skills gap: Developing a Digital Marketer Model for the communication industries. *International Journal of Information Management*, 34(2), 65–73.

Shakil, K. A., & Alam, M. 2014. Data management in cloud based environment using k-median clustering technique. *International Journal of Computer Applications*, 3, 8–13.

Shakil, K. A., Sethi, S., & Alam, M. (2015, March). An effective framework for managing university data using a cloud based environment. In *2015 2nd International Conference on Computing for Sustainable Global Development (INDIACom)*, pp. 1262–1266.

Shakil, K. A., Zareen, F. J., Alam, M., & Jabin, S. 2020. BAMHealthCloud: A biometric authentication and data management system for healthcare data in cloud. *Journal of King Saud University-Computer and Information Sciences*, 32(1), 57–64.

Siamagka, N. T., Christodoulides, G., Michaelidou, N., & Valvi, A. 2015. Determinants of social media adoption by B2B organizations. *Industrial Marketing Management*, 51, 89–99.

Simonson, I., 2005. Determinants of customers' responses to customized offers: Conceptual framework and research propositions. *Journal of Marketing*, 69(1), pp. 32–45.

Slater, S. F., & Olson, E. M. 2001. Marketing's contribution to the implementation of business strategy: An empirical analysis. *Strategic Management Journal*, 22(11), 1055–1067.

Smith, K. L. 2007. What Is Digital Marketing? Available at: http://digitalmarketing101.blogspot.com/2007_09_30_archive.html. Accessed on March 10, 2021.

Spilker-Attig, A., & Brettel, M. 2010. Effectiveness of online advertising channels: A price-level-dependent analysis. *Journal of Marketing Management*, 26(3–4), 343–360.

Sponder, M. 2012. The uses and accuracy of social analytics data and platforms. In C. Reiman (Ed.), *Public interest and private rights in social media* (pp. 175–196). Cambridge: Chandos Publishing.

Tam, K. Y., & Ho, S. Y. 2006. Understanding the impact of web personalization on user information processing and decision outcomes. *MIS Quarterly*, 30, 865–890.

Trainor, K. J., Andzulis, J. M., Rapp, A., & Agnihotri, R. 2014. Social media technology usage and customer relationship performance: A capabilities-based examination of social CRM. *Journal of Business Research*, 67(6), 1201–1208.

Vargo, S. L., & Lusch, R. F. 2011. It's all B2B… and beyond: Toward a systems perspective of the market. *Industrial Marketing Management*, 40(2), 181–187.

Verhoef, P. C., & Leeflang, P. S. 2009. Understanding the marketing department's influence within the firm. *Journal of Marketing*, 73(2), 14–37.

Verhoef, P., Kooge, E., & Walk, N. 2016. *Creating value with big data analytics: Making smarter marketing decisions*. Oxfordshire: Routledge.

Waisberg, D., & Kaushik, A. 2009. Web Analytics 2.0: Empowering customer centricity. *The Original Search Engine Marketing Journal*, 2(1), 5–11.

Wamba, S. F., Akter, S., Edwards, A., Chopin, G., & Gnanzou, D. 2015. How 'big data' can make big impact: Findings from a systematic review and a longitudinal case study. *International Journal of Production Economics*, 165, 234–246.

Wang, G., Gunasekaran, A., Ngai, E. W., & Papadopoulos, T. 2016. Big data analytics in logistics and supply chain management: Certain investigations for research and applications. *International Journal of Production Economics*, 176, 98–110.

Webmarketing123 2015. State of Digital Marketing. Available at: https://static1.squarespace.com/static/550c33c6e4b09fa40565c247/t/5575e652e4b0b131dad80a2e/1433790034752/State-of-Digital-Marketing-2015.pdf. Accessed on February 12, 2021.

Webster Jr, F. E., Malter, A. J., & Ganesan, S. 2005. The decline and dispersion of marketing competence. *MIT Sloan Management Review*, 46(4), 35.

White, T. B., Zahay, D. L., Thorbjørnsen, H., & Shavitt, S. 2008. Getting too personal: Reactance to highly personalized email solicitations. *Marketing Letters*, 19(1), 39–50.

Wiersema, F. 2013. The B2B agenda: The current state of B2B marketing and a look ahead. *Industrial Marketing Management*, 4(42), 470–488.

Wilson, R. (2010). Using Clickstream data to enhance business-to-business web site performance. *Journal of Business & Industrial Marketing*, 25 (3): 177–187.

Wind, Y. J. 2006. Blurring the lines: Is there a need to rethink industrial marketing? *The Journal of Business and Industrial Marketing*, 21(7), 474–481.

Winer, R. S. 2009. New communications approaches in marketing: Issues and research directions. *Journal of Interactive Marketing*, 23(2), 108–117.

Wright, L. T., Harrison, T., Waite, K., & Hunter, G. L. 2006. The internet, information and empowerment. *European Journal of Marketing*, 40(9/10), 972–993.

Wymbs, C. 2011. Digital marketing: The time for a new "academic major" has arrived. *Journal of Marketing Education*, 33(1), 93–106.

Zahay, D. 2014. Beyond interactive marketing. *Journal of Research in Interactive Marketing*, 8(4), 32–46.

Zarrella, D. 2009. *The social media marketing book*. Newton, MA: O'Reilly Media, Inc.

Zheng, S., & Zhang, L. (2010, July). Queueing models based performance evaluation approach for Video On Demand back office system. In *2010 IEEE International Conference on Software Engineering and Service Sciences* (pp. 303–307). IEEE.

Zhou, L., Zhang, P., & Zimmermann, H. D. 2013. Social commerce research: An integrated view. *Electronic Commerce Research and Applications*, 12(2), 61–68.

6

Smart Retailing: A Novel Approach for Retailing Business

Ghanshyam Parmar
Constituent College of CVM University
Natubhai V. Patel College of Pure and Applied Sciences
Anand, Gujarat, India

CONTENTS

DOI: 10.1201/9781003307761-6

6.1 INTRODUCTION: WHAT IS RETAILING?

Definition: Retailing is a process of finite activities to sell goods or products straight to the end user (final customer) who is intended to use that (Jargons, 2021). A point of purchase (POP) is where the retailer accommodates a place from where the customer will purchase the product.

In any retailing business, basically there are two or three entities called manufacturer, wholesaler, and/or retailer for selling products to the customer. These three or two entities are directly involved in the retailing process for selling products.

A retailer is an entity who is the final link between the manufacturer and the producer of a product with the final customer in the chain of selling product. Whatever revenue a retailer gets from the business is always from the retailing.

6.1.1 The Important Entities in a Typical Supply Chain of Retailing

Manufacturers: They produce the finished products using machineries, resources or basic materials, and manpower.

Wholesalers: A wholesaler is a mediator who purchases finished products in large quantities from the manufacturers and sells those products to retailers.

Retailers: They sell the products to the final customer as a single or in small quantities with the maximum retail price given by the manufacturers or with a minute discount.

Customers: They are final buyers who purchase the products from the retailer (Murry, 2021).

6.1.2 Characteristics of Retailing

1. It is a process of direct interaction with the end customers.
2. The revenue generated by selling products to the customers may be in large volume, but the revenue will be less compared to the gain with manufacturers and wholesalers.
3. In any retail business, the service provided by the retailer for customer satisfaction is the major part.
4. The discounts and the promotions are offered on the retailer side only.
5. Major factors that affect the success of any retail business are the layout of the retail outlet and the geographical location (yourarticlelibrary, 2021).

6.1.3 Types of Retailing

Store Retailing: The retail outlets are the actual form of store retailing. The other types are superstores or supermarkets, showrooms with specific products catalogue, malls with a retail outlet, discount shops or stores, discount superstores where customers get a minimum discount on each product, convenience store which contains daily use products, and off-price retailers who sell second handed or used, cancel ordered products at a discounted price. Different types of discount strategies are developed by retailers for competition.

Nonstore Retailing: This is the type of retailing where the selling process of the final products will take place, where there is no retail outlet called non-store retailing. It is classified as under:

1. *Direct marketing:* In this process of advertising, a product to the customer with direct channels where representative explains product features where both met the first time. Customers will purchase that product in future.
2. *Direct selling:* The salesperson or the representative of the manufacturer who has a personal connection with the customer will sell the product directly to the customer at the doorstep. There may be a chance that a customer who has invited relatives, friends, and neighbors to understand the features of a product, and then the representative takes the orders of that product.
3. *Automated retailing:* It is the type of self-service where vending machines are used. In past years, vending machines were found in candy and newspaper machines in restaurants, coffee or tea machines in offices and factories, beverages or soft drinks and gas filling vending machines at gasoline stations, and in banks customers can use ATM machines to get information about their account and deposit – and – withdraw, large retail stores, etc.

4. *Electronic or Telemarketing retailing:* When any firm uses a telephonic or an electronic network to communicate with the customer understanding the product details. Before buying services or products electronically or on a telephonic call, customers agree with product features and terms and conditions. These products or services are credit cards, subscriptions of magazines, club memberships, and insurance policies.

Corporate Retailing: Two or more retail outlets of one manufacturer or owner is called retail or corporate chain. The products offered by the stores are similar in all retail outlets with similar prices, offers, promotions, layouts, or ambiance. Examples are a franchisee, leased departments, and customer cooperatives. There is a contractual agreement between the corporate retailer and franchisee. The types of products sell by franchisees are fashions, food, medicines, shoes, gritting cards, etc. (Jargons, 2021).

6.2 WHY SMART RETAILING?

In the current scenario, eCommerce win the battle against the retail stores because there are many benefits a customer can get when buying products from e-Commerce websites. Nowadays, online retailing (Kiran Chaudhary, 2018) is increasing, where most probably all retailers have created their own websites and mobile application to maintain their current customers and attract new customers. But what else retailers can do so a customer who visits their stores but does not buy anything, just view physical product compare with another and then buy them from E-commerce sites. How to convert visitors to their customers is a challenge for retailers.

These are the reasons by which the necessity is created over the eCommerce to do something new with the use of technology with retail outlets, to convert viewers to customers.

1. Overcome geographical limitations
   In any business, the geography limits the selling of products in a specific area. If it is an e-commerce business with a website, customers can buy products from anywhere in the world. Customers can even buy the product from e-commerce websites using mobile devices, which remove the limitation of geography.
2. Vital role of search engines to make new customers
   Retailing business is based on the relationship, services, and branding with the customer. By searching products in a search engine

(website), customers can get links for the e-commerce website, which increases the customers in the business. The more index in the search engine of the website more customers get trust in the business.

3. Reduces overall cost

   The main advantage is that the geographical location is not required; therefore, the cost for buy or rent expenditure is removed. This increases profit, and an e-commerce merchant can give more discounts, which leads to more selling. Another advantage is that advertisement is online through a search engine and social media, so again the cost of advertisement is reduced. The employees required for check-in or check-out for billing (payment) and inventory management are also reduced.

4. Product search becomes quicker

   No worry about physically moving your trolley or a cart to a specific location to search and take the product. Every e-commerce website facilitates search and also compares products with different brands to help customers to take decision quickly. Some e-commerce sites show special offers for their valuable customers.

5. Not to visit multiple shops

   The product information is now in the hand using e-commerce sites. Not to west travelling time and cost for searching products. E-commerce helps to visit different stores from a single place.

6. Information on hand

   Detailed readable information is given by e-commerce sites compared to the retail store. Also, a video of product features is available to understand easily. These things are hardly customers can get at a physical store. Customers can find detailed information to compare products because at the store all brands are not available.

7. 24 × 7 Access

   E-commerce sites allow customers to purchase any product from anywhere and anytime. The customer service of e-commerce sites is also available 24×7, which is benefited a lot to customers.

8. Return or Replace

   There is a return policy in e-commerce, where customers can buy discounted products with a group of products, and if one of them is not suited, then it can be returned. Even customers can replace the product in case of fitting size. The return or replacement contains 7 or 10 or even 30 days. These advantages cannot be given in retail stores (Murray, 2021).

6.2.1 Trends in Retailing

1. Blockchain technology in eCommerce and retailing
   Blockchain technology helps secure money transfer from an owner (customer) to a seller in eCommerce as well as in retail outlets. The structure of the blockchain stores transactional records (called block) in a block until that block is not full. The full block connects to the previous block and creates 'chain'. Blockchain creates a ledger by which one can find his/her historical transactions. Transactions made using blockchain must be verified and agreed upon by the customer and seller before they are stored in a block. The approved transaction will be encrypted and linked with the previous transaction. These transactions are stored in distributed computer networks but not on a single server, so it is impossible to hack by hackers. Customers can view their purchase history also. The transaction cost charges bear by the seller must be reduced as a priority. Using blockchain, there is no third party or middlemen required for secure transactions. The companies which use blockchain technology are Amazon, Walmart, OpenBazar, Shopin, and Paytomat.

2. Augmented reality (AR) and virtual reality (VR) in stores
   AR reality provides customers to find their products through in-store navigation easily. VR makes customer engagement by showing a virtual tour of the store from their own location means not to visit a physical store. Customer engagement is also done by providing content through impressive 3D graphic banners instead of simple 2D banners. AR creates realistic products through projection, whereas VR headsets involve customers to get a great buying experience. Customer satisfaction creates a reduction in product returns. AR and VR are the best in digital marketing; it provides an interactive advertisement to create customer engagement. Employees can get training using VR technology by simulating real situations and environments. Applications of AR and VR are furniture, fashion, footwear, and beauty product industries. AR and VR are used by some brands like U.S. Army, Disney Coloring, Swedish furniture giant IKEA, Gucci – 'try on' shoes in AR, Dulux Visualiser, Modiface on Amazon, L 'O' real Makeup, and much more.

3. Google Shopping supporting the retail market
   Sellers or advertisers have to choose Google Shopping for selling their products. Customers can search for any product on Google and they get another tab as Shopping, where customer gets the product

and prices from different sellers. Google gets a commission for each purchase. The feature of Google Shopping Ads increases retailers' ratings (familiarity) with customers. This is done when keyword search by the customer for any product matches. The more matches, retailer's product appears above and above in search results, which increases retailer's ratings. Retail-centric reporting tools allow retailers to view the performance of the product campaign and manage and promote product's bidding and budget.

4. Retail robots

Robots are doing much more activities in retail. The technologies used in robotic assistants in a store are artificial intelligence (AI) and machine learning. Robotics is not new technology with humans, but for store operations, it's a great job. Amazon is using robots to manage inventory in their stores. Even Walmart has developed its own army for inventory management in the year 2019. Machine vision algorithms in robots can scan and analyze whether items on shelves are out-of-stock or not. They send images and information to associates who have hand-held devices or send this information to unloader robots that fulfill the requirements. Robots do different work like real-time tracking of product movement, stock management, labeling of price tags on products, and space management for placing more products in less space.

5. AI technology in retailing

Machine learning and deep learning technology of AI provide an interactive environment to the customer for a personalized experience with the product. AI technology gives prediction and enhances forecast about sales on real-time data using internal and external data including geographical information, sales performance of similar products in the market, and other environmental factors like social media and online reviews. AI and machine learning can identify data errors in the supply chain and correct them so it can optimize the delivery of products to customers, which creates proper logistics. It can forecast the demand for products from real-time data.

6. Smart devices and Internet of Things (IoT)

Smart devices or equipment like smart cameras, beacons, and microphones enabled with the IoT technology give detailed and accurate data of customers to the retailer about customers' likeness and behavior. IoT-enabled smart shopping carts facilitate to scan a product's barcode and put into the cart. Customers can pay bills through a debit/credit card or through mobile payment, which is not required to stay in a queue. Smart equipment like beacons and sensors are using proximity. When a customer is nearer to this device, they can get promotions and coupons as a discount on their mobile phones if they are Bluetooth enabled. IoT-enabled beacons can measure environmental factors like light, temperature, and humidity and control the use of intelligent lighting systems, air conditioners, and reduce power consumption, which emits less carbon dioxide. There are many areas in retailing where IoT and smart devices are used, which we will discuss later in this chapter.

7. Data science transforming the retail market

Customers are purchasing products from retailers and creating a history of their transactions with the preferences of products. Based on these historical data and the data-science technology, retailers can predict what the customer can purchase next, which helps retailers to price optimization and give promotional ads to customers. Customers can get extra benefits like discounts or offers from retailers based on the history of purchase or search, store visit frequency, average bill amount, etc. Customers buying history creates recommendations of other things they can buy with a particular product. Data science also helps retailers to take a decision on where (choose location) to open new retail outlets and the performance of current outlets. Using a data-science approach, retailers can get a deep understanding of what somebody/something is like, which improves the business efficiency (Sharma, 2021).

6.3 TECHNIQUES USED IN SMART RETAILING WHICH BENEFITS RETAILERS AND CUSTOMERS

TABLE 6.1

Benefits of Techniques to Customer and Retailers

Benefits of Techniques to	
Customer	**Retailers**
1. Customer groups	Insights
2. Indoor navigation	Interactive media campaigns
3. Smart fitting rooms	Virtual zones
4. Radio-frequency Identification (RFID) smart tags	Predictive equipment maintenance
5. Self-checkout	Demand alert warehouses

6.3.1 Benefits to Customer

6.3.1.1 Customer Groups

By the observations like interest, activities of them in store, roaming at a particular location, product interests, and context of visitors in store, as shown in Figure 6.1 (softwebsolutions, 2021), a retailer or an administrator creates specific customer groups. The basic reason for doing this process is to identify the likeness of a customer. To create such types of tags, the administrator does not require any coding skills or any technical knowledge because this is done by the smart retail. This type of segmentation of customers gives a clear idea of what a particular customer is interested in. The best part is that the administrator does not have to be a coder or require technical knowledge to create these groups since smart retail does this by itself. The retailer can create different types of tags based on reward points, visit frequency, purchase history, etc. These tags are assigned to customers, and based on the tags, they can avail benefits when they walked into the store or from the geofence area.

FIGURE 6.1
Customer groups.

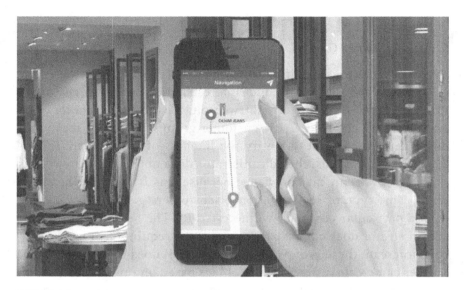

FIGURE 6.2
Indoor navigation.

6.3.1.2 Indoor Navigation

Figure 6.2 (softwebsolutions, 2021) shows that a customer has to use the mobile application of a particular store. In the mobile app, customers can view features and useful information regarding offers and discounts of the day, special number of days, or week. When customers enter into a store for purchase, they can view a map in their mobile app. The application navigates and shows the precise location of the specific product that the customer wants to purchase. The application uses an indoor positioning system (IPS) that creates a network of devices by which a person's location can be known where GPS is not reachable like multistory buildings, underground parking, and airports. In indoor navigation, 3D maps are used for navigation and finding routes.

6.3.1.3 Smart Fitting Rooms

In fitting rooms, customers take a trial of outfits and take decision to buy that outfit or not. So, for that, the retailer does not want to take any chance. As shown in Figure 6.3 (Beaconstac, 2021), a smart fitting room contains a smart mirror and integrated sensors (RFID or near-field communication (NFC)) with AI. When a customer enters into a fitting room, the devices

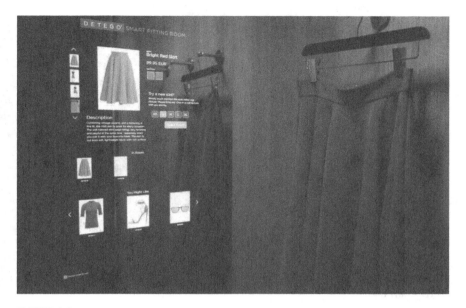

FIGURE 6.3
Smart fitting rooms.

automatically identify the exact outfit or artifact and show its details on a mirror. The smart mirror or display screen shows different colors, sizes, and designs that are available in the store. The smart fitting room shows combinations of other products like sandals or shoes, eye-wear, top or bottom outfit, jackets, etc. If a customer wants to try another size or color or design or other matching articles, they can send an e-request through a mirror to the store assistant. The sore assistant locates the product requested using a beacon and deliver to the customer. The other functionalities are the availability of articles, product recommendations, e-request as article delivery, direct purchase options, etc.

6.3.1.4 RFID Smart Tags

RFID contains digital data like barcodes where data can be read by a device. RFID smart tags are from the group of automatic identification and data capture (AIDC) technologies, where they automatically identify and collect the data of an object and store that data in the database. Figure 6.4 (Dudley, 2021) shows how RFID smart tags are used by various

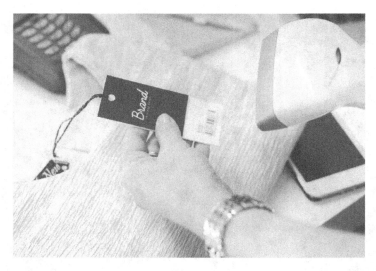

FIGURE 6.4
RFID smart tags.

retailers who sell their products directly to the customers called retail industry verticals.

A smart tag is used to basically show the information of a product in the customer's hand-held devices. The smart tags may be used in different ways like on shelves, giving authenticity by showing the origin and manufacturing of the product, and also in supply-chain management. This creates trust in the mind of customers, which promote the brands (Beaconstac, 2021).

6.3.1.5 Scan & Go or Self-Checkout

Figure 6.5 (Beaconstac, 2021) shows the technology where retailers provide different types of facilities like mobile point-of-sales (mPOS) self-checkout systems, vending machines, and self-checkout scan & go applications. In a self-checkout vending machine, customers have to scan their products one by one at the machine, and the amount will be deducted automatically from the balance of the retailer's mobile applications. Another way of self-checkout through vending machines is that each product is labeled with RFID tags. When customers put their shopping bag or all products on the counter of a machine, using RFID on products, it will check all products at once and create a bill. Customers pay bills using the app wallet or credit/debit cards. Another approach by retailers is that customers can scan QR codes on the products through the retailer's mobile app and camera and

FIGURE 6.5
Scan & go or self-checkout.

add products to their shopping cart. The payment will be done at the exit of a store using the NFC technology.

The associates can find products easily out of stock using smart shelves and cameras, and also mislocation of products, because checkout will not be done without a mobile app, so theft of products will not be done.

6.3.1.6 Face[note]

The biometrics platform of face recognition technology is used by face[note] in retail shops to identify their valuable customers, increase engagement, and give customer satisfaction by giving loyalty rewards. In face[note], customers take their selfie through the mobile application of the particular shop. Figure 6.6 (Rivara, 2021) shows that when a customer visits that shop the magic mirror at the shop identifies the customer and welcomes

FIGURE 6.6
Face[note].

her. The customer purchases the products and when the customer comes to the payment desk, there is a tablet where the customer has to show the face. The application of a tablet or any smart device detects the customer and shows one scratch card on the screen. The customer has to scrub the scratch card and he/she gets the discount coupon (Kostyushko, 2021).

6.3.2 Benefits to Retailer

6.3.2.1 Insights

The purchase details of products and customer's transaction records are useless without any useful analysis tools. Figure 6.7 (softwebsolutions, 2021) shows that business intelligence and data visualization tools give you clear insights into your campaigns. These analysis tools can give analysis like the how much time customers are visiting at a particular location. This can be achieved either by heat maps or by the number of footfalls at a specific area. Through this analysis, retailers can find the ratings of a particular product. Suppose in a particular area there are three outfits in display, customers viewing three of them take outfit-1 and outfit-2 in the fitting room. But somehow the outfit-2 is again put back on the shelves. The outfit-3 is somewhat untouched. Here, the movement of outfits is tracked by the RFID on those outfits. The analysis tools take the data of movement from shelves to a fitting room, and based on this, they can identify the reasons and take necessary decisions (softwebsolutions, 2021).

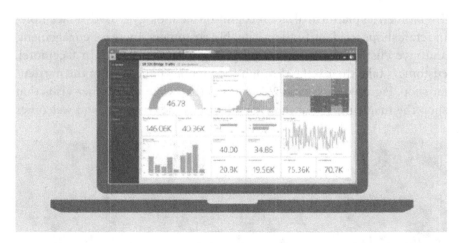

FIGURE 6.7
Insights.

6.3.2.2 *Interactive Media Campaigns*

An advertisement which is interactive will be created and directly delivered to the devices of customers. These advertisements are interactive so the customer gets curiosity about that product. These types of interactive ads in campaigns are created using AR, VR, AI, get responses to questions, and quizzes. Figure 6.8 (softwebsolutions, 2021) shows that the administrator creates a number of groups and a simple interface of software helps to create a customized campaign for all. So, an appropriate advertisement will reach a particular person who has likeness to that campaign.

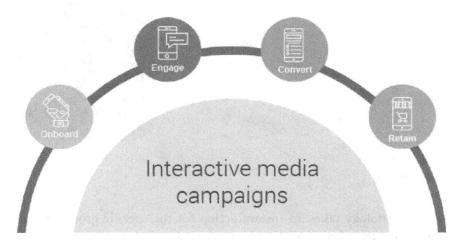

FIGURE 6.8
Interactive media campaigns.

Based on the visit to the store of the customer, they can get different ads, which means the first-time visitor gets different campaigns. This is useful for sending appropriate communication to customers at key points. The admin can set up some rules that if customers stay for more than some specific time, then they can get a message that buy 2 and get 1 for free within 30 min. By this, an eCommerce user can be converted into the customer of the store.

6.3.2.3 *Virtual Zones*

V-Zones means creating an area with the technology called Geofences, which is operated on GPS. The V-Zones can be created nearer to the store as well as different areas in the store. Figure 6.9 (D'Angelo, 2021) shows that when a customer passes from the V-Zone of a store by street, smart

FIGURE 6.9
Virtual zones.

retail technology takes an instant action for the specific group of customers that the admin had created or any action for a new customer. The actions may be some offers or discounts for their old customers, as well as an introductory offer to the new customers. The area covered by the V-Zone inside the store is few meters and outside the store is few hundred meters. As per the requirements, as many as sensors and beacons can be activated or deactivated (softwebsolutions, 2021).

6.3.2.4 Predictive Equipment Maintenance

The idea of predictive equipment maintenance is to identify behavioral patterns in components of machine failure or misworking in nearer future and prevent these problems (Conn, 2021). For example, in every grocery store refrigerator, HVAC (heating, ventilation, and air conditioning) are required to store products and foods which require cooling. When the sensors are attached to these units, they can sense and forecast maintenance. The sensors also identify power consumption and give or take necessary action for energy savings. The sensors also monitor temperature fluctuations and manage the temperature for food safety.

6.3.2.5 Demand-Alert Warehouses Using Smart Shelves

Smart shelves and sensors are used to track the consumption of a product in real time. Another scenario is that the product-1 is usually consumed in one week, but as per the increase of purchase, the smart retail gives an alert to the warehouse for purchase (Doles, 2021). RFID on product and NFC will help to find the movement, purchase of a product, and inventory management. The smart shelves create demand alerts to in-store smart retail, and this will send an alert to arrange delivery of specific products using the IoT order management system.

6.4 TECHNOLOGY AND DEVICES USED IN SMART RETAILING

A smart retail store leverages a number of technologies including the following.

6.4.1 BLE (Bluetooth Low Energy) Devices

Figure 6.10 (Matic, 2021) shows how the BLE device looks like. The continuous radio signals are emitted by BLE devices within a specified range to nearby smart/mobile devices. Smartphones/smart devices will listen to

FIGURE 6.10
BLE (Bluetooth low energy) device.

the radio signals given by the BLE devices within the range, which are in that range can listen and be triggered. The smartphones/device then sends a UUID (universally unique identifier) number through signals to the retailer's cloud server. As per the UUID, a server checks the activity associated with it and sends back appropriate data or action to the smart devices/phones.

The signal communicates to the smart device by sending its ID and giving the location information. BLE devices support mobile operating systems like iOS, Android, and Windows Phone, and for computer, it supports Linux, Windows 8, and Windows 10.

The BLE technology helps retailers for customizing the detail shown into the smart devices like visible properties like different colors and size, information on price and/or discounts, promotional offers, and available stock (Patel, 2021). Nowadays all have smartphones in their hand, so when they enter the smart retail store, they can immediately get discounts or coupons given by the retailer that will blink into their devices as per the campaign.

Benefits of BLE for Retail

1. *Smart device monitoring and product location services:*
   BLE devices can easily find the product movement into the store because it has real-time tracking and location intelligence capability, which tells smart retail that the product is on the premises or not.
2. *Proximity marketing:*
   The capability of BLE devices is to send signals to nearby smartphones/devices. Proximity (nearness) marketing means sending promotional information/discounts and advertisements to nearby devices to better engage the customers, which creates curiosity in customers and gets them into a store. Based on the previous transaction and behavior made with the store of the customer, BLE helps smart retail software to send useful information and personalized offers to the customer, which increases the customers' satisfaction and leads to more sales and more customers to the store.
3. *Customers need-based notification and alerts:*
   AI of smart retail software and BLE can detect the location and interaction of a customer with a specific area, and then based on the past billing transaction, they can understand the need of the customer and sends notification and alerts of specific discounts or availability of stock.

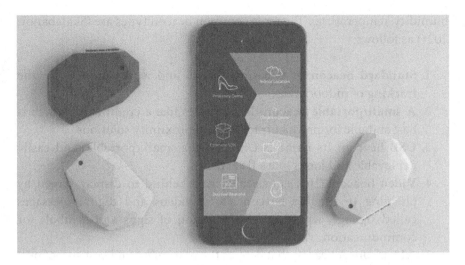

FIGURE 6.11
Beacon technology.

6.4.2 Beacon Technology

Beacon is a small size wireless transmitter that uses BLE technology to send signals to nearby smart devices. Figure 6.11 (Endive, 2021) shows the general design of beacons. In the location-finding technology and proximity marketing, beacons are the latest technology. They connect easily to nearby smart devices and transmit location-based information. Beacons are simple, more accurate, and their interaction is easy.

Beacons are assembled with a CPU for processing, radio for broadcasting signals, and batteries for giving power to all components. Beacons repeatedly broadcast its ID through radio signals. This ID is listened by the customers' smart device (mobile phone), and the location will be traced by the beacons. The ID of a beacon is unique and is recognized by the customers' smartphone. Once the connection is established, the program feed into the beacon sends information to the smartphone based on the smart retail software (Haines, 2021). The different manufacturers of beacons available are Apple iBeacon, PayPal beacon, Gimbal Proximity beacon (Qualcom), Samsung Proximity, Google Beacon (Eddystone), Radius RadBeacon, and GemTot. The range of the beacon is from 60 to 70 meters.

Types of beacons
The beacons are differentiated as per their size, type of use, battery performance, and the ability to resist environmental factors (dust, water,

humidity, temperature). The most common beacon types are (Skalabanov, 2021) as follows:

1. **Standard beacon:** It is a small Wi-Fi and works properly in the tracking of indoor areas.
2. **A small/portable beacon:** It is in sizes like a credit card, which is best suitable for product tracking and proximity solutions.
3. **USB beacon:** Its name is USB, so it is small, portable, and easily deployable and looks like a flash drive.
4. **Video beacon:** This is basically used behind to display screen by plugging in it. This beacon shows videos and digital messages called signage, which is a combination of signs and symbols for communication.
5. **AI beacon:** A beacon that detects the movement and gestures of persons using algorithms of machine learning.
6. **Sticker beacon:** The beacons are specifically used for product tracking in the store.
7. **Parent beacon:** By the name, it creates a network of beacons and acts as a big Wi-Fi router to manage and gather information from them and send it to the cloud server.
8. **Dedicated beacon:** This type of beacon is the best solution where the working environment is a harsh condition with the factors like water, UV, humidity, and dust.

6.4.3 Near-Field Communication

A short-range wireless communication technology called NFC connects compatible devices like handheld smart devices (phone, tablet), wearables, credit/debit cards, and other devices (Roberts, 2021). The information or action between the devices can be easily transferred by NFC technology by a simple interaction. The actions may be like bill payment, download, or use of coupons. Figure 6.12 (Rajiv, 2021) shows the application areas of the NFC technology.

NFC produces electromagnetic radio fields that allow two devices to communicate and transmit data with each other. To do this, both devices must be NFC enabled. The range of the NFC field is in few centimeters or the distance between two devices must be less than 10 cm to work efficiently for a proper transaction.

There are two type of NFC devices (Mikhail, 2021).

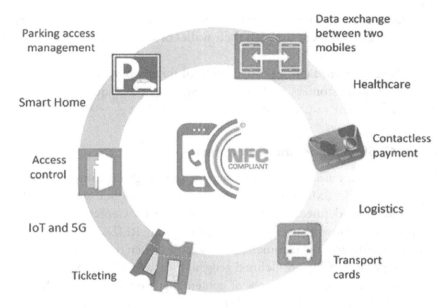

FIGURE 6.12
Near-field communication.

1. *Active NFC:*

   The handheld devices or smartphones are called active NFC devices, which require power and can read information from NFC tags and transmit information to other NFC compatible devices; to update any information on the NFC tag is only permitted if that device has the permission. All Android devices and new Apple devices are NFC enabled. Apple Pay and Google Wallet functionality is enabled with active NFC.

2. *Passive NFC:*

   The Passive NFC tags contains data or information, and they can only send these data to active NFC-enabled devices, but they cannot read any information itself. Because it did not require power to work so it can be embedded with all thing that wants to communicate with other devices.

   Passive NFC can be used with cloths and footwear where it can resist multiple washing and drying cycles. On shelves of supermarkets, NFC tags are attached to products and customers can touch their smartphones with NFC tags and get information about the product on their phones or add the product to their shopping cart.

Customers can use the facilities provided by the retailers like point of sale or payment through their wallet or credit/debit card.

These NFC tags are a cheaper solution than the use of a handheld or desk scanner. Also, customers are free from standing in long queues for checkout and save their valuable time.

6.4.4 Geofencing in Smart Retailing

Geofencing uses a location-based service to engage customers by sending messages like SMS, E-mail, or messages into a mobile app when they enter into a pre-defined specified geographical area. Geofencing platform or application software uses Wi-Fi or cellular data, RFID, and GPS to connect mobile devices of customers. This executes when the customer enters, exits, or present in the pre-defined geographical area (Priyam, 2021).

To create a geographical area of geofencing, first we have to define a virtual boundary or a region with center radios with the use of latitude and longitude to monitor. This can be done through marking on a map to create a digital barrier. Figure 6.13 (Brent, 2021) shows the working of geofencing. Android and iOS both allow the application to create a geofence.

After creating a virtual region, flags for notification are enabled true when a smartphone enters or exits the area. This all will be done if only if

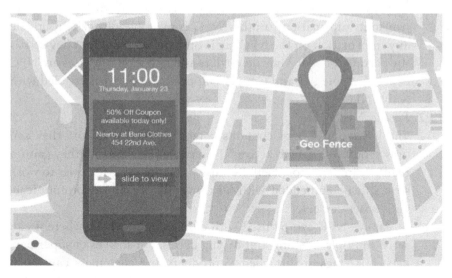

FIGURE 6.13
Working of geofencing.

the customer gives authorization to geofencing. By entering into the geofencing, a welcome message will be sent and by exiting the area a good by message will be sent.

6.4.5 QR Codes

The quick response, or QR, code is a machine readable two-dimensional array of the custom barcode with black and white square boxes (Nils, 2021). QR codes can store a wide variety of information. A simple (linear) barcode can hold approximately 20 characters, whereas a QR code can store up to 7089 digits or 4296 characters. The text stored in a code can also store special characters and punctuation marks, and it can also encode internet addresses. The main thing is that when more data will be stored in QR code, it means the size will increase and the complexity of the structure also be increased.

The QR code is made up of black and white blocks (squares or pixels). It can be read by an image sensor or by a camera of a smartphone, where a QR code scanner application is required and which can be interpreted by a processor of a device.

Figure 6.14 (Jumana Waleed, 2015) shows that each and every block has its importance in the respect of position and alignment. The series of squares and dots represent some details like version information, timing pattern, format information, data and error correction keys, separators, quiet zone,

1. Version information
2. Separators
3. Timing Pattern
4. Format information
5. Data and Error Correction
6. Quiet zone
7. Alignment Pattern
8. Postion Detection Pattern

FIGURE 6.14
Structure of a QR code.

alignment pattern, and position detecting pattern. The three large position detection squares help the QR code reader to identify and locate images quickly. Customers can hold the QR code reader-enabled smartphone against the QR Code, and the phone will automatically scan the details.

There are plenty of information that can be shared through QR code like pdf file, app store link, visiting card information, social media, Facebook likes, video link, website URL, images, events information, audio file, coupon, feedback, customer ratings, sending an email, and text message.

QR code used in smart retailing business

1. *Virtual Stores:*

   Amazon Go: When customers enter the store, they have to use the Amazon Go app and scan the QR code. They just pick up whatever products they want to purchase. The product is automatically added to the shopping cart. When the customer takes exit the store, the amount will be automatically debited from the Amazon account. This service is launched in the United States by Amazon with the name 'Just Walk Out'.

   Walnut Store: The first touch-and-feed smart grocery store in India was launched by Preethi Desai in 2016 in Bengaluru. The store is not a virtual store, the customer can taste, smell, and feel the product and then purchase it. Once the QR code of the product is scanned through the walnut app and purchased, the store gives the home delivery (Scanova, 2021).

   Tesco: Tesco has launched first time a smart store in the year of 2011 in South Korea's subway. Tesco has placed the banners of products with QR code in the subway; customers will scan and purchase the product delivered to home before they reach.

2. *Cashless Payments for Customers:*

   Stores provide digital wallet, which is connected with the customer's credit/debit card. Examples are **Walmart** (The biggest retail store in United States), **7-Eleven** (The Japanese-American international chain of convenience stores), **Starbucks** (The famous coffeehouse chain in the world), and **Dunkin Donuts** (The American multinational coffeehouse and donut company) (Scanova, 2021).

3. *Tags and Receipts:*

   Customers can view product details and its manufacturing process by scanning QR codes on product tags (Scanova, 2021). Customers purchase the products and gets receipts in their store app or by email. Examples are **Zara** (Fashion and clothing brand), **Decathlon** (A French sporting goods retailer), and **GaGa App** (QR code is printed on receipt and customer can scan that and get rewards. It is a Malaysia's Gaga Rewards app which is joined with local retailers).

4. *Location and Prevent from Fake Products:*
   Ralph Lauren: A UK-based luxury departmental store, partnered with Harrods, uses a QR code to give pathway to the customer on their mobile for finding a product. The products are made secured by adding a QR code with a product, which give authenticity against fake products in the market.

6.4.6 IoT and AI

Smart things which are the mixture of IoT devices with the technology of AI. Today, many IoT devices are converted to smart devices with the help of AI technology, which is called AIoT (Matthews, 2021).

1. *Smart Cameras:*
   For finding thieves, security cameras are the best solution in any retail or super stores, which are essential in the retail sector to deter thieves. Walmart uses smart cameras to identify the faces of shoppers who are trying to exit from self-checkout stations without scanning products.

2. *Intelligent Shopping Carts:*
   A shopping cart contains sensors and intelligent image recognition abilities which can identify that what products a have taken into shopping cart. The information like product details and bill amount of that product can be view by the customer on the display panel of shopping cart.

3. *Decision-Steering Sensors:*
   The retail managers make decisions from their experiences as how many employees are required on each weekend or on Christmas eve or on a special day. Nowadays, smart sensors are there, which count the number of customers entering. For example, the last 4 weekends were busiest in grocery department from 6 to 8 pm. The tool of AI gives suggestion to put more employees in that department.

4. *Mirrors with Shopping Suggestions:*
   The shoppers always require suggestions when buying outfits. Shopping can become a bit stressful for people who need to buy

things to wear. IBM has partnered with Vero Moda to find a solution for these hassles with a smart mirror, which gives suggestions to a customer that how the outfit will look alike on them. Also, retailers can get a clear idea that which product is sold more.

5. *Tools for Finding a Proper Parking Spot:*
Generally, people waste 10–12 minutes of time finding a location for parking. Overhead sensors on the parking entrance collect data about incoming cars and the current free location for parking. The digital signs guide the drivers to locate the nearest free space.

6.5 MOBILE APPLICATIONS FOR CONSUMERS AND RETAILERS FOR SMART RETAILING

Table 6.2 shows different mobile applications currently in the market, which are used to help customers and retailers as well to create a smart retailing environment.

6.6 TECHNIQUES AND SOLUTIONS IN SMART RETAILING

Table 6.3 shows that different IoT, smart, and sensor devices are used to create a different technological environment in smart retailing. For example, to create a smart fitting room, QR code, smart camera, smart mirror, NFC, and RFID are used.

TABLE 6.2

Mobile Applications for Consumers and Retailers

Customers	Retailers
Mobile point-of-sale (mPOS)	Role-specific solutions for employees
Self-service kiosks	Inventory management
Store assistants	Asset management
Mobile wallets	Digital signage
Loyalty and promotions	POS management

Source: Demichev (2021).

TABLE 6.3

Techniques and Solutions in Smart Retailing

	Solutions						
Techniques	**QR Code**	**Beacon**	**Smart Camera**	**Smart Mirror**	**NFC**	**RFID**	**GPS**
Indoor navigation		✓	✓				✓
Interactive digital signage	✓						
Smart fitting room	✓		✓	✓	✓	✓	
Self-checkout	✓	✓	✓		✓		
Virtual zone (Geofencing)						✓	✓
Demand-alert warehouses					✓	✓	
Proximity marketing		✓				✓	
Smart shopping cart						✓	

REFERENCES

Beaconstac. (2021, January 17). *Retail 101: How to Create a Smart Retail Store*. Retrieved from www.blog.beaconstac.com: https://blog.beaconstac.com/2019/11/how-to-create-a-smart-retail-store/.

Brent, L. (2021, February 7). *What Is Geofencing And How Does It Work?* Retrieved from www.propellant.media: https://propellant.media/what-is-geofencing/.

Conn, E. (2021, January 24). *IoT in Retail –- Applications, Benefits, Challenges, and Solutions*. Retrieved from www.iotforall.com: https://www.iotforall.com/retail-iot-applications-challenges-solutions.

D'Angelo, A. (2021, January 24). *Why Use Geofencing for Your App?* Retrieved from www.plotprojects.com: https://www.plotprojects.com/geofencing/.

Demichev, A. (2021, February 5). *Retail Software Development – Itransition*. Retrieved from www.itransition.com: https://www.itransition.com/industries/retail-wholesale.

Doles, D. (2021, February 1). *IoT in Retail: The Benefits to the Retail Employee*. Retrieved from www.iotforall.com: https://mojix.com/iot-retail-employee/.

Dudley, C. (2021, January 17). *7 Powerful Examples of How RFID Technology Can Be Used in Retail*. Retrieved from www.medium.com: https://medium.com/qash/7-powerful-examples-of-how-rfid-technology-can-be-used-in-retail-e3f5a711eb85.

Endive, S. L. (2021, February 4). *iBeacon Technology: Business Benefits for the B2B & B2C Industries*. Retrieved from www.endivesoftware.com: https://www.endivesoftware.com/blog/ibeacon-app-development-for-b2b-b2c-industries/.

Haines, E. (2021, February 5). *5 Things You Need to Know About Beacon Technology*. Retrieved from www.wordstream.com: https://www.wordstream.com/blog/ws/2018/10/04/beacon-technology.

Jargons, B. (2021, January 4). *What is Retailing?* Retrieved from www.businessjargons.com: https://businessjargons.com/retailing.html.

Jumana Waleed, H. D. (2015). An Immune Secret QR-Code Sharing Based on a Twofold Zero-Watermarking Scheme. *International Journal of Multimedia and Ubiquitous Engineering*, 10(4), 399–412.

Kiran Chaudhary, P. N. (2018, February). Factors Determining Customer Satisfaction, Customer Trust and Customer Loyalty in Online Retailing: An Empirical Study. *International Journal in Multidisciplinary and Academic Research (SSIJMAR)*, 7(1), 1–13.

Kostyushko, K. (2021, January 19). *Facenote – XRC Labs: Retail Tech & Customer Goods Accelerator*. Retrieved from www.xrclabs.com: https://www.xrclabs.com/facenote#:~:text=Facenote%20is%20a%20biometrics%20platform,engagement%2C%20and%20introduce%20biometric%20solutions.

Matic, N. (2021, January 26). *Bluetooth Low Energy – Part 1: Introduction to BLE*. Retrieved from www.mikroe.com: https://www.mikroe.com/blog/bluetooth-low-energy-part-1-introduction-ble.

Matthews, K. (2021, February 11). *5 Applications of AIoT in the Retail Industry*. Retrieved from www.iot.eetimes.com: https://iot.eetimes.com/5-applications-of-aiot-in-the-retail-industry/.

Mikhail. (2021, February 6). *How Does NFC Work?* Retrieved from www.bluebite.com: https://www.bluebite.com/nfc/how-does-nfc-work#:~:text=Active%20NFC%20devices%2C%20like%20phones,Apple%20devices%2C%20use%20active%20NFC.

Murray, J. (2021, January 7). *Advantages of E-Commerce over Traditional Retail*. Retrieved from www.thebalancesmb.com: https://www.thebalancesmb.com/advantages-of-ecommerce-1141610.

Murray, J. (2021, January 3). *Retail: What Is It?* Retrieved from www.thebalancesmb.com: https://www.thebalancesmb.com/what-is-retail-2892238.

Nils, D. (2021, February 8). *QR Code Basics*. Retrieved from www.qr-code-generator.com: https://www.qr-code-generator.com/qr-code-marketing/qr-codes-basics/.

Patel, M. (2021, February 3). *Bluetooth Low Energy (BLE) – The Future of Retail Technologies*. Retrieved from www.einfochips.com: https://www.einfochips.com/blog/bluetooth-low-energy-ble-the-future-of-retail-technologies/#:~:text=How%20it%20works%3F,number%20to%20the%20cloud%20server.

Priyam, J. (2021, February 7). *What Is Geofencing? Your Guide to Location-based Marketing*. Retrieved from www.webengage.com: https://webengage.com/blog/what-is-geofencing/#:~:text=Geofencing%20is%20a%20location%2Dbased,parked%20in%20the%20geographical%20location.

Rajiv, B. (2021, February 6). *Applications and Future of Near Field Communication*. Retrieved from www.rfpage.com: https://www.rfpage.com/applications-near-field-communication-future/.

Rivara, E. (2021, January 19). *Facenote*. Retrieved from www.facenote.me: https://facenote.me/.

Roberts, D. J. (2021, February 6). *Near-Field Communication (NFC)*. Retrieved from www.investopedia.com: https://www.investopedia.com/terms/n/near-field-communication-nfc.asp#:~:text=Near%2Dfield%20communication%20(NFC)%20is%20a%20short%2Drange,is%20the%20ultimate%20in%20connectivity.

Scanova. (2021, February 8). *QR Codes in Retail Stores*. Retrieved from www.scanova.io: https://scanova.io/blog/qr-codes-in-retail-stores/.

Sharma, S. (2021, January 8). *7 Amazing Trends to Watch in Retail Industry in 2020*. Retrieved from www.yourstory.com: https://yourstory.com/mystory/amazing-trends-watch-retail-industry-2020?utm_pageloadtype=scroll.

Skalabanov, A. (2021, February 6). *What Are Beacons and How Beacons Technology Works*. Retrieved from www.intellectsoft.net: https://www.intellectsoft.net/blog/what-are-beacons-and-how-do-they-work/.

softwebsolutions. (2021, January 14). *How the Smart Retail Helps Retailers to Convert Visitors to Customers*. Retrieved from www.softwebsolutions.com: https://www. softwebsolutions.com/resources/how-smart-retail-solution-benefits-retailers. html.

yourarticlelibrary. (2021, January 3). *Retailing: Introduction, Meaning, Definition and Characteristics*. Retrieved from www.yourarticlelibrary.com: https://www. yourarticlelibrary.com/retailing/retailing-introduction-meaning-definition-and-characteristics/47944.

7

Leveraging Web Analytics for Optimizing Digital Marketing Strategies

Sapna Sood
Accenture, Gurgaon, India

CONTENTS

DOI: 10.1201/9781003307761-7

7.1 INTRODUCTION

Web analytics is a crucial tool if a marketer wants to understand the impact of a marketing strategy in terms of acquisition, retention, and conversion of visitors into repeat visitors and thereby building a marketing strategy which is completely customer centric (Peterson, 2004; Kaushik, 2007). In the case of digital marketing, since Tim Berners-Lee came up with the first browser (1990), it has become very vital for a marketer to identify who are coming to their website, how are they using the website, what pages are they visiting, and how much time do they spend on the websites (Connolly, 2000; CERN, 2008).

Web analytics can be defined as tracking of the goals and objectives by collecting, measuring, reporting, and finally analyzing quantitative data from online sources for optimizing the websites (http://www.webanalyt icsassociation.org/, 2006). With the growth in technology, it has become very crucial for organizations to understand the visitors to their website, their needs, and if they are able to easily able to look for information that is of their interest in a website. Answers to all these questions will help marketers in building a user-friendly website, which is highly customized to the needs of the visitors (Kosala & Blockeel, 2000). Also, the interest of companies in gathering more and more data from their websites is also increasing and ultimately converting to business intelligence.

Technology and different web analytics tools are continuously changing providing a lot of options for choosing an analytics tool (Hassler, 2010). The important challenge that organizations are facing is to determine the software for understanding the difference between metrics/KPIs and to evaluate different needs to be emphasized when implementing an analytics program. Now companies have software for checking the traffic on web, but not all companies are able to utilize the analytics tools to their full potential (Gassman, 2009a). Small/medium-sized companies and NGOs that run websites for sharing knowledge are struggling; they frequently lack financial and personnel resources to successfully manage a web analytics program. A recent Gartner study reports that to adequately finance a WA program, organizations need a budget of at least $250,000 per year and some organizations a lot of money (Gassman, 2009b).

The literature on web analytics (academic) stresses and explains only the benefits or constraints of unique analysis through algorithms and the creation of advanced web mining techniques; giving negligible attention to customers and organizational perspectives of web analytics. In the case of data mining, the web analytics segment has its roots primarily in web mining. Two separate methods were described for categorizing web mining: content and use mining. Another group has been added to this: structure mining (Kosala & Blockeel, 2000).

Digital content mining makes use of the information shared online like text or photographs, which are accessible online for finding valuable data from online sources of information for enhancing the discovery of information (Kosala & Blockeel, 2000; Pierrakos et al., 2003). Structure mining in the case of websites mostly deals with the link structure of any online entity like websites, which is mostly used for the categorization of different web pages (Kosala & Blockeel, 2000). Lastly, how visitors are using a website helps in understanding the exploration and browsing trends (Cooley et al., 1997). The complete process of describing data, i.e., from the collection of the data to the redesigning of the website and other recommendations. Content mining, structure mining, and use mining are bundled together under a broad terminology of web analytics.

International business has become more dynamic and challenging because of the advancement of globalization in economic, cultural, social, technical, and political contexts (Chaudhary & Monica, 2014). According to the complex global marketing climate, the global marketing strategy must be revamped. While the ideals of domestic and foreign marketing are the same, administrators must always apply them differently due to environmental variations.

7.2 REQUIREMENT FOR WEB ANALYTICS

Recent growth in technology and specifically in domains like health care, supply chain, etc., have resulted in the inundation of data giving meaning to the buzzword "Bigdata." In comparison with data from traditional sources, Bigdata has many unique features: enormous, unstructured data which cannot be handled via traditional databases resulting in designs of new systems for collecting, transmitting, storing, and processing data (Malhotra et al., 2017).

Websites are a crucial medium for organizations to communicate, and enhancing web communication is very important for meeting the goals of the website and the audience targeted (Norguet et al., 2006, p. 430), which is important for understanding the purposes of every website in order to gain valuable insights. All websites have multiple and unique intentions and priorities in terms of WA and need various metrics to assess their performance. For example, web analytics is used for analyzing sales or profit from an e-commerce website, while this main performance will not be important information for website sharing government information. Targeted metrics vary from one website to another.

Analytics is a multidimensional and environmental field that makes use of mathematics, statistics, predictive modeling, and many other machine learning techniques for identifying relevant patterns and information in the data available. Recording data has become an easier job because of powerful computers with lots and lots of storage that run good algorithms. We can discover many things by applying data analytics and generate answers to questions that one has never thought of asking. The strength of data analytics is that all software that are being used now are a day-to-day web application that adds to the analytics data any time anyone taps, streams, downloads, submits, visits, shares, or otherwise interacts with some form of your digital involvement. There are six high-level fields of web analytics with respect to the internet, i.e., application analytics, social media analytics, advertisement analytics, viewer analytics, and big data analytics. The chapter aims on studying web analytics, which is now becoming increasingly useful.

Nowadays, with the aid of web applications, all data related to any form of sector, education field, health care, government data, etc., are all accessed and serviced from any cloud storage. A website provides an economical and a forum for contacting stakeholders in this digital age and for shaping and portraying an online reputation in this digital era. The designers of the website use multiple techniques for making a website more fun, accessible, efficient, stable, informative, and competitive. The use of the website is explained as a qualitative attribute describing easiness to navigate the website.

In addition to conventional website assessment approaches, expert-based and user-based testing for analyzing websites is conducted for making improvement. In general, web analytics is the method of gathering data on the behaviors of people visiting your website (visitors) – how they found you, what sites they accessed, what they purchased or downloaded, etc., when they visited, and how they mined the data for information that can be used for improvement.

Globalization has made foreign business more complex, i.e., economically, socially, culturally, politically, and technically. Considering the complex global marketing climate, global marketing strategy must be redesigned. While the concepts of domestic and foreign marketing are the same, administrators must always apply them differently due to geographical variations. Organizations can get a complete geography-wise and audience-wise view of their customers through different analytics tools like Google Analytics.

Customers prefer online shopping outlets over physical stores in today's digital world. Consumers have welcomed purchasing supermarket fruits and vegetables online despite initially being drawn to the clothing, accessories, and electronics categories. As a result, India's online shopping market is rapidly expanding. Consumers now have a broad range of options available online in terms of product types, number of items under each segment, payment options, discounts, e-coupons, and exclusive promotional offers, among other things. Customer satisfaction is described as "the fulfilment response of the customer." It's a decision that a product or service function, or the product or service itself, delivered a satisfactory degree of consumption-related fulfilment, with or without elements of under- or over-fulfillment. When a customer reviews a product or service, their preferences have an effect on their overall satisfaction. When assessing the difference between expectations for the service and the real performance experience, satisfaction is a customer's emotional answer. The customer's preferences are shaped first by their desires, beliefs, previous encounters, and extrinsic cues about the commodity. The company's-built confidence and perceived value greatly amplify the effect of satisfaction on e-commerce.

7.3 REVIEW OF LITERATURE

7.3.1 Evolution of Web Analytics

Web analytics simply saved internet data as log files in the early 1990s. This resulted in search engine spiders evolving. This method was refined by later Javascript tags. Such tags have made it easier to access website operations. Google Analytics joined the fight in 2005, and it made it possible to dig down into viewer behavior. There are two different categories of web analytics as explained in Figure 7.1.

Off-site web analytics, without taking into account whether we own or manage a platform, applies to web calculation and web data analysis. It

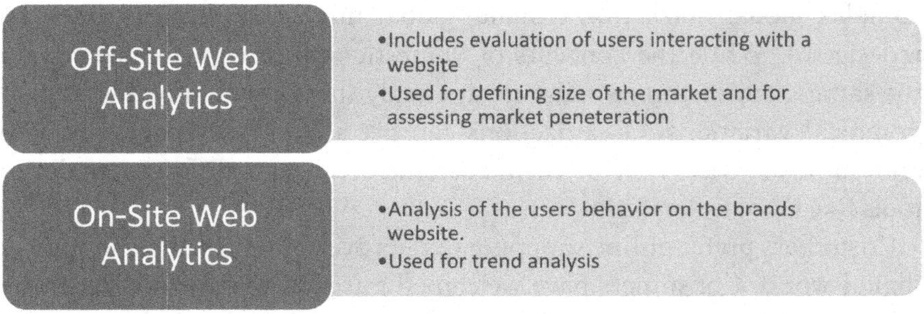

FIGURE 7.1
Off-site and on-site web analytics and its use cases.

involves the evaluation of the users of a website, exposure, and comments that take place on the Internet. For example, we can define the size of the market for an e-commerce website, identify competitors, assess market penetration for our business, perform surveys, and consult market research sources. Resources such as Google Search Insight and Compete. com share information on offsite web analytics.

On-site web analytics refers to the most common method of analyzing the actions of a page user for our website and performance in a commercial rather than conventional way. This includes its drivers and conversions. The numerous landing pages are, for example, correlated with online sales. Usually, this web data is compared to key performance metrics and is used to strengthen a website or marketing based on user reaction. It analyzes logs and pages tagged to understand and perform trend analysis.

To stay ahead of the race in this dynamic digital environment, marketers are leveraging upon several web analytics resources. Google Analytics and Adobe Analytics are the most used applications for on-site web analytics. Even as new technologies, such as heat maps and session replay, have come into being that provide additional detail.

In order to evaluate the marketing, Google Analytics alone provides thousands of data points. The most important information for any organization, of course, is that which drives revenue: leads and conversions. The source of those leads and sales is told by Analytics and gives us insight into how we can boost traffic and conversions. However, it's crucial that in a one-size-fits-all vacuum, we don't view data as metrics that are important to one company and are not relevant to another.

The bounce rate, for example, is a vastly misinterpreted metric. That might be a bad thing if your bounce rate is high or it might not matter. A visitor could read your article in its entirety if you are a publisher and then quit, resulting in a bounce, but they accessed the page at 4:00. Was that bounce or wasn't it a bad thing? But a high bounce rate for an e-commerce store means that you need to perform an audit of your marketing plan, website, or pay-per-click (PPC) advertising and decide:

- Do visitors see what they expect from the click of an ad or a keyword?
- Is the website design user-friendly, smooth, and clean?
- Is the path to conversion simple?

Many researchers have tried to figure out how to use a face recognition, a hybrid approach, that combines global (face information) and all local information. There are three steps to the suggested method: The input images are read in the first stage and enhanced using a filtering and clipping process. The second stage uses a Genetic Algorithm to derive image features in two forms: global and local. Images extracted are to feed-forward neural network–back propagation network for identification in the third step. The proposed approach was reviewed on images from the FERET (face recognition technology) collection, and it was found to be more efficient than the current method on both local and global features. Face detection technology is like what is used by social media firms.

7.4 HOW THE SUCCESS OF YOUR DIGITAL MARKETING PLATFORMS CAN BE VIEWED?

To evaluate the success of your different marketing channels, data analysis frequently begins with the Acquisition tab in Google Analytics. There you'll see how many visitors arrived from organic search, social media, PPC advertising, referrals from other websites, and other sources. This page also shows you the "quality" of those visits – how long a user stayed, how many pages they viewed, and if they completed a goal (like a form submission) or made a purchase. It's very important that you look at a breakdown of your audience in this way so you're not throwing money or effort away on marketing channels that aren't driving sales or goals.

Data analysis frequently starts with the Acquisition tab in Google Analytics to determine the performance of various marketing channels. You can see how many visitors from organic search, social media, PPC ads, referrals from other websites, and other sources have arrived there.

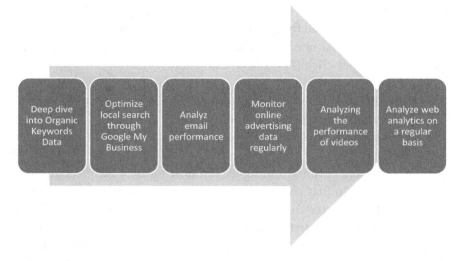

FIGURE 7.2
Performance checklist for growing digital presence.

This page would also show you the "quality" of such visits, how long a customer stayed, how many pages they visited, and whether a target (such as a form submission) was completed or a purchase was made. It is really important for a marketer that they look into a breakdown of their audience to make sure that they don't waste their money and efforts on marketing channels that don't give profitable results in terms of high sales.

Yet information is objective; in relation to the marketing, you have to see it. Perhaps your organic visitors declined from last month, for instance. There are many potential reasons: seasonal fluctuations, an algorithm upgrade strike, unexpectedly ranked above you by a rival, changes to the content of the website page, a PPC ad above the organic result, sudden website UX issues, and many other possibilities. Typically, a little investigation will reveal the cause quickly.

For a massive presence in the digital landscape, companies should revisit their digital marketing strategy. Some of these are shown in Figure 7.2.

7.5 DEEP DIVE INTO ORGANIC KEYWORD DATA

Keyword knowledge drives search engine optimization (SEO), so every SEO practitioner's best friend is Google Search Console or a similar platform. Here, you can see the output of your website-related keywords that drive traffic, find out which pages are indexed (or not the average rank for each page on your website, how your mobile and desktop search keyword information compares with many other data points. You will discover from this data whether new content or content improvements are successful in enhancing keyword search and uncovering opportunities to capitalize on new keywords.

7.5.1 Optimize Local Search through Google My Business

There is a tab called "Insights" on your Google My Company (GMB) account. Here, in local searches, you can find out the keywords that drive your GMB listing, what actions users take when your listing appears, whether they found your company looking for your address or your business category, how many images they viewed, and more. This information will tell you what information in your GMB listing you can update, add or delete to maximize these results.

7.5.2 Analyze Email Performance

Any details about your email campaigns can be found in Google Analytics, but you would need to log into your email management system for the most detailed review. In your email site, critical stats can be presented, such as open rates, which links get clicks, which users are the most active on your list, and more. For each email campaign, a marketer should analyze the disparity in outcomes and decide what was at the heart of it. Certain parameters should be deeply studied like the order of the information presented in the email, layout, the bids applied, and the discussion points.

7.5.3 Monitor Online Advertising Data Regularly

There are thousands of data points in Google Ads, but ROI is the most significant statistic the executives and owners would be concerned about How much did they invest on clicks vs. how much sales or leads were generated? You will need to dig in to see which commercials and campaigns fulfill your targets, and which ones do not and change your promotional and bidding strategy accordingly.

Google Advertising is a data repository that can be very overwhelming at first glance. But if you practice it in little chunks, you'll figure out pretty easily what's most important. Seeing which advertisements are working and producing revenue is pretty straightforward. But you might wonder, too, why don't the other ads convert? Before you set up an ad campaign, the building block for PPC advertising is keyword research – Google's keyword planner, along with SEM Hurry, MOZ, and other networks, is an excellent method for this.

7.5.4 Analyzing the Performance of Videos

On YouTube, metrics are released on your channel for each post. You will see how much the video has been shared, feedback, viewing time, and even other data points from these metrics. In order to boost search results and to analyze your advertising tactics around the video, this will advise your plan for inserting, removing, or modifying tags.

7.5.5 Analyze Web Analytics on a Regular Basis

It's time to bring it into perspective to advise your marketing plan after you've evaluated all of your details. Over the last week, month, quarter, or year, has your conversion rate increased or softened? If so, what campaign steps have been taken that have culminated in such peaks and valleys? Knowing that the X approach resulted in a conversion rise of 28 percent is useful material. With a tiny adjustment to the marketing strategy, would you build on that number? Can it be repeated on another medium or some other way?

It lets you make decisions on the next steps to provide a good view of how your marketing activities affect your conversions, site visits, leads, and overall results. To maximize your performance, can you make minor variations on landing pages or email text? Post a better ad for PPCs? Add a better photo to your ad on Facebook or Instagram? Write a piece of content that draws upon keyword search success?

But being able to acknowledge when your marketing instincts are flat-out incorrect is the most important thing about evaluating your results. You could have been off the mark if the adjustment you made to the plan resulted in a 10 percent strike. Data is for illumination, not support, it is meant to critically display the whole scene, not support your hypothesis or judgment (biasness).

For advertisers, acquisition, audience, and behavior are very important.

7.5.6 Audience

A large data about the visits to the website is given in Section 7.5.6. It includes numerous subsections that include details about the sex, age, and position of visitors to your website. Marketers will not only get information about the apps and mobile devices used for accessing the website but will also get information about their preferences.

Detailed details on how individuals come to your site will be given in the Acquisition section. Digging through the All Traffic tab will inform you just how individuals get to your page, and whether a user contributes to which platform.

7.5.7 Behavior Segment

The behavior segment allows you to understand how the platform communicates with users. This section becomes important for understanding which pages are the most popular among visitors on your website. When these are used together, the exposed data assist marketers in making decisions like which marketing activity drives maximum website traffic.

Inside Google Analytics, reviewing these parts will provide marketers with useful insights that will help them in making smart decisions about the style, language, and location of content to be used on a website.

7.5.8 Channels for Traffic

Before we look at who is visiting your website, it's interesting to think about how they got there. To see the various traffic sources for a specified/limited period, go to the Acquisition tab and pick All Traffic from the drop-down display. Click the "Channels" button, set the time limit at the top of the display screen, and scroll down to see the production timeframe. Here's a quick rundown of what each of these networks means:

Direct: Visitors who have used the platform directly like typing the URL into a tab, clicking a bookmark, or clicking a link in an email. Direct traffic is a strong indicator of a brand's power.

Organic Search: Marketers thank search engines like Google and Bing for bringing prospective users to their websites. An organic traveler is someone who visits a website after clicking on a link from a search engine's result list. A large amount of organic traffic is a clear indicator of the importance of the content and SEO strategy.

Paid Search: Businesses paying advertising promotions (think Google AdWords) on websites are bundled under this option.

Referral: Visitors who clicked on a link and landed on a marketer's web page on another domain are considered as referrals. Initially, all traffic that was not direct or organic was bundled under referrals before the growth of social media platforms. Google has developed a separate social traffic tab in the last two years, making it easier for advertisers to concentrate on only the pages that bring traffic to their pages. This is the section to visit if you guest blog to see how much traffic is being guided to your website.

Social: This is my favorite part of Google Analytics as a social media marketer, since it tells me just what social media platforms generate much of the traffic to my website. To influence the social media approach, this knowledge can be used.

Email: The number of people who have visited a website can also be attributed to an email campaign. If a company does a lot of email marketing, marketers want to look into the performance of the campaigns. Marketers can see which channel is their site's primary traffic driver by looking at the traffic channels. They will notice that the channels are classified in order of driving power; the channel at the top is the one that drives the majority of web traffic. Analyzing the effect of different networks will help advertisers assess which campaigns to focus on and, potentially, create ideas for increasing traffic from other outlets.

To maximize traffic across all channels, Table 7.1 shows some important mediums to consider.

Direct: When people type the link of your website directly in the browser and visit the website is all what is considered as a direct source of traffic.

Organic Search: Ensured that H1 and H2 tags, meta descriptions, and keywords are included on all domain pages and content updates. The bigger the website's SEO, the more likely it is to be found by a search engine.

TABLE 7.1

Medium and Explanation

Medium	Explanation
Direct	People directly visiting a website
Organic searches	People coming to a website after typing in Google searches
Paid searches	Online paid campaigns for meeting an objective
Referral	Guest blogging for improving referrals
Social	Traffic from social media platforms
Email	Traffic through email campaigns, retargeting existing users

TABLE 7.2

Targeting Options Availability

Targeting	Options	Details
Audience	Gender	Landing page views, purchases
	Age	Landing page views, purchases

Paid Search: Consider updating your keywords and/or targeting options to make your advertising more relevant.

Referral: Request a guest post on popular websites. Contributing content on other sites is a great way to increase referral traffic.

Social: That will almost undoubtedly boost social traffic by increasing the number of posts and the number of contacts posted on social media. Social media influences almost all to purchase a product and spend more money on it. They used social media to gather intelligence about consumer behavior. Data from Facebook, Twitter, LinkedIn, and YouTube users are taken into account. They used big data technology, and the data from social media were diverse and high speed, high volume. Big data is a comparatively modern technique that is being used in a wide range of scientific areas. Researchers used big data analytics to process and interpret data in order to predict consumer activity on social media in this post. They used a series of criteria and specifications to examine consumer behavior. They looked at consumer expectations and views about social media and had to preprocess the data to ensure it was of high quality so they could make an informed decision based on their conclusions.

Email: Increase the number of calls to action and links in your email promotions. Be sure that the call to action sticks out in the email templates and continues to attract users to the website.

Once a marketer has put an ad/post or any video online, the next is to deeply study the reach of the post as shown in Table 7.2.

7.6 AUDIENCE DEMOGRAPHICS

Consider who is viewing the website in terms of age, location, and gender is the simplest way to tailor content to meet the preferences and expectations of the target audience. A marketer must understand who the target audience is in order for the material and images on the website to cater to and resonate with them. To find this detail, go to the audience page.

7.6.1 Age and Gender Demographics

In this tab, it can be viewed that out of the total visitors who landed on your website, how many of them were female vs male, what age group is more inclined toward the content being shared on the website, and more. To see what pages users are landing on when they get to your web, marketers can head over to landing pages. A clear measure of the success of the social media and advertising campaign is the view of the landing pages.

7.7 CONCLUSION

Web analytics tools like Google Analytics and Adobe Omniture are incredibly powerful tools. Marketers would be able to develop content and imagery that their audience needs by paying attention to the audience's demographics. This helps them to build for their audience a personalized and meaningful web experience that will keep them coming back for more.

Marketers can also check which guest bloggers are helping to improve their web exposure as they start tracking their referral traffic. This would save their time by encouraging them to concentrate their content creation efforts entirely on guest bloggers who have a return in the form of website visits. Similarly, they would be armed with information from their social referrals, helping them to determine which social media sites are suitable for posting their blog posts. They would provide a thorough understanding of who their client is, what they want, and how they locate them by using, analyzing, and focusing on these various components within analytics systems.

REFERENCES

CERN (2008). CERN – Where the web was born. *CERN – Where the web was born.* Available at: http://public.web.cern.ch/public/en/About/Web-en.html. Accessed on January 3, 2020.

Chaudhary, K., & Monica, M.. (2014). Global marketing–A comparison of domestic and international marketing. International Journal of Management Research, Volume 2, Issue 4, pp. 34–45.

Connolly, D. (2000). A Little History of the World Wide Web. *W3C: A Little History of the World Wide Web*. Available at: http://www.w3.org/History.html. Accessed on September 21, 2019.

Cooley, R., Srivastava, J., & Mobasher, B. (1997). Web mining: Information and pattern discovery on the World Wide Web. In *Proc. of ICTAI*, p. 558.

Gassman, B. (2009a). *Five Best Practices for Web Analytics Initiatives*. Stamford, CT: Gartner Group.

Gassman, B. (2009b). *Key Challenges in Web Analytics, 2009*. Stamford, CT: Gartner Group.

Hassler, M. (2010). *Web analytics: Metriken auswerten, Besucherverhalten verstehen, Webseiten optimieren*, 2nd ed., mitp.

Kaushik, A. (2007). *Web Analytics an Hour a Day*. Indianapolis, IN: Wiley Publishing.

Kosala, R., & Blockeel, H. (2000). Web Mining Research: A Survey. SIGKDD Explorations, Volume 2, Issue 1, pp. 1–15.

Malhotra, S. Doja, M.N. Alam, B. & Alam, M. (2017). E-GENMR: Enhanced generalized query processing using double hashing technique through MapReduce in cloud database management system. Volume 13, Issue 7, 234–246.

Norguet, J.-P. Zimányi, E., & Steinberger, R. (2006). Improving web sites with web usage mining, web content mining, and semantic analysis. J. Wiedermann, G. Tel, J. Parkony, M. Bielikova, J. Stuller (Eds.), *SOFSEM 2006, LNCS 3831* (pp. 430–439). Berlin/Heildelberg: Springer.

Peterson, E. (2004). Web analytics demystified. Available http://www.Webanalytics demystified.com/about_wad.asp. Accessed on 15 January 2019.

Pierrakos, D. et al. (2003). Web usage mining as a tool for personalization: A survey. User Modeling and User-Adapted Interaction, Volume 13, pp. 311–372.

8

Smart Retailing in Digital Business

S.R. Mani Sekhar, Tarun Krishnan, Louie
Antony, Sandeep B.L., and Siddesh G.M.
Department of Information Science and Engineering
M. S. Ramaiah Institute of Technology
Bangalore, India

CONTENTS

8.1 INTRODUCTION

Before we delve into the enthralling topic of smart retail, imagine the present day scenario where we depend on the shopping staff to ask for a size bigger or smaller for whatever we are shopping for, let's say a bright blue

DOI: 10.1201/9781003307761-8

Hawaiinshirt! The staff member first of all is probably going to get confused over the name 'Hawaiin,' then has to look for the unique code on the shirt, after which the employee has to ask the person sitting at the system to go through the records if the same shirt is available in a size smaller or larger. After acquiring the confirmation on the availability of the shirt, the employee finally has to search through the store containing numerous products consisting of pants, shirts, shoes and other such commodities, which would require a colossal amount of time and effort.

After all this time of confusion, the customer is likely to either be frustrated over the incompetence of the employee or has already left the shop. Now imagine if there was an intermediate between the customer and the employee, first something that could help improve customer experience which in our case could be to immediately display whether the shirt of a smaller or larger size is available or not; this would not frustrate the customer and would maybe prompt the customer to purchase more items and hence increase sales; second, for instance, they could provide assistance by acting as a warehouse for the store's collection and hence help the employee to quickly gain information on the spot, finally they can even act as a replacement for the staff. This however does seems quite daunting considering the loss of jobs that would occur as a process but would definitely boost sales.

So from the above example, we should be able to answer a few fundamental questions regarding "Smart Retail."

8.1.1 What Is Smart Retail?

Smart retail can be defined as a term used to describe a set of smart technologies that are designed to give the consumer a greater, faster, safer and smarter experience when shopping. Let's go over this definition, smart retail is basically a process using modern or new-age technologies that have been designed specifically to aid the consumers' experience while they shop [1]. The customers' experience can be improved by providing them with faster services such as immediate product replacements, quick check-outs, instantaneous product locations and so on. Working hard is very beneficial in a general sense, but working smart can help in reaping benefits in a shorter period of time; considering the above example, smart retail could be used to immediately scan the consumers' body and predict which of the available products would fit on the customers' body and show them the route to the product.

They could moreover be used to predict which products might appeal to consumers based on their previous activity using inbuilt artificial intelligence (AI) and deep learning. Using these above ideas, for example, would not only save the employee's time, but more importantly, the consumers who are the main motive for creating such devices. And finally with the emergence of the Coronavirus pandemic and other frequently common transmittable diseases, smart retailing products can also help by reducing or completely removing human interactions, which would definitely keep consumers away from harmful diseases or even a simple case of common cold.

8.1.2 Impact of Smart Retail on the Modern Society

As time goes by, technology seems to be increasingly moving onto online platforms, which in turn forces retailers to move along with the technological revolution. As the world is entering an era of a technology-driven world, the amount of data that is being collected from each user is immense. Consequently, it arises the concept of Big Data.

The workflow of an industry cannot undergo any change in the technological revolution if there isn't a change in the amount of manual labor that goes into it and the introduction of technology-driven devices such as Internet of Things (IoT) and the application of AI in them. This certainly would have an immense blow on the availability of jobs [2]. Nevertheless, this would have an enormous impact on the amount of sales and in turn result in huge profits for the industry and would also help customers get what they desire in an ample amount of time.

For instance, Amazon had its first public opening of Amazon Go also known as walk-out technology on the 22nd of January 2018 where customers just have to scan their Amazon app on the entry of the store and they can choose any item they wish and walk out of the store without having to wait in long queues to pay for their purchases as the total amount of the purchase would be automatically debited from the customers' Amazon account as they walk out of the store.

With the integration of sensor fusion, deep learning and openCV, the sensors would be able to recognize which item the customer has chosen and add it to their virtual cart on the app. Customers can conclude their purchases without having to make any physical contact with a cashier ever again. This would eventually encourage more customers to use such automated stores.

8.1.3 Benefits of Smart Retail

The concept of smart retail evolves daily because it is beneficial to the customer as well as to the retailer. As we all move on daily with our busy schedules, we seek to save as much time as possible and this would include having to wait in long queues, having our needs met at the very moment when needed, etc. [3]. All these issues would be solved by the application of smart retail integrated into the world around us as a customer. Even as a retailer of a store, it would in turn assist them by not having to keep numerous employees, and sales would definitely reach heights that were never seen before. By adhering to modern and upcoming technologies such as smart retail, it would give retailers a better insight into the products that are in high demand to customers such as the demand for winter clothing which would rise during winter or how customers are responding to the sales during festive seasons and so on. Nevertheless, it would help industries to reap profits and more importantly keep customers pleased.

8.2 APPLICATION OF SMART RETAIL

This section discusses various applications [4] which can be incorporated by a retailer using the latest computing technology such as AI, machine learning (ML) and IoT named as smart retail.

8.2.1 IoT in Smart Retail

IoT for many years has started to revolutionize retail experience in a number of ways, some of which are stated below [5]. IoT is a network of objects or sensors that are interconnected to devices so that they can communicate with each other over a network. Efficiency and accuracy are the major factors when it comes to IoT devices as many applications and industries are now completely dependent on them.

IOT connected devices such as beacons, digital signages, smart shelves, etc., being set at retail stores make it easier for customers to locate the item that they are searching for or to find a particular shop in a mall. Just finding the product quick isn't enough to boost sales nowadays, questions such as

- How long a customer waits in an aisle?
- When the customer bought a particular product?
- Which product was bought by the customer?

These can be answered by the assistance of IoT devices which can help by stocking up if a particular product is in high demand or even by sending a discount coupon for a product to a regular customer which would encourage customers to make more purchases in turn increasing the store's profits.

Integrating IoT devices with an app for the store would also help customers to have an enhanced and more detailed description of a particular product, for example, in the case of a grocery store, details of products such as availability, expiry date, nutritional value and so on would be available to the customer with much ease.

Few real-life applications of IoT devices in smart retail are discussed below:

i. Smart mirrors – Smart mirrors are two-way mirrors having an inbuilt display behind the glass. The mirror lets you check your notifications over various platforms while you are dressing up or looking at yourself in the mirror. This is also integrated with a virtual google assistant which can connect to your smart home and provide many other features such as taking photos, acting as a surveillance system in your house and also giving you the ability to watch makeup videos while putting on makeup, for example.

   In the retail industry, for customers who prefer trying on clothes before buying them, smart mirrors make it considerably easier as the mirror would scan the various physical features of the customer such as height, physique, etc., of the body; the mirror would subsequently show customers how they would look in the dress without having to try it on. This would play a huge role in the future of smart retail.

ii. Beacons – Beacons are miniature sensors that can be placed anywhere and have the ability to sense if a particular item is being moved away from its position. This would help retailers get notified immediately when an item is going out of stock and would help by sending notifications to stock up [6]. It could also provide assistance by sensing whether a customer is choosing a particular product and can communicate to the customer's app, which would add the product to the virtual cart, so the customer doesn't have to wait in a queue to pay for the item's purchase and can directly be charged through the app.

iii. RFID tags – Inventory management has always been one of the major issues faced by retailers. Improper management of inventory can cause multiple problems such as employees not being able to find a particular product in time for the customer, which leads to inefficiency and a decrease in sales [3]. Inventory management started in the old-fashioned way with retailers having to write down on a piece of paper to manage the products moving in and out of the store. This was highly tedious and required tiresome manual labor. Then came the innovation of barcodes that are commonly used nowadays but possess disadvantages such as having to place the barcode within 15 feet of the barcode scanner; moreover, barcodes are printed on a paper or plastic, which make them highly prone to damage.

From the above examples taken, it is evident that barcodes only partially solve the problem at hand but still do not completely eradicate the complications that we face. As the concept and implementation of RFID tags have been rising day by day, it would help retailers to be able to track each and every product in their warehouse with ease. With the help of such scanners, it could even show the direction towards the location of a particular product in the warehouse.

8.2.2 ML and AI in Smart Retail

ML and AI are the most rapidly growing transformative technologies in the industry [4] because of their ability to skillfully handle large amounts of data and find hidden patterns in the received data, something which humans struggle to achieve. ML and AI have the ability to learn valuable behavioral information about users and customers on their own by analyzing data and providing user-specific experiences. Additionally, ML and AI help retail companies to adhere to their customers' needs, which can help by reducing the purchase of unnecessary stock and increasing the sales of in-demand products.

Big data in smart retail is and always has been one of the biggest assets and greatest challenges faced by retailers [7]. The below section provides insights into how retailers can increase their revenue by analyzing customer purchases and provides graphical representations of various parameters that would help in satisfying customer requirements as well.

i. Product Pricing

One of the major benchmarks is choosing an optimal price for each product depending on customer interactions [8]. According to some research groups, even a 1% increase in prices would increase 8.4% of the company's revenue (i.e., if the volume remains the same). ML can be used to cross reference and analyze various factors such as identifying in-demand products or recognizing the prices of the individual items that yielded the highest returns, which in turn would help finding the ideal price that would bring about maximum profits.

ii. Forecasting

One of the essential features provided by ML is the forecasting of desired or relative information obtained from historical data [9]. Every AI-powered forecasting is adjusted based on reviews, seasonal trends, geographical locations and other factors specific to the store. For retailers, forecasting can be used to predict the number of items to be purchased based on the users' spending behavior so as to keep sought-after products in stock. Forecasting can also be used to foretell whether the store undergoes a loss-making cycle that can help the store to plan ahead for the losses that are soon to be encountered. Based on various researches conducted, it is estimated that about 85% of the demand forecasting process will be performed by the AI in their respective businesses.

iii. Marketing

AI-driven automated methods are required by marketing teams in the present day to obtain up-to-date information on the customers' requirements and behavior [6]. AI allows these teams to create a highly personalized approach to clients by minimizing manpower required to crunch enormous amounts of data. AI moreover can help by reaching a narrower and targeted population efficiently, which can help in saving lots of time and resources. According to statistics, the adoption of AI by marketers has grown by 44% since 2017 and is increasing at a rapid rate.

iv. Manufacturing

AI is not only used to perform tasks related to data processing, they are also used in the field of manufacturing through their presence in robots. Implementation of robots in the field of manufacturing allows companies to reduce employee costs, gain more efficiency and productivity, reduce production times, etc. For example, AI has been used extensively in the widely famous shoe manufacturer Nike; their startup called Grabit Nike creates the top of shoes 20 times faster than a human employee would.

v. Customer Relationship Management (CRM)

CRM [10] deals with strategies, techniques, tools and technologies use by companies with the main motive of developing, retaining and acquiring customers. Every company requires a good CRM to prosper.

However, in the modern world, a truly efficient CRM system can turn out to be a very expensive solution for most companies. Using the capabilities of AI, and integration of natural language processing technologies, they allow the CRM system to directly answer to the customers' needs and can hence build traction which can develop, retain and acquire new customers. For example, in automated customer care services, these CRM systems are used to prevent human interventions and prevent unnecessary conflicts.

vi. Delivery

Three vital points for making any delivery efficient are reasonable pricing, reliability and speed. It is very difficult in the present day to maintain high-quality service on power with high delivery speed. A brand reputation might be determined by the efficiency of the delivery service. Nowadays, for modern customers, the speed of delivery is the paramount factor. A recent statistic showed that 16% of the people would leave the cart or cancel their order if the delivery time was slow [11]. With the proficiency of AI, we are able to run delivery services with high efficiency and speed. For instance, the AI system can help by providing the shortest possible route or can even change the route based on real-time occurrences, which in turn reduces the delivery time. Moreover, by reducing the distance to be travelled by the delivery associate, the fuel charges also subsequently reduce.

AI can also use clusters to determine which orders are at close proximities to each other, which can also help in reducing the distances travelled. In addition, AI provides a very high standard of reliability and helps in cutting out human errors such as delivering to an incorrect address or even delivering the wrong item to customers. For example, Flipkart automated guided vehicles to help in delivering products on time. The workers at the sorting center just need to place the packages on these CoBots which in turn use AI and ML to drop the packages at their designated pincode pin for the final delivery, hence removing any man-made errors while designating packages to their destinations. These CoBots can handle sorting 4500 packages per hour in comparison to the 500 that can be sorted by humans per hour.

8.3 SECURITY AND PRIVACY ISSUES IN SMART RETAIL

In [12], the author uses various IoT-based devices to make smart homes, smart fridges, etc., indeed make our lives easier and stress free; however, all these devices come along with the cost of privacy which may not be immediately evident to the people who choose to use them. Various devices which have sensors have the ability to collect information and share it across the cloud, which yield large amounts of data that can be combined, analyzed and acted upon to understand human behavior.

8.3.1 Security in Smart Retail

As the majority of IoT devices such as medical sensors, smart watches, smart security [2] systems, etc., that we use nowadays are connected to the internet and usually most of these devices are interconnected to each other, hacking even a single device can lead to the disclosure of the personal information of all the interconnected devices.

One of the main reasons why hackers are attracted to IoT devices is because most of the data is stored on public cloud services which makes it easier to get information without having to access the device itself [13, 16]. Routers are becoming a very attractive target to hackers as they are usually always on and moreover possess outdated software that are difficult to upgrade and are hence left idle by their owners, hence making it easier to hack the routers to which the IoT devices are connected to, making routers very vulnerable. When it comes to devices such as smart health devices, tampering with them could be harmful to patients in cases such as delivering an overdose of medication to a patient.

Smart home devices usually lack proper secure designs and implementations, this may be due to the objective of minimizing costs and ensuring that these devices can reach the hands of the common man. A 2014 HP study revealed that about 70% of IoT devices such as home alarms, door locks, TVs, webcams, etc., have vulnerabilities that could easily be exploited. One common occurrence across these devices is that around 80% of these devices are guarded by rather weak passwords, 70% of devices did not encrypt communications, 60% lacked encryption for software updates and another 60% had insecure web interfaces. All of these vulnerabilities can be easily exploited with a person having the right skill set.

Reasons why IoT is not available in every household is the general perception among people that their information can be easily stolen or tampered with. A recent survey conducted in 2015 by Icontrol State of the Smart Home study found that around 44% of Americans were "very concerned" about the idea that information could be stolen from their smart homes, and 27% were "somewhat concerned." With the above levels of uncertainty, it is fair to say it is not a surprise why IoT devices are not present in each and every household.

8.3.2 Privacy in Smart Retail

Location data is primarily the geographical location of a particular device. Location data is the most essential information that has the ability to link individuals and interests. The number of devices using location-based data is increasing exponentially, and data collection in most cases occurs without prior knowledge of the user [7]. Taking this into account, all the location data of places that the user frequently visits can be sold to marketing companies for the purpose of sending advertisements based on assumptions made on fondness for the places the user has visited.

i. Excessive data: The amount of data that is generated by IoT devices is staggering. According to researchers, it was found that a little less has 10000 households generate about 150 million data points every day [14]. This leaves a large amount of sensitive information at risk.

ii. Unwanted public profile: Reports have found that companies use personal data that is offered by consumers freely when they accept the terms and conditions. For instance, an insurance company can use the data collected about a person when the person is driving through a connected car while calculating an insurance rate. The same goes for health insurance companies with the help of fitness bands.

iii. Eavesdropping: Hackers or manufacturers could use smart home devices to virtually invade a person's home. Intelligent personal assistants such as Alexa could be used to eavesdrop on conversations that are taking place at a business meeting or conference.

8.4 FUTURE OF SMART RETAIL [14]

There are many ideas and fascinating thoughts about how smart retail might appear in the future, but the real question to be asked is, will these thoughts turn into reality and will these ideas be implemented in various locations around us?

• By 2025, at least two of the top 10 global retailers will establish robot resource organizations to manage nonhuman workers. Over the past several years, large retailers like Walmart, Target and Walgreens have announced the use of smart robots and AI for performing tasks such as delivery, store cleaning and product assistance. With the soon to be an emergence of robots in stores around us, it would be up to the retailers to redeploy their human workforce in value-adding fields that cannot be performed by AI so as to prevent wide-scale unemployment, something which our world already has enough of. By 2021, it is estimated that around 77% of retailers plan to deploy AI, with robotics for warehouse picking as the top use case.

- Meanwhile, the top 10 retailers globally will leverage AI to facilitate prescriptive product recommendations, transactions and forward deployment of inventory for immediate delivery to consumers [15]. It is believed that once AI has been properly implemented in stores around us, tasks such as product recommendations would be already performed as we walk into a store based on our previous transactions and personal information. Moreover, instead of waiting in long queues for getting our items billed, we can directly have the power of walking out of stores and have the money to be paid be right away deducted from our accounts as we saw from the Amazon Go example. Finally, delivery of goods from the stores would probably get completely automated as already seen from small instances of drones flying to deliver food items like pizza or robots that parcel food from restaurants and deliver them to your doorstep.

- By 2024, Tier 1 retailers in North America and Europe will reduce inventory carrying costs by 30%, dramatically improving free cash flow for digital investment, while revamping balance sheets. Major sources of funds are getting placed in digitalization. Retailers would have to realize that digitalization is the way to move forward, which is already being visibly noticed by few of the top retailers in the world. Retailers will leverage AI to drive more-accurate demand forecasting, create tailored market assortments and forward-deploy inventory to localized fulfillment centers to maintain inventory flexibility, which can help in boosting sales to heights that have not been reached before. Another advantage of having IoT technologies in stores is that they will help in improving on-shelf availability which would help in reducing the required safety stock of products and help in accurately depicting the required stock, thereby reducing losses that would occur either when the remaining stock goes unsold or are sold at a discount.

8.5 CASE STUDIES

This section discusses the latest case studies in the area of smart retailing.

8.5.1 Levi Strauss Company

According to McKinsey & Co, inventory distortion [9, 15] due to over-stocking, shrinkage and stock-out leads up to over 1 trillion dollars' worth of losses for retailers globally. They estimate that by 2025 with the help of IoT retail will range over 1 trillion dollars.

In 2015, Intel collaborated with the clothing manufacturing company Levi's to help implement a smart inventory system. RFID tags were attached to all items in the store. The data that is collected is sent to the cloud for cloud-based analysis. RFID antennas are always on which continuously keep scanning for products and would be able to locate and keep an account for every item on a floor at any time. The system was also designed to provide alerts to stock-up when a particular product in the store is going out of stock. The sensors provided by Intel also have the ability to analyze the way customers move in the store, to help retailers optimize the placement of the products.

Some of the benefits of the system are discussed below:

- Improved efficiency in inventory management: The management now has an accurate insight into what is on the shelf or which merchandize might be running low. Now, when a customer walks into the retail store looking for a specific fitted pair of jeans in a specific color and size, it can be found instantly on the shelf without the employees having to waste time in searching for the product.
- Reduced inventory costs: Reducing overstocking and stock outs can help lowering inventory costs. Having an inventory tracking system also lets the management know about the theft of products by both customers and staff.
- Insights into customer behavior: The system not only keeps track of items being sold but also what items have been touched or tried on. Through this retailers are able to identify premium traffic areas and track which item is abandoned and which is preferred.
- Identifying new usage models: This platform also helps to collect data from multiple edge sensors on how inventory moves as a part of the supply chain. This could help in suggesting new usage models.

- Improved customer experience: Privacy is a major factor, with the help of a smart fitting room app, customers can view their selected merchandize to be viewed in a fitting room on the screen. If required, the customer can request a different size from the employee without leaving the fitting room.

8.5.2 Costa Coffee

The International Vending Alliance (IVA) has grown anxious with the decline of the vending industry as customers prefer new methods of buying such as touchscreen kiosks [15]. The IVA collaborated with Intel to come up with a 'smart black box' technology to overcome vending machines. This aims to implement new features such as touchscreens, cashless payments, etc. The 'smart black box' technology lets you use multiple hardware-based components on a single software-based platform.

Some of the features that are in favor of both customer and retailers are listed below:

Customer related

- Options for cashless payments.
- Interactive digital signage.
- Touch screen mechanisms for better usability.

Vendor related

- Remote management with online monitoring.
- Tracking temperatures for warm or cool beverages.
- A smartphone app that allows machines to communicate with customers with beacon technology.

Here, the hardware uses an Intel's low-power dual-core i7-3517UE processor with integrated graphics and supports several display interfaces. The coffee machines also give customers abilities such as Bluetooth connectivity and links to social media and also allow payment through credit and debit cards. The buttons were replaced by touchscreens to allow users to navigate through product information and place orders.

The analytical part consists of the Intel Audience Impression Metrics suite. The Intel AIM Suite Audience Counter is a software-based technology that uses a camera to gather viewership metrics for signage. It gives retailers the ability to record and analyze impressions and demographics, which would help them make it user friendly according to the results obtained from the analysis.

Some of the benefits of the present system are discussed below:

- The system provides real-time data by sending notifications on when to collect cash or when to restock.
- The analytics tool enables retailers to tighten the supply chain, so as to ensure in-time delivery, which also reduces losses due to overstocking.
- Retailers gain significant insight into customer preferences and behaviors.
- The optical sensor views customers and detects purchase choices thus enabling the brand marketers to ascertain from the collected data, the effectiveness of their ads.

8.5.3 Axonize Company

Axonize is an upcoming company in the field of smart retail that has the main motive of transforming everyday locations like offices and buildings into smart spaces. They provide their customers with end-to-end solutions to tackle the new age software by providing necessary devices and sensors to quickly launch their secure IoT projects within a few days.

Below points illustrate the key concept of the projects that they had helped to set up for one of their large customers dealing in fast-food chains

- Phase 1: Before starting to evolve the work space, Axonize first confirmed whether they would obtain positive return on investments (ROI) for the project that they were about to carry out in two branches. Subsequently, various energy sensors were installed on electric devices such as refrigerators, lighting devices and air conditioners. After researching energy consumption patterns that were displayed by the branches, they observed that there was faulty equipment in the refrigeration unit in one of the branches where few of the compressors were overworked. This prompted them to provide maintenance and fix this issue, which led to significant energy savings, hence leading to a green light for the commencement of the project.
- Phase 2: Next, electricity monitoring system was installed in all their customers' branches and locations. Door sensors were placed

in refrigerators to send alerts if the doors were not fully closed after a set interval of time. This was done as, in general, employees would simply push the door without the door actually sealing, which would require the refrigerator to spend more energy and work harder to keep the food cold. Another reason why these sensors were placed was that if the door was not fully shut overnight, this would result in food wastage which would eventually account for loss of potential revenue. The alerts that were being sent by these devices were delivered to the respective store managers and were also customized as per the branches opening hours. Another application was installed which sent alerts if lights and air conditioners were left on after closing hours on accident; employees with access to these new smart devices were allowed to remotely turn these devices off.

- Phase 3: The next requirement of the customer was to install a "customer-facing application" using IoT devices. The main objective was to develop a guest 'Comfort Score,' which was obtained by placing sensors around the store that monitored smell, noise, air quality and the temperature in the restaurant. From each sensor, data was obtained which were given individual scores based on a certain criterion. Finally, all the individual scores from each sensor were tallied up to create a guest Comfort Score, which could be proactively monitored across the various branches to see that their users were satisfied with their service, which is most important when it comes to the restaurant industry or business. If this Score dropped below a certain level on any particular day, desired actions could be taken at that particular branch.

- Phase 4: Continuous advances are being made to improve guest satisfaction by this system integrator. Their latest project is on researching technology to track the time taken for the meal to reach the guests from when they enter the restaurant; lowering these times would help in drastically improving customer satisfaction rates.

Sensors that were installed in their customer's modules are illustrated below

- Waste Bin Detectors: These sensors use ultrasound to measure and detect filing levels in waste and recyclable containers.
- Door and Window Open Sensors: They measure door movements and determine whether the doors are opened or closed. These are extremely

useful when it comes to refrigerators as seen in the second phase above. Moreover, in case of the presence of a faulty door or a window in an air-conditioned-filled restaurant, this would cause undesirable external conditions affecting the restaurant's temperature.

- Sound Detectors: These are used for detecting and identifying different sound types, which can be helpful when it comes to event triggers. Increasingly, sudden changes in sounds can provide insightful information as to whether an incident or accident might have occurred, which would require immediate attention and care.
- Brightness Sensors: These sensors measure light with data measurements taking place over 3-minute periods. This would be helpful to the customers in case there would be any faulty bulbs or lighting, which would lower the customer experience.
- Occupancy Sensors: These are used to measure movements specifically in checkout areas or tables that can help in alerting the staff to clear the tables quickly in order to allow the new guests to be seated quickly rather than standing for unnecessary extra time in the waiting line.

Benefits to food chain and customers:

- Fast scaling: As IoT projects do not require engineers or DevOps to be involved, each phase takes a shorter span of time to implement.
- Obtained positive ROI: As there were quick development times and low investments in DevOps which usually takes up a lot of the budget, the branches showed positive ROIs quickly.
- Provided a unified platform: Their customers could access whatever outputs that they desired through a single app that connected to different parts of the building, restaurant equipment and could moreover help with analyzing customer interactions, hence leading to the improvement in customer satisfaction rates.

8.6 CONCLUSION

Researchers' study reveals that IoT is on the verge of fundamentally changing how retailers emerge in the future. The retailers who move forward along with these technologies will have a better insight into all areas of their business. On the other side, retailers who don't move along with the technological revolution are likely to disappear altogether and stand no chance among the data-centric retailers. This perspective of business has always been used by Tech giants such as Amazon, Facebook, etc., who have been pioneers of the Big Data era for years. This chapter provides a platform where a reader is able to understand smart retails, its advantages and how smart retail is integrated with smart technologies. The case studies discussed help the reader in understanding how AI, ML and IoT are integrated with smart retails and how they help to overcome the current trends. Even so, it is not an easy road to success in the field of smart retail with major issues such as technology integration, security, privacy, etc. These issues will have to be intercepted as you move on to become an experienced retailer.

REFERENCES

1. Hagberg, J., Sundström, M., & Egels-Zandén, N. (2014, November). Digitalization of retailing: Beyond e-commerce. In The 4th Nordic Retail and Wholesale Conference (pp. 4–6).
2. Pantano, E., & Timmermans, H. (2014). What is smart for retailing? Procedia Environmental Sciences, 22, 101–107.
3. Đurđevíc, N., Labus, A., Bogdanovic, Z., & Despotovíc-Zrakíc, M. (2017). Internet of things in marketing and retail. International Journal of Advances in Computer Science & Applications, 6(3), 7–11.
4. Vakulenko, Y., Shams, P., Hellström, D., & Hjort, K. (2019). Online retail experience and customer satisfaction: The mediating role of last mile delivery. The International Review of Retail, Distribution and Consumer Research, 29(3), 306–320.
5. Jayaram, A. (2017). Smart Retail 4.0 IoT Consumer retailer model for retail intelligence and strategic marketing of in-store products. Proceedings of the 17th International Business Horizon-INBUSH ERA-2017, Noida, India.
6. Dimitris, M., Ekaterini, V., & Zogopoulos, V. (2018). An IoT-based platform for automated customized shopping in distributed environments. Procedia CIRP, 72, 892–897.
7. Malik, A., Magar, A. T., Verma, H., Singh, M., & Sagar, P. (2019). A detailed study of an internet of things (IoT). International Journal of Scientific and Technology Research, 8(12), 2989–2994.
8. Aktas E, Meng Y. (2017). An exploration of big data practices in retail sector. Logistics, 1(2), 12.
9. Elgendy, N., & Elragal, A. (2014, July). Big data analytics: A literature review paper. In Industrial Conference on Data Mining, pp. 214–227. Cham: Springer.
10. Anderson, J. L., Jolly, L. D., & Fairhurst, A. E. (2007). Customer relationship management in retailing: A content analysis of retail trade journals. Journal of Retailing and Consumer Services, 14(6), 394–399.
11. Kumar, V., Anand, A., & Song, H. (2017). Future of retailer profitability: An organizing framework. Journal of Retailing, 93(1), 96–119.

12. Venus K., Khullar V., & Verma N. (2020). Review of artificial intelligence with retailing sector. Journal of Computer Science Research, 2, 1–7.
13. Bradlow, E. T., Gangwar, M., Kopalle, P., & Voleti, S. (2017). The role of big data and predictive analytics in retailing. Journal of Retailing, 93(1), 79–95.
14. Dhruv, G., Noble, S. M., Roggeveen, A. L., & Jens, N. (2020). The future of in-store technology. Journal of the Academy of Marketing Science, 48(1), 96–113.
15. Intel (2016). The future of retail through the internet of things (IoT). https://www.intel.com/content/dam/www/public/us/en/documents/white-papers/future-retail-through-iot-paper.pdf
16. Alam, M. (2012, October). Cloud algebra for cloud database management system. In Proceedings of the Second International Conference on Computational Science, Engineering and Information Technology, 26–29.

9

Business Analytics and Performance Management in India

Pavnesh Kumar and Siddhartha Ghosh
Mohan Malaviya School of Commerce & Management Sciences
Mahatma Gandhi Central University
East Champaran, India

Kiran Chaudhary
Shivaji College, University of Delhi
New Delhi, India

CONTENTS

DOI: 10.1201/9781003307761-9

9.1 INTRODUCTION

A term that entered the forefront in the late '90s and became widely used over the last decade is 'Analytics'. It all happened because of the rapid growth of the internet and related information technologies. It is a must for organisations to leverage analytics as an integral part of their current practices.

Predictive approaches (particularly in the field of data analytics), information technology, predictive analysis and the use of computer models are used together to process consumer and company information and data to perform necessary analysis. These studies include all of the different scenarios to allow knowledgeable decision makers to draw on all of their available resources to produce a well-informed decision based on the computer-based model that assists those who make decisions at the top level of business management to visualise the output of any particular decision under different circumstances.

The practice of doing business analytics has been around for a long time and will be necessary as long as new and improved tools are made available due to the digital revolution. It originated from information analysis by the allies deployed during World War II. As time went by, this approach was increasingly applied to industry. Once the economy started to take off and corporations began to become more commercially viable, management science began to enter into the realm of business analysis, and support software for decision making started emerging.

There are many uses of business analytics. This model can be applied to both historical data in order to better explain previous situations, as well as modern-day situations in which new data is being gathered. Statistical study of current industry status and past corporate strategies can also help companies figure out where they are, and which business approaches will be most beneficial for them.

An estimate can be made of the company's future success by doing this, so it is common to do so prior to opening a new branch or department. An important function in market analytics is predictive analysis, which is employed to come up with improvement strategies for better results.

Performance monitoring entails practising to ensure objectives are fulfilled regularly and effectively. Performance assessment can be used to assess an organisation's performance, a department's performance, the procedures used to create a product or service, or the performance of individual employees. Performance management can be characterised as an effort to identify competent and committed individuals who work collaboratively to achieve mutual meaningful goals within an enterprise that promotes and facilitates their accomplishment.

With the evolution of performance management as a philosophy, the role of human resource management in organisations has shifted dramatically in recent years. Performance assessment is also a widely recognised method in human resource management in a large number of organisations. The focus has shifted away from the 'command and control structure' in favour of a 'system based on commitment'. This shift reflects the increasing emphasis placed on employees' responsive perspectives and job success in achieving an organisation's goals and strategy.

Performance management's primary objective is to cultivate and nurture an organisation's talents. Job performance used to be formerly considered as a subgroup of psychological assessment because it presented an objective definition of the degree to which people revealed certain qualities, properties or behaviours.

Performance assessment denotes the processes and practises used to reveal the degree to which workers exhibit specific job behaviours and the results of those behaviours. Business analytics is applicable and useful in a wide variety of situations. It may be used for descriptive research, which makes use of data to make sense of the past and present. This type of descriptive research is used to determine the company's overall market place and the efficacy of prior management decisions.

It is also used for statistical analysis and is often used to evaluate a business's historical results. Additionally, business analytics is used for prescriptive analysis and is used to develop optimisation approaches that result in increased business efficiency.

9.2 UNDERSTANDING BUSINESS ANALYTICS

By using analysis of its raw consumer and business data points, an organisation can better understand its overall market performance. Data is gathered using mathematical models, operating methods and optimisation methods to extract information that can be used to adjust the company's operations, in real time.

Data is the paramount part of a business analytics application and its interpretation is essential. Large institutions, including universities, governments, NGOs and corporations collect vast amounts of information through a variety of channels to gather large quantities of data. When this data increases exponentially in a rather short time, it is said to become 'Big Data'. For all intents and purposes, big data is identical to any set of standard data. A variety of consumer data sources are often used in combination with business intelligence (BI) data to get real-time updates, which can then be used to make necessary business applications in the market.

BI is a mechanism by which organisations analyse their own data in order to get a better understanding of their results. Organisations are concerned with determining how things occur and what they should do to boost the results and prevent any errors wherever possible. The focus is on the internal review in this case. By contrast, business analytics reports on the "why" aspect of an event. Organisations, in this case, concentrate on the external influences affecting the organisation's internal efficiency.

Economic intelligence, along with external environmental evidence, technological instruments, quantitative models and statistical analytical processes, may be considered one of the many aspects of market analytics. By combining internal and external organisational research, brands can extract useful and actionable lessons.

Business analytics provides brands with many advantages, including persona development and demographic segmentation, content strategy development, business extension and growth forecasting, resource optimisation and order fulfilment and increased customer value adding.

9.3 UNDERSTANDING PERFORMANCE MANAGEMENT SYSTEM

The goal of performance management systems (PMSs) is to compare an employee's work with their set task and objectives and evaluate whether they are meeting the needs of the job. The system generally uses the year-end data to assess the past year's performance of the employees and set new goals for the next year.

In certain instances, the person is asked to self-evaluate and meet with their boss about any perceived differences. The PMS system ensures that the company's priorities are achieved in an effective, timely and profitable manner. Typically, these targets are defined by the top management and passed down to be applied by various divisions and individuals.

It is a must for a company to have some sort of standard to define the minimum expected performance of the employees. It applies equally in the case of promoting or firing some employees. For promoting an employee, he/she ought to have a reputation for achievement which can be properly backed by data. Management would typically look for proof that the individual has been consistently outperforming the goals of his/her current position for promotion.

When an individual isn't doing well in his/her job, an in-depth analysis will produce a strategy for his/her development. Managing an employee who is regularly underperforming requires time and commitment from the management as well as discovering possible improvement; detailed evaluation reports are vital in the process.

PMS is a part of an interaction between an employee and their immediate supervisors with the motive of improving the overall performance. Many workers have an ingrained fear that their work can be overlooked, but building a relationship with their bosses can offer them the affirmation which can be essential for them to stay motivated. Hence, the PMS incentivises workers to perform well. PMS has advantages like higher employee happiness and satisfaction, higher-performing individuals and teams which thrust the business on the path to success.

9.4 LITERATURE REVIEW

Business analytics can be considered as consisting of a broad array of processes as well as applications of newer technologies, which are utilized for gathering and storing data which is in turn analysed for assisting businesses in reaching improved decisions (Watson, 2009).

The terms "Business Intelligence", "Big Data" and "Business Analytics" are interchangeably used for topics that are similar in nature. For example, the business community prefers using the term "Business Analytics", while the community of information technology professionals stresses upon using the term "Business Intelligence" (Sircar, 2009).

Businesses globally have been increasingly using information technology solutions, which have led towards the making of complex and larger than ever datasets pertaining to various functions of an organisation. It has become an uphill challenge for organisations to make some sort of sense out of these datasets to make better business decisions based on them. These large and complex datasets are often referred to as "Big Data" by IT companies and working individuals. The existing IT solutions are inadequate to process and synthesise these datasets, which need newer, better and advanced computational power to process and arrive to understand more about these big data sets while also assisting businesses as to what to do next (Wicom et al., 2011).

Business analytics as a field is undergoing a phase of swift growth due to the gradual increase of structured and unstructured data, which has been aiding this growth. This is supposedly the business trend of the last decade having the maximum potential due to massive investments being made in the IT sector, which in turn is expected to aid the field of BI. This also provides the company with the necessary tools to inspect and process newer types of data such as images, voice, log files and videos to reach better decisions. (Davenport & Dyché, 2013)

Organisations are expected to deploy and harness the fruits of business analytics in those areas which predominantly depend on the information of quantitative nature, like finance divisions, marketing departments and the strategic planning section of an organisation. The work done in these departments generally requires both analysis and, in turn, prediction, suggesting their inclination towards using business analytics (SAS, 2011).

It was found that organisations investing in upcoming technologies saw a positive impact on their employees' performance. There was an observable increase in the productivity as well as efficiency of employees. The organisation as a whole is also seen to become strong in providing customer services. All these observations were made in a case study done on Allied Bank Ltd, Pakistan with the title "Impact of Technology on Performance of Employees" (Jawad et al., 2014).

It has become a necessity on the organisation's part to conduct a review of their employees after a fixed time period, which ensures to cover the gap between the actual performance of the employees and set organisational standards of individual employees' performance (Rohan Singh et al., 2013).

It was observed that by giving specific goals of challenging nature to employees, a motivational effect is observed in them when compared to the circumstances when an easy, somewhat vague goal has been asked of them. This is in accordance with goal setting theory, which establishes that goal setting is directly linked with task performance (Hamumokola, 2013).

It was established that PMS plays a vital role in enhancing the effectiveness of any organisation. The systems help in fulfilling key expectations of the business while also assisting in boosting market expectations. It also assists the management of the organisation to make decisions regarding employee promotions, while employees of the organisation remain satisfied with the PMS system in place (specific to the IT industry) (Gudla, 2012).

Business analytics is an obvious tool that can be used for making key decisions in an organisation relating to costing, pricing, planning, reporting and performance measurement. Various techniques of analytics can be utilised in these imperative decision areas to reach better decision making. Today's businesses need fluidity and need to react to the movements in key areas of business. As a result, an increased demand has been felt for a faster cycle to scrutinise the performance of employees against the set expectations across all levels like strategic, operations or tactical (Nielsen, 2017).

An increased application of analytics and its integration with businesses has been observed. There is a gradual transition of organisations functioning in a reactionary mode to a predictive analysis mode while better harnessing the power of business analytics. The operational and business executive level is provided with extended information access with performance analysis. There is also an increased alignment of analytics and performance management with business plans and strategies (The Asian Banker, 2007).

The study shows that there exists a great potential for business performance analytics in addressing the challenge of the restricted capability to quantify the cause–effect relationship between the organisation's performance and the value drivers. Business performance analytics can help improve the understanding of descriptive, predictive and prescriptive analytics. This can enhance the PMS (Anna Raffoni et al., 2017).

9.5 OBJECTIVES OF THE STUDY

The objectives of this research study are as below:

- To examine the role of business analytics and performance management, which makes it stand apart from the regular processing of data.
- To understand how business analytics and performance management technology is being implemented in the industry.
- To suggest a model to better understand how business analytics lays the foundation of a PMS in an organisation.

9.6 RESEARCH METHODOLOGY

A thorough review of the literature on the title and related concepts was conducted. Secondary data of both qualitative and quantitative nature was analysed. The latest information was sought from technology journals, research publications, news reports, books, magazines and various websites. Libraries and corporate reports were also consulted while writing this chapter. The collected literature was cross checked and properly validated to provide the latest information.

9.7 UNDERSTANDING THE RELEVANCE OF BUSINESS ANALYTICS IN TERMS OF PMS

The immediate need for quicker decision making has emphasised the need for market intelligence (monitoring), i.e., business analytics. Planning anticipates potential changes in business procedures and processes and encourages the adoption of change and optimisation of organisational processes, which are critical. Integrating business analytics and PMSs is essential to attain this.

In general, businesses accept the fact that their decision-makers should base their decisions on facts rather than gut feelings. Using new data with the help of business analytics and PMS can help develop newer insights for the business.

There are a host of noteworthy global software and data processing changes occurring at the moment, all of which are the result of these emerging changes. Furthermore, the use of quantitative databases is helping to build upon the data collection foundation for other data analytics projects.

In order to prevent lengthy and erroneous data transfer procedures, the centralised database allows for business analytics and performance management software solutions to build on a strong foundation. Centralised master data is particularly useful for the planning process as well as data analysis, financials, as well as performance management techniques such as restructuring and risk assessment. Based on this, a modular data model can be developed to accommodate varying time frames for short-term organisational needs, mid-term tactical decisions and long-term strategies to be adopted.

Hence, we see that business analytics and PMSs go hand in hand in current digitally driven e-commerce-based times. Since a lot of purchases are happening in the digital domain, it is beneficial for the company to carefully analyse and better its offering wherever deemed necessary. Also, an efficient company will also be looking to maximise the efficiency of their employees and the PMS will be helpful in mitigating this need.

9.8 MODEL

The above model is an attempt to understand how business analytics is actually the driving force to lay the foundation of standards that are set by organisation and then, accordingly, individual employee expectations are communicated (Figure 9.1). This individual employee expectation serves as the base over which the PMS weights out the performance of the employees with subsequent analysis of performance giving the top-level management the necessary understanding of whom to promote or put into PiP (performance improvement programme).

The model tries to highlight both the aspects of business, namely, the business analytics part (on the left) and the PMS part (on the right).

The organisation is divided into three levels of management; each assigned to different tasks. The operational level of the management faces customers directly and is also responsible for achieving their expected target goals. The targets can be in the form of revenue generation, lead

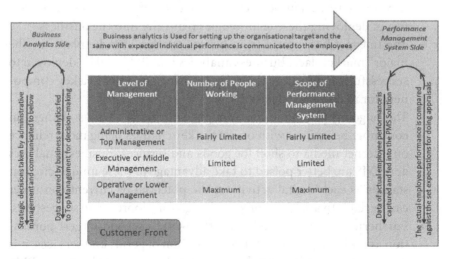

FIGURE 9.1
A model of business analytics and PMS.

conversion to actual sales, consumer query numbers managed or any such quantifiable number.

The set targets are then compared to the actual performance of the employees using the PMS, and appraisals are performed, with good performing employees receiving rewards in the form of promotion or bonus, and those employees receiving feedback who were unable to meet the target for various reasons.

The administrative and executive levels are also within this circle, with each level further synthesising the available business analytical information to derive further meaning in order to make better decisions. The PMS is also used for both levels, though the number of employees at both levels is fairly limited when compared to the organisational level. Managers working at executive levels are generally responsible for a team or departmental targets, while administrative level managers are responsible for overall business or a division of business.

Thus, both the systems, namely, business analytics and PMS run complementary to each other and not in isolation.

9.9 FINDINGS

- The use of business analytics and PMSs will form a key component in various aspects of business as India already possesses the expertise in deploying these technologies fruitfully into the business.
- The internet has moved from being "another" marketplace to "the major" marketplace. Business analytics and PMS will be deployed to successfully manoeuvre the business using analytics as a key component for making fast decisions.
- The ongoing pandemic has brought with itself various changes in consumer behaviour, with one of the key changes being more reliance on internet media to shop for goods and services. Business analytics and PMS are better poised to take advantage of these unique circumstances as each digital activity of the potential or current consumer can be fed into analytics for suggesting more appropriate suggestions.
- Furthermore, because India has the world's second-largest population and a large potential for consumption of goods and services, it is very likely that new technologies such as business analytics and PMS will remain in the long run as consumers gradually shift to online mediums to purchase their requirements.

9.10 SUGGESTIONS

We have the below suggestions for business analytics and PMS for business in India:

- Since business analytics uses consumer data and purchase behaviours in finding and suggesting product offerings, there must be some legislation that can be enacted for ethical use of consumer data as there has awareness internationally of potential data leaks or unauthorised data processing. Indian government's proposed *'Personal Data Protection Bill'* is one right step in this direction.
- Since business analytics and PMS is in the early developmental stage in India, it is worthwhile that companies of Indian origin prefer employing Indian individuals and software for business analytics and PMS, which can protect India's interests in future from the dangers of using Indian data for promoting foreign product offerings in India.
- The government must also consider developing world-class facilities for the development of business analytics and PMS tools using already available Indian expertise. Such an initiative will ensure India's upper hand in the coming days and will prepare for the digital leap of the future.

9.11 CONCLUSION

In earlier days, managers used their experiences, instincts and observation in making decisions, which never had analytics. Business analytics is about how to influence decisions rather than relying on the previous way, as well as how well they can be done with the presence of data and facts. More businesses today have a need for quick and better decision making due to the rapid evolution of the dynamic industry and expansive data sets, and the fact that such decisions are made in a sophisticated computing environment is characteristic of today's era.

When businesses see that technological developments can help them to improve their productivity as well as being a key to profitability, they attempt to employ them in the first place. A corporation's wish is to look to incorporate knowledge of the future into its current policies and structures. As corporate leaders come to grasp the significance of data analytics, the number of people in roles related to it is increasing, thereby generating greater demand for those who possess these skills. The mix of industry and nontechnical analysts provides corporations with a critical competitive edge over their rivals who do not possess either the skills or the resources and necessary tools, thus giving the business using business analytics an upper hand.

Also, the firm's performance management strategy would allow it to meet the long-term needs of its stakeholders. The company will closely monitor all critical phases associated with the current approach and ensure that the framework is consistent with the long-term goal that drives its industry activities. More specifically, the firm's performance management programmes would emphasise the decentralisation of decision-making processes in order to allow workers to improve their technical skills over time. As a result, workers will be encouraged to contribute to the organisation's long-term sustainability by offering valuable solutions that will increase the level of outcomes achieved. The organisation's appraisal processes would empower it to be equal to all of its workers and to motivate them to do well at their assigned workstations.

REFERENCES

A. Raffoni, Visani, F., Bartolini, M., & Silvi, R. (2017, October 11). Business Performance Analytics: Exploring the Potential for Performance Management Systems. *Taylor and Francis Group Online*. doi:10.1080/09537287.2017.1381887

Gudla, S. (2012). The Study of Performance Management System in IT Organizations. doi:10.9790/487X-0633752

Hamumokola, N. N. (2013). *The Contributions of Performance Management Systems to Performance in the Namibian Context*. University of the Witwatersrand, Johannesburg, Faculty of Commerce, Law & Management. Retrieved April 24, 2021, from http://wiredspace.wits.ac.za/jspui/bitstream/10539/14001/2/MCom%20 Dissertation%20NN%20Hamumokola%20Final%2018092013.pdf

Jawad, A., Muzaffar, A., Mahmood, H. K., Ramzan, M. A., & Rizvi, S. S. U. H. (2014). Impact of Technology on Performance of Employees (a Case Study on Allied Bank Ltd, Pakistan). *World Applied Sciences Journal*. doi:10.5829/idosi.wasj.2014.29.02.1897

Nielsen, S. (2017, May 20). Business Analytics and Performance Management: A Small Data Example Combining TD-ABC and BSC for Simulation and Optimization. Retrieved April 24, 2021, from https://pure.au.dk/portal/files/113728189/Working_ paper_BA_and_Man_Acc_Final_2017.pdf.

Singh, R., Mohanty, M., Mohanty, A. K. (2013). Performance appraisal practices in Indian service and manufacturing sector organizations. *Asian Journal of Management Research*, 4(2). Retrieved April 24, 2021, from http://citeseerx.ist.psu.edu/viewdoc/ download?doi=10.1.1.587.1326&rep=rep1&type=pdf.

SAS (2011). The Current State of Business Analytics: Where Do We Go From Here? Retrieved April 24, 2021, from https://www.sas.com/content/dam/SAS/bp_de/doc/studie/ba-st-the-current-state-of-business-analytics-2317022.pdf.

Sircar, S. (2009, February). Business intelligence in the business curriculum. *Communications of the Association for Information Systems, 24*(17). Retrieved April 24, 2021, from https://aisel.aisnet.org/cgi/viewcontent.cgi?article=3413&context=cais

The Asian Banker (2007, March). Successful Implementation of Analytics and Performance Management in Financial Institutions. Retrieved April 24, 2021, from https://bit.ly/3aFxtuJ

Davenport, T. H. & Dyché, J.. (2013, May). Big Data in Big Companies. International Institute for Analytics. Retrieved April 24, 2021, from https://www.iqpc.com/media/7863/11710.pdf

Watson, H. J. (2009, November 1). Tutorial: Business intelligence – Past, Present, and Future. *Communications of the Association for Information Systems, 25*. Retrieved April 24, 2021, from https://aisel.aisnet.org/cgi/viewcontent.cgi?article=3490&context=cais

Wicom, B., Ariyachandra, T., Goul, M., Gray, P., Kulkarni, U., & Phillips-Wren, G. (2011). The Current State of Business Intelligence in Academia. *Communications of the Association for Information Systems, 29*(16), 299–312.

10

Parameterized Fuzzy Measures Decision-Making Model Based on Preference Leveled Evaluation Functions for Best Signal Detection in Smart Antenna

Seema Khanum, Rajiga S.V., and Mathanprasad L.
Department of Computer Science, Government Arts College
Salem, India

M. Gunasekaran
Department of Computer Science, Government Arts College
Dharmapuri, India

Firos A.
Department of Computer Science and Engineering, Rajiv Gandhi
University
Doimukh, India

CONTENTS

DOI: 10.1201/9781003307761-10

10.1 INTRODUCTION

10.1.1 Basic Concept of Antenna Engineering

An antenna has an input and an output. Input is basically an electrical signal. The output is basically an electromagnetic free space signal. The nature of this input and the output is different [1]. In the input, the signal is of electrical nature, and at the output, the signal is of wave nature, which is an electromagnetic signal, which is nothing but waves in free space. The very basic definition of an antenna is nothing but a device that converts an electrical signal into a free space electromagnetic wave. It converts the electrical signal into the wave. That's the concept of the transducer. The transducer converts an electrical quantity to a nonelectrical quantity, for example, a speaker.

In the speaker, the input is an electrical signal, for example, our speaker on the mobile device. The signal is electrical in nature. But in the output, we hear the voice. So, the output is a sound. It's a nonelectrical quantity. So, our speaker is a transducer. It converts the electrical signal of the mobile phone inside the mobile chip and creates the sound wave. The transducer converts the electrical quantity into nonelectrical quantity. The antenna is also a transducer, and the concept is also applicable for the vice versa case. For example, in the microphone, the input is a nonelectrical quantity which is a sound wave, and then the microphone will create a voltage based on the input sound wave, which is electrical in nature. So, the concept could be interchanged. Any device that converts electrical to non-electrical quantity or vice versa is nothing but a transducer. An antenna is one kind of transducer. If we analyze the nature of an electrical signal mathematically, an electrical signal is basically a sinusoidal current of the voltage signal [2]. An antenna radiates electromagnetic waves. Assuming that the input electrical signal is sinusoidal in nature, if we provide this signal the DC voltage which is fixed over time, the antenna cannot radiate this signal. What an antenna can do is it can radiate or it can create this electromagnetic wave only when the input electrical signal is sinusoidal in nature. Electromagnetic wave does not need any medium to propagate [3]. It can travel in free space, and it travels with the speed of light in vacuum.

Whenever we talk about the antenna, we felt that any antenna could be very bulky and very large metallic in nature. It was true in the past. The antennas were mostly metallic, large, and bulky in nature. However, things have changed a lot. Now the concept of the antenna can be translated to the microscopic level. Even there are nanoantennas that we cannot even see with our naked eye [4]. We have these classifications based on several scenarios. For example, the first one is a dish antenna and the second one is a space antenna being used for a satellite. Space antenna being powered by the solar power energy, the signal can travel billions of miles away. So, in that case the receiving antenna would be big large antenna. In astronomical antennas, the size of the dish is very huge. It's like thousands of feet in diameter; it's very huge and very powerful. It can transmit signals billions of miles away to distant galaxies and stars [5]. It can also receive signals from those distant places. The largest the size of the antenna the more powerful it is. Wi-fi is the third category of antenna, which is wi-fi antenna. It is attached to a wi-fi router.

10.1.2 Application of Machine Learning in Antenna Design

Machine learning is an approach where it takes a huge amount of data set and then produces an output. The output is a mathematical model [6]. A machine learning algorithm can operate on these data sets, which can be labeled or can be clearly defined. Machine learning is very intelligent in the sense that it can also create its own pattern to identify the input data and then generate a predictive mathematical model. Under this machine learning, we have another subset called deep learning, so deep learning is somewhat smarter than machine learning. It's much more intense in one sense because it mimics the functionality of the human brain. In the human brain, we have billions of neurons. A single neuron is useless. But with the combinations and the interactions between these billions of neurons, these interactions are the key [7]. So, with the deep learning approach, it mimics the multilayered structure of neurons in our brain and then operates on the input data sets and then generates the output data sets [8].

At the heart of machine learning, we have algorithms where we train algorithms by using training data sets. The input data is provided to AI algorithms, and based on the training data sets, it will generate a mathematical model [9]. So, it's very useful in those scenarios where we do not have any closed form of an analytical model of any system. In summary, the machine learning algorithm operates on input data, and we also need to train it by using training data sets. Then, in the output, it generates a mathematical model. The quality of the training data sets will determine how accurate our mathematical model is in the output if we provide enough data sets in training [10]. If we provide good quality data sets in the training, it will generate a very precise mathematical model in the output.

The machine-learning algorithms can be primarily of three types, supervised learning, unsupervised learning, and reinforcement learning [11]. In a supervised learning algorithm, the training data sets are labeled. They're very well defined; the input and the output data sets are present in the training data. We have this clear distinction that if the input is from a known dataset, then the output would be the anticipated result. The training data set is the combination of input and output data that are labeled and are clearly defined. High-quality data sets are used to train this algorithm.

So, supervised learning can create this excellent predictive mathematical model if we provide enough amount of training data sets. In the case of unsupervised learning algorithms, the training data sets are unlabeled data. We do not have any information about the data sets. It creates a pattern and a clustering way to classify this unlabeled data. It's intelligent enough to understand and distinguish between the commonalities of the existing data sets, which are unlabeled. It creates its own pattern so that it can generate a mathematical model based on the clustering effect [12]. It would classify the data sets into several clusters, which have some commonalities in terms of characteristics. In an unsupervised learning algorithm, we need a huge amount of data sets for an accurate mathematical model. In the reinforcement learning algorithm, we do not have any training data sets. It must face the environment with an agent that is the entity learns. For example, the agent must face the environment through its action. It would interact with the environment, and then it would generate this reward; it could be positive or negative. A positive value is a reward and a negative value is a penalty.

In another example, two kinds of experiences are generated after interacting with the existing environment. Based on these experiences, good experience and bad experience, the agent learns continuously. It learns to know what is what, and if it learns, what would be the consequence, etc. Based on this learning experience, it performs.

It generates its own experiences, and then based on those good and bad experiences, that is the reward and the penalty, it would learn. This is very powerful and that is why Google has created AlphaGo [13], which has mastered the chess playing and can defeat any chess master in the world.

10.1.3 Deep Learning versus Machine Learning

Although these two terms are used very interchangeably quite often in the literature in the context of scientific discussion, there is a slight difference between these two things. Machine learning is the superset and deep learning is a subset of machine learning. Both of them actually belong to a similar kind of domain, but there's a subtle difference. The difference is, in machine learning, we have training data sets and algorithms and we can apply different approaches of the algorithm to generate mathematical models. In machine learning, we generate models from data. But in deep learning, we have a neural network in the core that is trained using learning rules and the input and output actually are both data. It's not a model. So, based on the training data sets and on its learning experience, it would create the best combination of input parameters and the output. Learning implies a deep neural network or DNN, which is a multilayered structure. The more the layers are the higher the complexities.

In DNN, the node is equivalent to a neuron in our brain. We have backpropagation to the millions of neurons, and when they interact with one another, they create electrical signals. We have hidden layers and billions of interconnections of neurons, represented by arrows. From the input to the first hidden layer, we have interaction. Then, we have this w1 which is our weighted matrix. This matrix is used to determine what value is given as the input to the first hidden layer. From the first to the second hidden layer, we have several interconnections. We also have another weighted matrix which is w2. For each level of hidden layers, we have this different weighted matrix. These matrices define the input value to the next hidden layer. Finally, at the output, we have the final weighted matrix. The output is the combination of these complicated interconnections of nodes and weighted matrices. The deep neural network operates quite similarly to the way our brain works. Billions of neurons work together to create a gigantic network. Output is not always what we want. So, there is a slight margin of error which is represented by delta, δ. This margin of error is feedback to what's the hidden layers in a backward fashion. This mechanism is called the backpropagation algorithm. This is used to minimize the error. Depending on this error, the weight of matrices is adjusted. The backpropagation algorithm fixes this margin of error, so that at the output, we get the nearest optimum values. One problem that this DNN suffers from is overfitting. For example, if it is following the training data sets very closely, it is overfitting.

The solution to this overfitting problem is a dropout. Dropout is a mechanism where we train the node of the hidden layer randomly, not all of them. We pick up any random node in the hidden layer, and then we train it. In that way, we actually minimize the number of hidden layer nodes being trained simultaneously. This is how we minimize the overfitting problem in DNN.

10.1.4 Application of Machine Learning Algorithm in Smart Antenna

We notice a weak Wi-Fi performance in places where a number of APs are available. Even after adding new wireless access points (APs), especially, will not always enhance the Wi-Fi performance. Cochannel interference is one of the reasons for this. If multiple neighboring APs operate on the same channel, it can lead to interference problems and lead to low performance. A smart antenna technology is proposed here, where a smart antenna AP detects a neighboring AP signal, and with the back propagation neural network (BPNN) model that uses the parameterized fuzzy measure decision-making model clustering method (PFMDMM) system for signal classification, it identifies the best signal for a WLAN node.

The rest of this chapter is structured as follows: Section 10.2 presents the background of smart antenna, the difference between conventional array and beamforming array, a comparison between switched and the adaptive array antenna, and some basic idea about the preference leveled evaluation functions method to construct fuzzy measures [14]. The proposed parameterized fuzzy measure decision-making model based on preference leveled evaluation functions [15] for best signal detection in smart antenna employs BPNN algorithm is given in Section 10.3. The experiment is presented in Section 10.4 in which we collected and preprocessed the cu/antenna data set (v. 2009-05-08) data set provided by Community Resource for Archiving Wireless Data (CRAWDAD) to evaluate our proposed method, and Section 10.5 includes the conclusion and main contributions of this study.

10.2 THE BACKGROUND

10.2.1 The Smart Antenna

The smart antennas are also known as adaptive array antennas [16]. As the name indicates, adaptive and array antenna elements put together to form an antenna array. Adaptive adjusts the pattern of the array. So, its name is adaptive array antenna. It is also recently called MIMO (multiple input multiple output antenna array), with smart signal processing algorithms used to identify spatial signal signatures, which shows the direction of an arrival signal [17]. The arrays are used with signal processing algorithms for the detection of the direction of arrival of the signal [18]. These are used to calculate beamforming vectors that are used to track and locate the antenna beam on the mobile or target. Smart antennas are different than reconfigurable antennas. Most of the time, it happens that reconfigurable antennas are confused with smart antennas. But they are different from smart antennas. Both of them have similar capabilities. Single-element antennas are called reconfigurable antennas and not antenna arrays [14]. When it comes to antenna arrays, it's a smart antenna, but when it comes to a simple element, then it comes to reconfigurable antennas. The objective is to maximize the gain in the desired direction. Another objective is to minimize the gain in the direction of interference. In the direction of interference, we are going to nullify, or we want the null, or we want the minimum radiation. Whereas in the direction of maximum gain, wherein the direction is not mentioned the actual target is there in that direction [19]. We want the maximum gain. So, in smart antenna, when we say we want the maximum gain in the desired direction, this is the desired user.

So, in this direction, we want maximum gain. Whereas in interference, in the interfering user, we want null in that case.

The objective working of smart antenna technical aspects involves number of elements made with the signals which are adaptively processed. The signals are adaptively processed one after the other in space with space-time filtering [20, 21]. There are basically two types of smart antennas: adaptive array antenna and switched beam array antenna. The adaptive array antenna is the core system component in mobile networks [22]. It allows the antenna to steer the beam to any direction of interest while simultaneously nulling the interfering signal. Adapting in the sense that it allows or steers the beam in the direction of interest, nullifying or nulling the beam in the direction of interfering signals. This adaptive antenna array can track and locate the signals. There is the adaptive algorithm which is involved in smart antennas. The output of it is a beamforming signal. The input signal when feeds to the adaptive algorithm, the adaptive algorithm will adapt in such a way that it provides the maximum gain in the desired direction and null in the interfering direction. So, it can locate and track the user signals, that is, users as well as interferences. It can customize an appropriate radiation pattern for each individual user. So, for each user, it can create or customize the radiation pattern.

10.2.2 The Difference between Conventional Array and Beamforming Array

There are individual radiation patterns for antennas. If we see all the antenna radiation patterns, this is a complete one. It is a case of a conventional array. But if we say this is of the beamforming array, the beamforming array is making the radiation increase or the more is the gain in the desired direction. The main beam is where the target is in. In case where we can see the main beam, we can see the higher gain. On the contrary, in the other directions, we can see the side lows which have very less gain. So, this is the difference between the conventional array and beamforming array in terms of radiation.

Another type of antenna is a switch to beam array antenna. As the name indicates, switch the beam. That means the radiation beam is getting switched. So, the switch beam array antenna has several fixed beam patterns and only the decision needs to be made on which beam is to be accessed at a given point of time [23]. The aim of the switched beam system is to increase

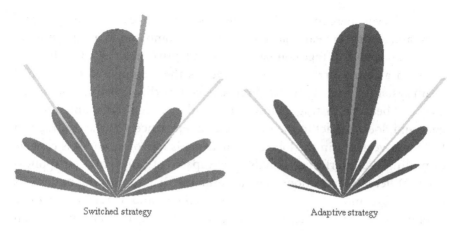

Switched strategy   Adaptive strategy

FIGURE 10.1
Difference between switched beam and adaptive beam.

the gain according to the location of the user. Based on the location of the user, the gain of that particular beam increases. Let us show it here diagrammatically. These are the multiple beams that can be seen in Figure 10.1. But the only one active beam is expected by the node. These beams are formed due to an antenna array [24]. If a user is there, this beam is active at a particular point in time. So, there are multiple fixed beams, with one beam turned on toward the desired signal. That is, the switch to beam antenna or switch to the beam array or single beam is steered to the desired signal. A single beam is getting steered to the desired signal.

10.2.3 Comparison between Switched and the Adaptive Array Antenna

Switched beam array antenna will be giving the maximum gain for the desired user for interfering users or for interference [25]. There are minor loops, but in the case of the adaptive scheme, for the desired user, the maximum gain is there. But at the same time, for interfering users, there is a null. This is the adaptive scheme. This is the difference between the switched antenna and adaptive antenna. Based on the criteria, we can differentiate between the switch to beam and adaptive array [26]. Based on the integration switch, the beam is easy to implement and it has a low cost. On the contrary, in the adaptive antenna array system, the transreceiver complexity is there, so that the cost is high and hard. Less hardware redundancy is there in adaptive arrays based on range and coverage. If we compare, switch to beam has more coverage compared to a conventional system and less coverage compared to the adaptive array [27]. On the contrary, in adaptive arrays, more coverage is there compared to switched beam systems. In terms of interference rejection, there is a difficulty in the switched beam in distinguishing between the desired signal and interference and doesn't react to the moment of interference. On the contrary, in the adaptive array, in the lobe also, focusing is narrower and it is capable of nulling the interfering signals. It is capable of nullifying the applications. Different applications of smart antenna that are coming under this category are mobile communications, cellular and wireless networks, satellite communications, wireless sensor network, military application and electronic warfare. A typical representation of the difference between switched beam and adaptive beam is given in Figure 10.1.

10.2.4 Preference Leveled Evaluation Function Method to Construct Fuzzy Measures

This section discusses a method to construct parameterized fuzzy measures based on preference leveled evaluation functions. The practical meanings of some parameters can also be found in the numerical instance that follows.

This study considered 2.4 GHz (802.11b/g/n/ax) range WLAN. Spaced with 5 MHz, 14 channels are there in 2.4 GHz (802.11b/g/n/ax) range WLAN. Fourteen channels in 2.4 GHz range are given in Table 10.1. A representation of overlapping channels within the 2.4 GHz band is given in Figure 10.2.

10.2.5 Construction Method Using Preference Leveled Evaluation Functions

With a normalized weight function $b = B^{\langle x \rangle}$ having the complementary preference $\hat{\lambda}_b \in [0,1]^x$, and let $(F, 2^F, t_X)$ be a given fuzzy frequency measure space where $F = \{x(1), \ldots, x(n)\}$. The x values that are the channel values in 2.4 GHz range are given in Table 10.1. Here, B is the bandwidth and $B^{\langle x \rangle}$ is the x-ary aggregate function. t_X is the space of all fuzzy measures on X [28, 29].

Let us identify a parameterized fuzzy measure $t_G^{\varphi_1, \ldots, \varphi_s}$ for parameterized fuzzy measure space $(G, 2^G, t_G^{\varphi_1, \ldots, \varphi_s})$, where $G = \{1, \ldots, x\}$ [30].

TABLE 10.1

Fourteen Channels of 2.4-GHz Range

Channel (x)	Frequency (F) (MHz)	Frequency Range
1	2412	2401–2423
2	2417	2406–2428
3	2422	2411–2433
4	2427	2416–2438
5	2432	2421–2443
6	2437	2426–2448
7	2442	2431–2453
8	2447	2436–2458
9	2452	2441–2463
10	2457	2446–2468
11	2462	2451–2473
12	2467	2456–2478
13	2472	2461–2483
14	2484	2473–2495

We denote by $([0, 1]^n)^G$ the space of all mappings,

$$\varphi : G \rightarrow \left([0, 1]^n\right) \tag{10.1}$$

We denote parameterized fuzzy measure $t_G^{(b,\varphi)} : 2^G \rightarrow [0, 1]$ such that for any $C \in 2^G$ ($C \neq \varphi$), we have

$$t_G^{(b,\varphi)}(C) = t_F(\{f \in F \mid \left(\vee_{g \in C}\varphi(g)\right)(f) \geq \hat{\lambda}_b(|C|)\}) \tag{10.2}$$

and still define $t_G^{(b,\varphi)}(\varphi) = 0$ for all b and φ. This is adjustability conferring to an expected preference b.

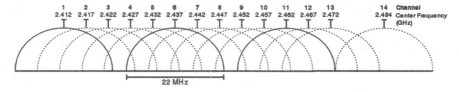

FIGURE 10.2
Overlapping channels of 2.4-GHz band.

Different complementary preference $\hat{\lambda}_b$ aid as diverse thresholds to be surpassed by union assessment $\vee_{g \in C} \varphi(g)$.

Also, when C = G, it follows $\{ f \in F \,|\, (\vee_{g \in C} \varphi(g))(f) \geq \hat{\lambda}_b(|C|)\} = F$,

$$\text{then } t_G^{(b,\varphi)}(G)) = 1, \text{ always.} \tag{10.3}$$

Usually, the greater the conservativeness, the lesser the parameterized fuzzy measure $t_G^{(b,\Theta)}$, but it is not always the case. Usually, we will get the expected results, if b and b', the two preferences, satisfy some special relation.

$(B^{\langle x \rangle}, \prec)$ gives a whole lattice with ordering $\prec$ demarcated such that for any two $b, b' \in B^{\langle x \rangle}$, $b \prec b' \Leftrightarrow \lambda_b < \lambda_{b'}$ [28].

For any two $b, b' \in B^{\langle x \rangle}$, if $b \prec b'$, then $\lambda_b(j) = \sum_{m=1}^{j} b(m) \leq \sum_{m=1}^{j} b'(m) = \lambda_{b'}(j)$ for all $j \in \{1, ..., x\}$. So, the relation about conservativeness [31], cn, is

$$cn(b) = \sum_{j=1}^{x} b(j) \cdot \frac{j-1}{n-1} = \frac{1}{x-1} \sum_{u=1}^{x} \sum_{m=s}^{x} b(m) = \frac{1}{x-1} \sum_{u=1}^{x} \left[1 - \sum_{m=1}^{u-1} b(m) \right]$$

$$= \frac{1}{x-1} \sum_{u=1}^{x} \left[1 - b(u) - \sum_{m=1}^{u} b(m) \right]$$

$$= \frac{x}{x-1} - \frac{1}{x-1} - \frac{1}{x-1} \sum_{u=1}^{x} \sum_{m=1}^{u} b(m)$$

$$= 1 - \frac{1}{x-1} \sum_{u=1}^{x} \sum_{m=1}^{u} b(m) \geq 1 - \frac{1}{x-1} \sum_{u=1}^{x} \sum_{m=1}^{u} b'(m) = cn(b') \tag{10.4}$$

Also,

$$\text{for any two C, C}' \in 2^G \text{ with } C \subset C', t_G^{(b,\varphi)}(C) \leq t_G^{(b,\varphi)}(C'); \tag{10.5}$$

$$\text{for any two b, b}' \in B^{\langle x \rangle} \text{ with b} \prec b', t_G^{(b,\varphi)}(C) \leq t_G^{(b',\varphi)}(C); \tag{10.6}$$

for any two $\varphi, \varphi' \in 2^F)^G$ with $\Theta < \Theta'$ (here "$<$" is $\varphi(j) < \varphi'(j)$ for all $j \in$ G),

$$t_G^{(b,\varphi)}(C) \leq t_G^{(b,\varphi')}(C). \tag{10.7}$$

Readers may refer the paper [32] for proof of the equations (10.1)–(10.7).

10.3 PROPOSED MODEL

The proposed parameterized fuzzy measure decision-making model based on preference leveled evaluation functions for best signal detection in smart antenna employs the BPNN algorithm, which is depicted in Figure 10.3. Input channels of 2.4-GHz range signals are fed to the model for identification of the best channel for the node. Signal range detection is done with the range-based received signal strength indicator (RSSI)

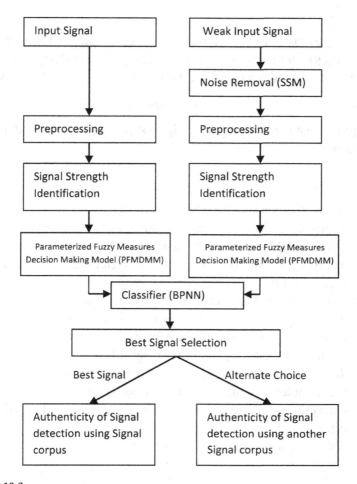

FIGURE 10.3

Block diagram of the proposed parameterized fuzzy measure decision-making model based on preference leveled evaluation functions for best signal detection in smart antenna.

method. Then, the PFMDMM is employed to identify best signals for the node, arranged in a proper format to feed into the artificial neural network for classification. In the training stage of BPNN, signal weights are given by some arbitrary values as per the x values in Table 10.1 and are then tuned for optimal during the iterative learning procedure with the help of the back propagation algorithm. At the testing stage, the neural network is tested against a variety of test samples of signals, to ensure whether the acquired system correctly categorizes the signal to the best preferred signal and other signal parts.

ALGORITHM 10.1: DECISION-MAKING MODEL BASED ON PREFERENCE LEVELED EVALUATION FUNCTIONS FOR BEST SIGNAL DETECTION IN SMART ANTENNA

Input: Input channels of 2.4-GHz range signals.

Output: Categorizes the signal to the best preferred signal and other signal parts.

Start

1. Input channels of 2.4-GHz range signals
2. Signal range detection with the range-based RSSI method.
3. The PFMDMM to identify best signals for the node, arranged in proper format to feed into the artificial neural network for classification.
4. *Training stage:* Weights of the feed forward neural network are given by some arbitrary values as per Table 10.1 and are then tuned for optimal during the iterative learning procedure with the help of the back propagation algorithm.
5. *Testing stage:* The neural network is tested against a variety of test samples of signals, to ensure whether the acquired system correctly categorizes the signal to the best preferred signal and other signal parts.
6. Categorizes the signal to the best preferred signal and other signal parts.

Stop

10.3.1 Signal Range Detection

Readers can refer to the steps for signal range detection with the range-based RSSI method in [33].

10.3.2 PFMDMM for Signal Detection

With $\varphi: G \to [0, 1]^4$, assume that the normalized weight function $b \in B^{(3)}$ is assigned to be w = (0.1, 0.4, 0.6).

We calculate λ_b = (0.1, 0.3, 1) and $\hat{\lambda}_b$ = (0.9, 0.6, 0), with $cn(b)$= cn (λ_b) = con($\hat{\lambda}_b$) = 0.75 showing a fairly added conservative measure in our preference. Then, using (10.2), we have t_G:

$$t_G^{(b,\varphi)}(\{1\}) = t_F(\{f \in F \,|\,(\varphi(1))(f) \geq \hat{\lambda}_b(1)\}) = t_F(\{4\}) = 0.2,$$

$$t_G^{(b,\varphi)}(\{2\}) = t_F(\{f \in F \,|\,(\varphi(2))(f) \geq \hat{\lambda}_b(1)\}) = t_F(\{4\}) = 0.4,$$

$$t_G^{(b,\varphi)}(\{3\}) = t_F(\{f \in F \,|\,(\varphi(3))(f) \geq \hat{\lambda}_b(1)\}) = t_F(\{3\}) = 0.4,$$

$$t_G^{(b,\varphi)}(\{1,2\}) = t_F(\{f \in F \,|\,(\varphi(1) \vee \varphi(2))(f) \geq \hat{\lambda}_b(2)\}) = t_F(\{1,2,3,4\}) = 1,$$

$$t_G^{(b,\varphi)}(\{1,3\}) = t_F(\{f \in F \,|\,(\varphi(1) \vee \varphi(3))(f) \geq \hat{\lambda}_b(2)\}) = t_F(\{1,3,4\}) = 0.9,$$

$$t_G^{(b,\varphi)}(\{2,3\}) = t_F(\{f \in F \,|\,(\varphi(2) \vee \varphi(3))(f) \geq \hat{\lambda}_b(2)\}) = t_F(\{1,3,4\}) = 0.9,$$

$$t_G^{(b,\varphi)}(\{1,2,3\}) = t_F(\{f \in F \,|\,(\varphi(1) \vee \varphi(2) \vee \varphi(3))(f) \geq \hat{\lambda}_b(3)\}) = t_F(\{1,2,3,4\}) = 1.$$

10.3.3 Deep Learning Model for Best Signal Selection

Deep learning or machine learning basically employs a DNN in the heart of this structure. We have training data sets and learning rules; we give some input parameters to DNN, and at the output, we get some optimized parameters based on training data sets. If we want to apply this concept of deep learning into smart antenna design, then at the input side, we can define five variables or five parameters, Inp= {W, L, h, ϵ_r, f} = {Patch width, patch length, thickness of dielectric substrate, dielectric constant, operating frequency}. If we provide this input (Inp) data to this deep neural network, at the output, we should expect optimized values of these five parameters. Notice that deep learning network will only perform well if we provide enough training data because based on those training data, which are of very high quality in nature, this deep neural network will learn. The proposed model's implementation used cu/antenna data set (v. 2009-05-08) provided by CRAWDAD to train the BPNN with anticipated/best permeates for any AP. In the proposed model, we used BPNNs to suggest the best signal for the AP.

10.4 EXPERIMENTAL RESULTS

In the study, signal vectors are categorized into the best-preferred signal and other signal parts with the help of the PFMDMM algorithm devised in MATLAB®. Input channels of 2.4-GHz range signals are fed to the model for the identification of the best channel for the node. Signal range detection is done with the range-based RSSI method. Then, PFMDMM is employed to identify the best signals for the node, arranged in a proper format to feed into the artificial neural network for classification. In the training stage of BPNN, the signal weights are given by some arbitrary values as per the x values in Table 10.1 and are then tuned for optimal during the iterative learning procedure with the help of the back propagation algorithm. At the testing stage, the neural network is tested against a variety of test samples of signals to ensure whether the acquired system correctly categorizes the signal to the best preferred signal and other signal parts. The PFMDMM is used to obtain efficient and speedy signal detection of an architecture. The study claims that for signal recognition, the system is 94% efficient in the average case.

10.4.1 Data Source

The study uses the cu/antenna data set (v. 2009-05-08) provided by CRAWDAD [34]. This data set contains collected signal strength data to descend a parametric model for 2.4 GHz directional 802.11 ad hoc antennas. To optimize these training data sets, we have tested this antenna for many times for different parameters and then created training data sets from the simulation data. With the exclusion of the location patterns, all the dimensions were created with commodity hardware by transporting numerous measurement packages among two antennas and logging received signal strength (RSS) at the end. In order to collect data sets, the three antenna configurations used are as follows:

- 8-degree horizontal beam-width hyperlink 24-dBi parabolic dish,
- 30-degree horizontal beam-width hyperlink 14-dBi patch with
- main-lobe beam width of approximately 52 degrees with a Fidelity Comtech Phocus 3000 8-element uniform circular phased array.

TABLE 10.2

Examples Data of cu/Antenna Data Set (v. 2009-05-08)

Id	rss	Batch	Position	Tag	norm.rss	norm.diff
1	48	parabolic-field2	0	default	−2.660532267	2.660532267
2	53	parabolic-field2	0	default	2.546716223	−2.546716223
3	51	parabolic-field2	0	default	0.463816827	−0.463816827
4	51	parabolic-field2	0	default	0.463816827	−0.463816827
5	50	parabolic-field2	0	default	−0.577632871	0.577632871
6	51	parabolic-field2	0	default	0.463816827	−0.463816827
7	50	parabolic-field2	0	default	−0.577632871	0.577632871
8	49	parabolic-field2	0	default	−1.619082569	1.619082569
9	50	parabolic-field2	0	default	−0.577632871	0.577632871
10	52	parabolic-field2	0	default	1.505266525	−1.505266525
11	51	parabolic-field2	0	default	0.463816827	−0.463816827
...	...	...	...	...	...	...
8715891	1.237726	patty-field	225	default	−9.639062036	−10.82143414

The data set mainly provides two information that is packet RSS and normalized RSS (norm.rss). norm.rss is the absolute RSS subtracted with the "reference maximum" for that trace. Greatest mean value for any angle within the trace is fixed as the reference maximum. A subset of the content of the cu/antenna data set (v. 2009-05-08) is given in Table 10.2.

10.4.2 Illustrative Example

The screenshot of the PFMDMM-based signal detestation simulation application is given in Figure 10.4. The signal depicted in blue color is the preferred signal suggested by the system for a node.

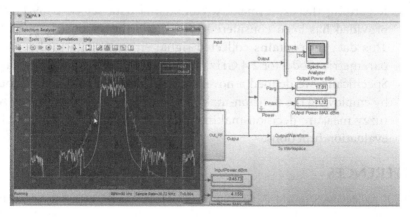

FIGURE 10.4
PFMDMM- based signal detestation simulation application.

Experiments with Laboratory Data. In order to verify the performance of BPNN models, that is, using the PFMDMM system for signal detection, experiments are realized on the laboratory data. For accurate signal detection, metal determination accuracy, namely, producer accuracy, user accuracy, and overall accuracy was 91.50, 95.32 and 94.99%, respectively.

10.5 CONCLUSION

A novel BPNN model that uses the PFMDMM system for signal classification to identify the best signal for a node is presented in this chapter. The results provided from the experiments proved that the parameterized fuzzy measure decision-making model based on preference leveled evaluation functions for best signal detection in smart antenna shows encouraging performances in terms of best signal suggestion for a WLAN node.

To the best of our knowledge, this is the first study making use of parameterized fuzzy measures decision-making model based on preference leveled evaluation functions for signal classification.

Specifically, the main contributions of this study are as follows:

- The proposed approach is able to provide satellite-based image clustering decisions making within narrow time intervals, which helps in addressing geological decisions more systematically.
- We propose a new use of parameterized fuzzy measure decision-making model based on preference leveled evaluation functions for signal classification-based BPNN architecture for the feature extraction process.
- Regarding the experiment, a cu/antenna data set (v. 2009-05-08) provided has been considered to evaluate the proposed approach. This data set contains collected signal strength data to descend a parametric model for 2.4 GHz directional 802.11 ad-hoc antennas.
- Specifically, we defined a novel automated signal suggestion model by employing the decision-making capabilities of the parameterized fuzzy measure decision-making model based on preference leveled evaluation functions.

REFERENCES

1. B. Aghoutane, S. Das, M. EL Ghzaoui, B. T. P., Madhav and H. El Faylali, A novel dual band high gain 4-port millimeter wave MIMO antenna array for 28/37 GHz 5G applications, AEU – International Journal of Electronics and Communications, Volume 145, 2022, p. 154071, ISSN 1434-8411, https://doi.org/10.1016/j.aeue.2021.154071.

2. K. D. Ayinala and P. K. Sahu, Isolation enhanced compact dual-band quad-element MIMO antenna with simple parasitic decoupling elements, AEU – International Journal of Electronics and Communications, Volume 142, 2021, p. 154013, ISSN 1434–8411, https://doi.org/10.1016/j.aeue.2021.154013.

3. M. A. Ashraf, K. Jamil, A. R. Sebak, S. Alshebeili, M. Shoaib, M. Alkanhal and Z. Alhekail, Evaluation of a single-input multiple-output antenna array for ultra-wide band applications, AEU – International Journal of Electronics and Communications, Volume 79, 2017, pp. 291–300, ISSN 1434–8411, https://doi.org/10.1016/j.aeue.2017.06.019.

4. S. R. Ostadzadeh, M. Soleimani and M. Tayarani, Prediction of induced current in externally excited dipole antenna using fuzzy inference, 2008 Second Asia International Conference on Modelling & Simulation (AMS), 2008, pp. 1039–1042, doi: 10.1109/AMS.2008.66.

5. T. A. B. Alves and T. Abrão, Massive MIMO and NOMA bits-per-antenna efficiency under power allocation policies, Physical Communication, Volume 51, 2022, 101588, ISSN 1874-4907, https://doi.org/10.1016/j.phycom.2021.101588.

6. A. Mahmood, M. Bennamoun, S. An, F. Sohel, F. Boussaid, R. Hovey, G. Kendrick and R. B. Fisher, Chapter 21 – Deep Learning For Coral Classification, Handbook of Neural Computation, Cambridge, MA: Academic Press, 2017, pp. 383–401, ISBN 9780128113189.

7. C. Wei, T. Chen and S. Lee, K-NN based neuro-fuzzy system for time series prediction, in Proc. International Conference Software Engineering, Artificial Intelligence, Networking and Parallel/Distributed Computing, Honolulu, 2013, 569–574.

8. G. Angiulli, Comments on "A hybrid method based on combining artificial neural network and fuzzy inference system for simultaneous computation of resonant frequencies of rectangular, circular, and triangular microstrip antennas", IEEE Transactions on Antennas and Propagation, Volume 57, Issue 1, p. 296, Jan. 2009, doi: 10.1109/TAP.2008.2009786.

9. J. Zhang and A. J. Morris, Recurrent neuro-fuzzy networks for nonlinear process modeling, IEEE Transactions on Neural Networks, Volume 10, Issue 2, 1999, pp. 313–326.

10. W. Orozco-Tupacyupanqui, H. Pérez-Meana and M. Nakano-Miyatake, A new method for searching the optimal step size of NLMS algorithm in intelligent antennas arrays based on fuzzy logic and artificial neural networks, 2014 IEEE Central America and Panama Convention (CONCAPAN XXXIV), 2014, pp. 1–6, doi: 10.1109/CONCAPAN.2014.7000421.

11. Y. Tawk, J. Costantine, S. E. Barbin and C. G. Christodoulou, A multi-band microstrip antenna design using cellular automata and fuzzy ARTMAP neural networks, 2009 3rd European Conference on Antennas and Propagation, 2009, pp. 3511–3514.

12. P. K. Guru Diderot, N. Vasudevan and K. S. Sankaran, An efficient fuzzy C-means clustering based image dissection algorithm for satellite images, 2019 International Conference on Communication and Signal Processing (ICCSP), 2019, pp. 0806–0809, doi: 10.1109/ICCSP.2019.8698054.

13. F. Li and Y. Du, From AlphaGo to power system AI: What engineers can learn from solving the most complex board game, IEEE Power and Energy Magazine, Volume 16, Issue 2, March-April 2018, pp. 76–84, doi: 10.1109/MPE.2017.2779554.

14. B. Kadri, F. T. Bendimered and E. Cambiaggio, Modelisation of the feed network application to synthesis unequally spaced microstrip antennas arrays, International Conference on Electromagnetics in Advanced Applications (ICEAA 99), 13–17 September 1999, pp. 371–374.

15. M. Grabisch, J. L. Marichal, R. Mesiar and E. Pap. 2009, Aggregation Functions. Cambridge: Cambridge University Press.
16. R. N. G. Robert, C. A. Pitz, E. L. O. Batista and R. Seara, An? 0-norm-constrained adaptive algorithm for joint beamforming and antenna selection, Digital Signal Processing, Volume 126, 2022, p. 103475, ISSN 1051-2004, https://doi.org/10.1016/j.dsp.2022.103475.
17. S. Jaisiva, T. Rampradesh, P. Vimala, P. Pugazhendiran and S. Karuppanan, Epoxy based on low profile MIMO antenna for cellular systems, Materials Today: Proceedings, Volume 46, Part 9, 2021, pp. 4099–4101, ISSN 2214-7853, https://doi.org/10.1016/j.matpr.2021.02.628.
18. B. Kadri and F. T. Bendimered, Fuzzy genetic algorithms for the synthesis of unequally spaced microstrip antennas arrays, 2006 First European Conference on Antennas and Propagation, 2006, pp. 1–6, doi: 10.1109/EUCAP.2006.4584907.
19. B. Kadri and F. T. Bendimered, Linear antenna synthesis with a fuzzy genetic algorithm. EUROCON 2007 – The International Conference on "Computer as a Tool", 2007, pp. 942–947, doi: 10.1109/EURCON.2007.4400530.
20. S. Bodjanova and M. Kalina, Approximate evaluations based on aggregation functions, Fuzzy Sets and Systems, Volume 220, 2013, pp. 34–52, doi: 10.1016/j.fss.2012.07.014.
21. P. Diniz, Fundamentals of adaptive filtering, in Adaptive Filtering Algorithms and Practical Implementation, 4th ed., New York, NY: Springer, 2013, pp. 152–154.
22. T. Su, H. Hung, J. Cheng, C. Lu and C. Hung, Fuzzy theory application to the satellite antenna controller, 2014 International Conference on Information Science, Electronics and Electrical Engineering, 2014, pp. 690–693, doi: 10.1109/InfoSEEE.2014.6947753.
23. Z. Xu, On method for uncertain multiple attribute decision making problems with uncertain multiplicative preference information on alternatives, Fuzzy Optimization and Decision Making, Volume 4, Issue 2, 2005, pp. 131–139.
24. M. M. Sani, R. Chowdhury and R. K. Chaudhary, Design and analysis of multiple input multiple output antenna for wideband applications using cylindrical dielectric resonator, AEU – International Journal of Electronics and Communications, Volume 131, 2021, p. 153598, ISSN 1434–8411, https://doi.org/10.1016/j.aeue.2020.153598.
25. A. Asrokin, M. K. A. Rahim and M. Z. A. A. Aziz, Dual band microstrip antenna for wireless LAN application, Proceedings of the 2005 Asia Pacific Conference on Applied Electromagnetics, December 2005, pp. 10698–110701.
26. J. Wu, C. Y. Liang and Y. Q. Huang, An argument-dependent approach to determining OWA operator weights based on the rule of maximum entropy, International Journal of Intelligent Systems, Volume 22, Issue 2, 2007, pp. 209–221, doi:10.1002/int.20201.
27. S. Chen, S. Liu and L. Hanzo, Adaptive Bayesian space-time equalisation for multiple receive-antenna assisted single-input multiple-output systems, Digital Signal Processing, Volume 18, Issue 4, 2008, pp. 622–634, ISSN 1051-2004, https://doi.org/10.1016/j.dsp.2007.09.012.
28. K. Wang, A new fuzzy genetic algorithm based on population diversity, International Symposium on Computational Intelligence in Robotics and Automation, July 29–August 1, 2001, pp. 108–112,.
29. B. Llamazares, Choosing OWA operator weights in the field of social choice, Information Sciences, Volume 177, Issue 21, 2007, pp. 4745–4756, doi:10.1016/j.ins.2007.05.015.

30. B. BharathiDevi and J. Kumar, Small frequency range discrete bandwidth tunable multiband MIMO antenna for radio/LTE/ISM-2.4 GHz band applications, AEU – International Journal of Electronics and Communications, Volume 144, 2022, 154060, ISSN 1434-8411, https://doi.org/10.1016/j.aeue.2021.154060.

31. L. Jin and R. Mesiar, The metric space of ordered weighted average operators with distance based on accumulated entries, International Journal of Intelligent Systems, Volume 32, Issue 7, 2017, pp. 665–675, doi:10.1002/int.21869.

32. C. Zhu, L. Jin, R. Mesiar and R. R. Yager, Using preference leveled evaluation functions to construct fuzzy measures in decision making and evaluation, International Journal of General Systems, Volume 49, Issue 2, 2020, pp. 161–173, doi:10.1080/03081079.2019.1668384.

33. T. Junchao and J. Han, An improved received signal strength indicator positioning algorithm based on weighted centroid and adaptive threshold selection, Alexandria Engineering Journal, Volume 60, Issue 4, 2021, pp. 3915–3920, ISSN 1110-0168, https://doi.org/10.1016/j.aej.2021.02.031.

34. E. W. Anderson and C. Phillips, CRAWDAD dataset cu/antenna (v. 2009-05-08), traceset: rss, downloaded from https://crawdad.org/cu/antenna/20090508/rss, https://doi.org/10.15783/C7VC7V, May 2009.

Index

Printed in the United States
by Baker & Taylor Publisher Services